Survival Along the Continental Divide

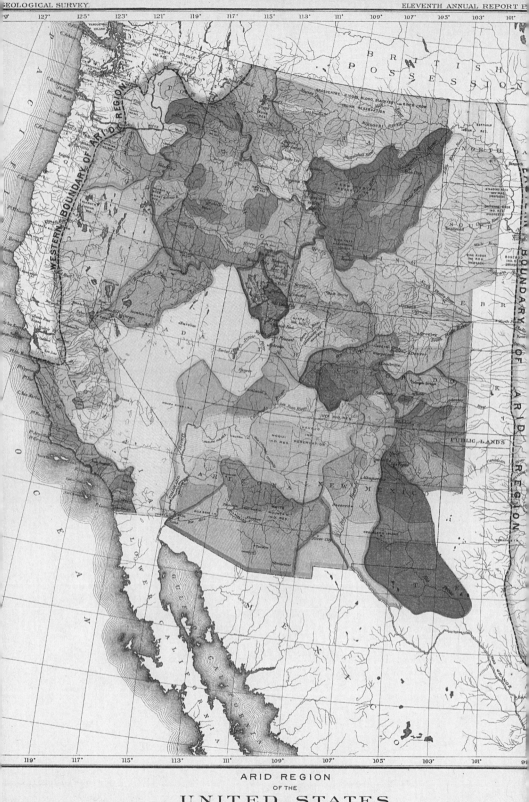

ARID REGION

OF THE

UNITED STATES

Showing Drainage Districts.

Scale

100   50 25   0   50   100   200   300 STAT. MILES.

SURVIVAL ALONG THE CONTINENTAL DIVIDE

An Anthology of Interviews

JACK LOEFFLER

UNIVERSITY OF NEW MEXICO PRESS
Albuquerque

A Project of the New Mexico Humanities Council
funded by a grant from The National Endowment
for the Humanities with additional support
from The Ford Foundation

Frontispiece: Map—Arid region of the United States showing drainage districts, entire. From *Eleventh Annual Report of the United States Geological Survey, 1889–90*. Courtesy of the Office of the New Mexico State Historian

13 12 11 10 09 08   1 2 3 4 5 6

Library of Congress Cataloging-in-Publication Data

Loeffler, Jack, 1936–

Survival along the Continental Divide : an anthology of interviews / Jack Loeffler.

     p. cm.

ISBN 978-0-8263-4439-7 (cloth : alk. paper)

1. New Mexico—Civilization.

2. Southwest, New—Civilization.

3. Pluralism (Social sciences)—New Mexico.

4. Pluralism (Social sciences)—Southwest, New.

5. New Deal, 1933–1939—New Mexico.

6. New Mexico—Economic conditions—20th century.

7. Social problems—Southwest, New.

8. Southwest, New—Social conditions.

9. Southwest, New—Economic conditions.

10. Interviews—New Mexico. I. Title.

     F796.5.L64 2008

     978.9'004—dc22

          2008001842

Designed and typeset by Mina Yamashita.

Composed in Minion Pro, an Adobe Original typeface

designed by Robert Slimbach.

Printed by Thomson-Shore, Inc. on 55# Natures Natural.

To the memory

of Lee Udall,

my great and dear friend

who long ago

cast light on the path of

a young aural historian

Contents

Foreword

Craig L. Newbill

Between Fences was originally a project conceived by the Smithsonian Institution's Museum on Main Street (MoMS) program as a traveling exhibition for smaller communities. The New Mexico Humanities Council (NMHC) sponsored Between Fences in seven communities across the state: Belen, Española, Ruidoso, Hobbs, Raton, Las Vegas, and Columbus. The NMHC supported the endeavor for communities "to discuss historic events that draw the state's diverse communities of humans together and divide them from one another." The project traveled the state from July 2005 to August 2006 with funding support from the National Endowment for the Humanities We the People initiative.

When the NMHC met at its summer board meeting in July 2005 in Ruidoso, no one participating in the planning session would have predicted that one of the final outcomes for Between Fences would be the publication of *Survival Along the Continental Divide: An Anthology of Interviews*. All of the participants at the board meeting recognized the public-humanities potential of projects related to "fences." Such fences included the obvious physical forms of fencing Americans had used for more than two hundred years, but also some not so visible barriers and the effects that both have on human interactions. Yet the NMHC board was also committed to public programs, which centered on discussions about what unites people in New Mexico—what is our shared legacy, or, as one member suggested, "We all know too well what divides us from one another. Why can't we also discuss what brings us together as human beings?"

During the board meeting, we outlined plans and ideas to bring many issues related to fencing to public audiences. Although we discussed and approved many formats and means of engagement, we left the meeting with the challenge of how to bring together many complicated perspectives related to fences in New Mexico. We agreed that fences and other not so obvious forms of demarcation continue to influence and determine how people define space, move across it, and relate to it (or not). At the time, the relationships and similarities among various human habitats were our primary focus. As I drove home along the Sierra Blanca mountain range and emerged in the Tularosa Basin, a Cooper's Hawk began to circle in front of me. I thought of Jack Loeffler.

Jack Loeffler is a former jazz trumpet player, reforming anarchist, and former traveling companion to Ed Abbey. A self-taught aural historian (one who also records all sounds, including the biotic and the mechanical), he has become someone I simply refer to as "the Studs Terkel of the Southwest." I do so because he has recorded hundreds of interviews throughout North America, but primarily in the American Southwest. He is well known both as a student and as a teacher. He has just recently donated his archival record of human interactions and recordings of the biotic community to the Museum of New Mexico. There, thousands of hours of recordings will ultimately become the core of the history museum's oral histories archives.

I set out to recruit Jack to the project knowing full well that he "hated fences," that earlier in life he was known for climbing them and occasionally cutting them down. But I also knew he was my first choice to conduct oral history workshops in the MoMS project because, at this point in his forty-plus years of studio and fieldwork, he seemed more on a path of mending fences among the wide range of people he has come to know in his endeavors as an historian, folklorist, and ethnomusicologist. Jack is a scholar not only "for the public," but "from the public." He has lived among Navajo sheepherders, camped with and run rivers with

Native people, ranchers, environmentalists, writers, poets, and photographers. He has produced an impressive number of radio programs and recorded opera, chamber, jazz, and folk concerts and performances. Making him an even better choice for this place-centered project, Jack does not hold humans apart as distinct from the places they inhabit, so the future public discussions for Between Fences would naturally involve his ongoing work on species interactions.

Fortunately for the NMHC and me, Jack patiently listened to my suggestions of how we could help prepare the seven towns in the MoMS exhibition to host the project. Teaching them how to conduct oral history projects in their own communities to explore what fences mean would come first. In addition to conducting workshops and overseeing the consultation process during oral history projects, Jack would be interviewing a wide range of people on the topic of fences so that those interviewed could be recruited to address public audiences. Jack improved the idea by suggesting a radio series consisting of fifteen or sixteen interviews with people from all walks of life around the state. He could record their different perspectives on fences, fence making, and community building, and produce a radio series that addresses fences both literally and figuratively. As if these projects were not challenging enough, I asked Jack to consider including some interviews about one of the century's greatest unifiers during a time of crisis, the New Deal. Especially crucial to New Mexico's history and cultural development during the twentieth century, the New Deal celebrates its seventy-fifth year in 2008. And so a collaborative endeavor to discuss fences and bridges was reshaped to better explore current and abiding issues facing New Mexicans in the twenty-first century. Complex issues in the anthology are discussed in accessible, informative, and delightful ways.

Another important person in this collaboration is Beth Hadas, former editor in chief for the University of New Mexico Press. When Beth heard that the radio series was being planned and saw for herself the incredible range of topics and perspectives addressed, she suggested that Jack write and edit the companion anthology you now hold.

So the idea for the exhibition project started with what divides New Mexicans from one another and what brings them together as a community. Jack responded with a project that meets the NMHC board's overriding concern that we continue to explore what unites us all as human beings and at the same time makes us distinct as New Mexicans. I believe this project captures some of the distinctiveness of our collective experiences and encourages the reader to explore further some of the issues presented in the interviews.

Acknowledgments

Many minds and many voices contributed to this book, which has been a joy for me to prepare. First, I thank my friend Dr. Craig Newbill, executive director of the New Mexico Humanities Council, who first conceived of this project in early 2006 and asked me if I would be willing to take it on, which I heartily agreed to do! I am also grateful to all my friends who staff the council, including Michelle Quisenberry, Nancy Brouillard, Susan Simon, and Jessica Billings, each of whom has nurtured this project in her own way.

My friend Beth Hadas, the finest of editors, read these words, applied her special magic, and made them presentable in spite of the author. My daughter, Celestia Peregrina Loeffler, and my old friend Yvonne Bond shared the task of transcribing the interviews, a chore beyond the ken of normal mortals. Copy editor Annie Barva filled in the potholes and paved over the cobblestones to allow the reader a smooth passage. My friend Dr. Claude Stephenson, our New Mexico State Folklorist, steered me past some critical forks along the trail. My *compañeros* from the board of directors of the Lore of the Land—Jim McGrath, Enrique Lamadrid, Sue Sturtevant, Suzanne Jamison, and Rina Swentzell—continue to provide deep friendship and support. Mimi Roberts and Drummond Hadley provided insights that helped clarify the process. And I am especially grateful to each of the seventeen participants who contributed their words and thoughts to this book.

Funding for this project was provided by a grant from the National Endowment for the Humanities and the ongoing support of the Ford Foundation. Thank you.

And finally, to my wonderful wife and partner in life, Katherine, *muchisimas gracias, mi amiga.*

Jack Loeffler
Los Caballos
2007

Introduction

In 2005, the New Mexico Humanities Council (NMHC) joined Smith-sonian Institution's Museum on Main Street traveling exhibition program to bring the exhibition entitled Between Fences to rural com-munities throughout New Mexico. Exhibit designers and curators had taken cues from the famous line "Good fences make good neighbors" that appears in Robert Frost's poem "Mending Wall." The line is spoken by Frost's neighbor to Frost himself as the two of them mend the rock wall that separates their rural properties in Vermont. Frost notes to him-self, "Something there is that doesn't love a wall, that wants it down," but his neighbor continues to mend the wall.

Eighty-one years after the poem first appeared in Frost's antho-logy *North of Boston*, the Between Fences exhibit opened in the Harvey House Museum in Belen, New Mexico, and thereafter visited museums in several small communities throughout the state, including Española, Ruidoso, Hobbs, Raton, Las Vegas, and Columbus. Although the West was represented, the exhibit had a distinctly eastern flavor, and there was a verdant cast to many of the displays that portrayed aspects of American life east of the hundredth meridian, the dividing line that separates the humid East from the arid West.

Dr. Craig Newbill, executive director of the NMHC, invited me to be the lead scholar and lecturer for the New Mexico displays of Between Fences. I was honored, flattered, and puzzled. There's something in me that doesn't love a wall. I actually heard Robert Frost read "Mending Wall" when I was a student at Ohio State University in 1959. It was apparent that he didn't love a wall, either. I told Craig that I wasn't particularly fond of fences, and he replied that that was why he had asked me to be the lead scholar. I accepted. A few months later Craig asked me to produce an anthology of interviews that would combine elements from the Between Fences project and another NMHC project that focused on the Great Depression and the New Deal in New Mexico. The leitmotif that I found in contemplating these themes was the landscape itself and how it was reflected in the particularly diverse cultures that abide here. Although thousands of miles of barbed-wire fences crosshatch the American West, the truer boundaries lie within watersheds and cultures.

For more than forty years, I have been an aural historian wandering the West and beyond, engaging people in conversation about their own perspectives, and recording these conversations for posterity. I have also recorded thousands of traditional songs as well as the sounds of many natural habitats and the species that wander therein. My archive already contained several interviews appropriate for this work, and I made a list of others that I wanted to conduct. The collection of interviews here reflects the points of view of people who live in the American Southwest on either side of the Continental Divide, the backbone of our homeland, east of which water flows toward the Atlantic, and west of which it flows to the Pacific. Hopi, Navajo, Río Grande Puebloan, Hispano, and American Anglo cultures are represented in this anthology, which is intended to reveal elements required of both individuals and cultures to survive in this arid landscape, not the least of which is reverence for the land itself.

The book is divided into three sections. Part I comprises excerpted interviews that I think convey individual and cultural perspectives concerning the shifting cultural mosaic of the larger homeland. Most of the boundaries reflected in this section are cultural boundaries rather than hand-wrought fences and walls. The interviews in part II address the presence of Franklin Delano Roosevelt's New Deal in New Mexico during the Great Depression of the 1930s, when the federal government sought to reinvigorate both the U.S. economy and mainstream American culture, which remain inextricably intertwined. The interviews in part III take the broadest possible perspective and suggest some ways to attack the extraordinary dilemmas that face the West today.

I begin with an essay I wrote at the inception of my involvement with the Between Fences project. Each interview also begins with an introductory narrative that includes modest reflections on the cultural and physical geography of this landscape, whose spirit snapped me into perfect accord half a century ago. I've grown to love my adopted homeland and now regard myself as a family member of its greater biotic community.

Jack Loeffler, photo
by Katherine Loeffler

PART I

Between Fences
and Beyond

All living organisms are territorial. The *Encyclopedia Britannica* defines the word *territory* very well: "in ecology, any area occupied by a home or defended, or both, by an organism or a group of similar organisms for such purposes as mating, roosting, or feeding. The type of territory varies with social behavior and environmental requirements of the particular species and often serves more than one function. Most vertebrates and some invertebrates such as arthropods, including insects, have territorial spacing mechanisms that prevent harmful overcrowding effects such as exhaustion of food supply. Some authorities also consider plants or micro-organisms that secrete repulsive chemicals into their immediate environments to be territorial, because the substances space individuals of species apart from one another."

In other words, the territorial imperative is as basic as hunger and sex. All living creatures claim their respective space and defend it vigorously. I am in awe of the creosote bush that predominates in many of the desert regions of North America. This plant is said to secrete a chemical that defines its immediate territory and thus cannot be encroached upon by other creosote bushes.

Songbirds announce their territories through song and defend their air space against raptors. Canines and other creatures mark territorial boundaries with urine. Ants of different species engage in mortal combat. All the while, life feeds on life within every earthly habitat, every territory, and every bioregion or ecosystem. Every species relies completely on its habitat for survival. Each habitat is a composite of living organisms collectively contained within a landscape or seascape or atmosphere. The surface and atmosphere of our planet are composed of an ever-shifting mosaic of ecosystems aswarm with myriad species that survive by means of competition or cooperation or a combination of both strategies.

Lest we forget, we are but one of those species, a biological phenomenon with a level of consciousness as yet unparalleled, as far as we know.

We humans gradually achieved our specieshood (and our proclivity for consciousness) some four to five hundred thousand years ago. There may have been eight to ten thousand generations of true humans since our emergence from the biological realm of our predecessors. It was colder then; it was the time of the Pleistocene, an age of glaciation when it was possible to wander afoot across a landmass that extended from what is now Siberia to what is now Alaska. Our ancestors seeded every continent but one. With the gradual warming trends of the Holocene epoch, we blossomed and little by little became the dominant species on our planet. Over the past ten thousand years or so, we have gradually all but abandoned our hunter-gatherer practices in favor of a more agrarian and community-oriented life-style. We have also grown in numbers. A few years ago I realized that in my lifetime the human population of our planet, Earth, had trebled.

Our ancestors ranged in tiny bands far and wide through a seemingly endless landscape, only occasionally encountering one another— just enough to spice up the gene pool and avoid giving birth to identical cousins. They marked their territorial rangeland with rock art and cairns, burial sites and waterholes, especially in arid habitats such as the American Southwest.

As the great human ecologist Paul Shepard points out, we began our specieshood as hunter-gatherers on intimate terms with our respective homelands. "Prehistoric humans . . . were native to their place. They possessed a detailed knowledge that was passed on from generation to generation by oral tradition through myths—stories that framed their beliefs in the context of ancestors and the landscape of the natural world. They lived within a 'sacred geography' that consisted of a complex knowledge of place, terrain, and plants and animals embedded in a phenology [periodic biological phenomena such as flowering, breeding, and migration] of seasonal cycles. But they were also close to the Earth in a spiritual sense, joined in an intricate configuration of sacred associations with the spirit of place within their landscape" (from *Coming Home to the Pleistocene*). As they wandered through the mysteries of habitat, they engaged in a form of geomythic mapping that defined their territories in a sacred manner.

Agriculture caused an enormous shift in human culture. Tiny villages came to dot a still seemingly endless landscape. As Lewis Mumford points out, "War was not yet in evidence. Such Neolithic villages as have been exhumed show a remarkable lack of anything that could be called weapons" (from *The City in History*).

Only when the city evolved and with it a complex system of human hierarchy that resulted in social boundaries did the surrounding landscape come to be fiercely defended against encroachment by so-called interlopers. That territorial imperative remains a major force in human nature.

In the five hundred or so human generations since the end of the Pleistocene epoch eleven thousand years ago, countless cultures have evolved, flourished, and withered, each having contributed to the sum of the human endeavor we know as culture. Inevitably, a major factor in cultural evolution is the shaping influence of natural habitat. The Inuit became specialists in hunting sea mammals for food, clothing, and bone and in using ivory to fashion tools. The Hopi perfected the art of desert farming and continue to perform annual cycles of ceremonials celebrating the local deities and Nature spirits whose presence is critical for the continued well-being of the Hopi people. The Seri of Sonora are among the last of the hunter-gatherers in North America. They fish, hunt, and gather edible desert plants, recalling their Seri-brand taxonomy in songs that define the characteristics of individual species. Biodiversity and cultural diversity have always been inextricably interlinked.

Differences in language, mythic history, and custom determine cultural boundaries between indigenous peoples. Geophysical boundaries are determined by watersheds and landforms wherein shrines of human provenance mark mythic moments in cultural recollection. Walls were part of the architecture of domiciles and storage areas among some cultures, but fences were rare in North America until after 1492, when domesticated livestock were introduced along with the notion of private ownership of land.

Before European contact, less than ten million people lived in what are now the contiguous forty-eight states. In the ensuing five hundred years, the human population of our homeland has become more than thirty times greater, and much of the landscape has been transformed by civilization and its attendant agriculture and extraction of natural resources. Some North American boundaries were created within the Spanish colonies that originated in the sixteenth century, when the king of Spain granted enormous tracts of land to specific individuals. Two centuries later the U.S. settlement of the West brought with it the meticulous surveying of the landscape.

The Mexican-American War of the mid-nineteenth century created an international boundary between the two nations. West of the Great Lakes, the boundary between the United States and Canada mainly follows an east–west survey line that is finally broken by the presence of Puget Sound. As the countryside filled in with farms in the East and with cattle and sheep ranches in the West, fences crisscrossed the landscape, apportioning the land into privately owned and deeded rectangular parcels. Larger areas of so-called public lands were also fenced and highways were constructed, thus blocking wildlife corridors.

The dividing line between the verdant East and the arid West is the hundredth meridian, which runs north to south through the Dakotas, Nebraska, Kansas, Oklahoma, and Texas. Though rarely fenced, state lines, county lines, and city and village boundaries are legally recognized. Private ownership of land is frequently defined by fences constructed along property lines.

Indeed, we humans are master fence builders, and our existence takes place between boundaries, both real and imagined. We Americans believe ourselves to have achieved the sort of domination of the land and its creatures that is promised in the biblical Book of Genesis. We have translated the territorial imperative into every aspect of existence. We have created giant bureaucracies to ensure that our respective territories have credibility, just as we have developed an ever more complex legal system both as a means of protection and as a justification for invading someone else's territory.

Our political systems legislate our secular behavior, and great religious systems have emerged to tend to our spiritual needs and shape our cultural practices. Enormous military organizations have existed for millennia both to invade someone else's territory and to thwart invasion from without. The Industrial Revolution and its technofantastic aftermath have created a boundary between ways of living. Most of us have gradually come to abandon the handcrafted life-style of our not-too-distant ancestors, collectively opting for a consumer-oriented life-style. Television has accustomed us to being entertained from without rather than being individually or collectively creative. It has erected a boundary between passivity and activity.

The arid paradise now known as the American Southwest is one of the most varied and fascinating landscapes on our planet. Three of the dozen or so distinct geophysical divisions of the North American continent coincide here just southeast of what is now Santa Fe, New Mexico. They are the Great Plains, the Rocky Mountains, and the Inter-Mountain Plateaus. The Inter-Mountain Plateaus are further divided into three provinces: the Columbia Plateau, the Colorado Plateau, and the Basin and Range. The provinces of the Basin and Range and the Colorado Plateau compose most of the American Southwest. The Basin and Range province contains the Chihuahuan, Sonoran, Mojave, and Great Basin deserts, which differ in prevailing vegetation and fauna, although there is some overlap. The overlapping natural boundaries between each of the great ecosystems are called *ecotones*, areas where committed bird-watchers may have a field day and botanists may be put to task.

During the most recent ice age, wildlife was abundant. Since then, many species, including much of the megafauna such as the woolly mammoths and woolly rhinos, have blinked into extinction. As the sun baked the landscape with the coming of the Holocene, entire forests migrated to higher, cooler elevations, forming mountaintop "sky islands" where isolated biological communities continue to evolve independently. Indeed, within the natural world, boundaries shift as climates are affected by weather patterns or by geophysical rearrangements such as volcanic eruptions or even by the introduction of exotic plants and animals. Water is a critical factor.

New Mexico, an area presently defined by a geopolitical boundary of human invention, has less surface water, relatively speaking, than any other state. It has about 230 square miles of surface water, depending on how much precipitation is yielded by the mostly clear heavens. The aridity allows the eye to see far for lack of tall trees and dense atmosphere. New Mexico is bisected north to south by the Río Grande, itself a natural boundary marker. West of the Río Grande is the Continental Divide. Watersheds are natural drainage systems that may either empty into larger watersheds and bodies of water or be totally self-contained, as is the case with the Great Basin Desert of Nevada.

New Mexico has been an intercultural proving ground for millennia. Humans are known to have existed here for at least twelve thousand years, as evidenced by the presence of Clovis points wrought by ancient hunter-gatherers. Cultures gradually shifted into a more agrarian mode and moved into clearly defined territories wherein complex structures were built, the remains of which still exist at Chaco Canyon, Salmon Ruins, Aztec Ruins, and surrounding outliers. The people who lived in these areas are thought to be among the ancestors of today's Puebloans, who live in communities near the Río Grande and farther west at Laguna and Acoma. Sometime during the past millennium, Athabascans moved in from the north and evolved into the Navajo and Apache tribal groups.

In 1598, Juan de Oñate, son of a Basque silver baron living in Zacatecas, Mexico, led a group of Spanish colonists northward to settle near the confluence of the Río Chama and Río Grande, where he established the first community of European provenance in the Southwest. He had moved into the heart of the Puebloan territory of Oke Oweenge, better known to outsiders as the San Juan Pueblo. Three months earlier, having crossed the Río Grande near today's El Paso, he claimed the entire region to the north in the name of the Spanish monarch in spite of the presence of many indigenous peoples living in communities throughout the region. Oñate was accompanied by a retinue of hundreds of colonists, thousands of head of livestock, and a coterie of Catholic missionaries intent on luring Indian souls into the Christian fold. Cultural boundaries were violated time and again, both within the landscape and within point of view.

The conquistadors had entered the New World in quest of mineral riches and glory. As they penetrated what is now New Mexico, a landscape held sacred by virtually every Native, they paved the way for secularization of the land, hence breeching the boundary between sacred and profane. As time wore on, they cohabited with the Natives, resulting in the *mestizaje*, or mixture of bloodlines, that altered biological boundaries established in antiquity.

Hispano communities were founded, and new territories staked out. There was conflict, not only with the Puebloans, but also with Apaches, Navajos, Utes, and finally the Comanches. The arrival of the horse profoundly affected Apaches, Navajos, and Comanches, who almost immediately became first-rate horsemen and thus expanded their respective territorial purviews by several magnitudes.

With the coming of the Americans in the nineteenth century, territorial boundaries were rearranged yet again, and by the twentieth century the landscape was a crosshatch of fences set in soil to accommodate ranchers whose livestock grazed grasslands. Waterholes in New Mexico were monuments to territoriality, and more than one gunfight resulted in death when one man's cow slurped from another man's waterhole. Fences of every nature were now to be found in abundance.

Our proclivity for claiming space and establishing boundaries runs deep. Each of us is confronted with rules and regulations, every form of prejudice, political points of view, communities of practice, religions, cultural mores, institutional bureaucracies, corporate dogmas, scientific disciplines, and the law of the land—to name but a few boundaries.

Our cultural attitudes are presently shaped in part by media funded and designed to engage us in a paradigm of world corporate economics, a fundament of which is the goal to turn habitat into money. This goal may well pose the greatest threat to life on our planet since the last significant spasm of extinction sixty-five or so million years ago. Fortunately, these same media are available to us to advertise the errors of our collective ways and to reactivate our imaginations in response to what many regard to be the greatest crisis ever faced by humanity: global warming and climate change.

We are obliged to expand our collective range of vision. While we look to science to solve our problems, we mustn't neglect the wisdom inherent in attitudes long held by cultures indigenous to homeland or the wisdom spun in the minds of writers, thinkers, and other explorers who have dedicated their lives to becoming as conscious as possible. Many contend that if indeed our species has a purpose, it is to evolve a level of consciousness that includes recognition of humankind's membership in the community of life, the enormity of our responsibility to our planet, and our great privilege to explore the mysteries of existence in this universe.

Paul Horgan, photographer
unknown. Photograph courtesy of
Michael Hurd, Hurd–La Rinconada
Gallery, San Patricio, New Mexico

Paul Horgan

Introduction

Paul Horgan, a twentieth-century American author of both fiction and
nonfiction set mostly in the American Southwest, was born in 1903
in Buffalo, New York. He moved to Albuquerque, New Mexico, with
his family in 1915. For years, he served as the faculty librarian at the
New Mexico Military Institute in Roswell. It was there that he wrote
Great River: The Río Grande in North American History (1954), which
remains the greatest overall human history of the watershed of the Río
Grande. Horgan received Pulitzer Prizes for both *Great River* and *Lamy
of Santa Fe* (1975), his biography of Jean-Baptiste Lamy, first archbishop
of Santa Fe.

He spent his later years as writer-in-residence at Wesleyan University
in Middletown, Connecticut. It was there that I interviewed him in his
book-strewn home in the university carriage house in 1987. He was the
most erudite person I had ever met, with the demeanor of a nineteenth-
century classicist. Paul Horgan passed from this world in 1995.

In the interview, Horgan delves into many of the cultural and environmental issues that helped shape his thinking over the course of his
long life. I'm sure that many readers (and listeners to his recorded interview) will detect a note of pomposity and possibly a tone of cultural prejudice in his expression. Bear in mind that he arrived in Albuquerque as

a twelve-year-old boy from the East in 1915, when Albuquerque was but a tiny city by today's standards. He was accustomed to a level of sophistication and urbanity, and so experienced culture shock at having been transplanted. He transcended many of these biases by virtue of his great intellect, boundless curiosity, and humaneness. After serving in World War II, he lived for years in the Roswell area and enjoyed an enduring friendship with artists Peter Hurd and Henriette Wyeth. Horgan was uninspired by the artist colonies of Santa Fe and Taos. He gained enormous respect for Archbishop Lamy and must have been affected by his perception of the rivalry between the French priest Lamy and Padre Antonio José Martínez of Taos, a local hero of the Hispano population who challenged Lamy, his ranking superior in the Catholic Church.

Horgan said that he abhorred revisionism. His writing reflects the enormity of his research in pursuit of the truth. He was possessed of a subtle and wonderful sense of humor that frequently cut through his formal demeanor. The influence of New Mexico's special light and the rugged luster of its landscape appears throughout his writing.

Paul Horgan

JL: Could you provide a sense of your earliest years in New Mexico and how they felt to you and how they may have influenced you?

PH: I was twelve years old when my family removed to Albuquerque from Buffalo, New York, and Albuquerque then was a Río Grande small city of fourteen thousand people. Its main concern economically was the Santa Fe Railroad, which was a division point and had great shops. The great transcontinental line was the lifeblood of the city, going east and west many times a day—many trains a day. It was a local rite to go and visit the arrival of the important train, the California Limited, one east and one westward every day. Celebrities would disembark and stroll the platforms at Albuquerque and visit the Indian exhibits and the Fred Harvey establishment with its collection

of regional antiques and so forth. So it became a citizen's prom-
enade, really, to go and witness this every day as the great trains
went east and west.

This is more than romantic to me. It was a great vein of contact with the farther world. Albuquerque felt very isolated to me
and, I think, to my family, coming from the metropolitan East.
But it wasn't long before the landscape, even in an unsophisti-
cated way, began to speak to me quite directly, and aside from
the benefits that resulted [for] my father's health—this family
removal, I know, gave him ten more years of life that he might
not have had otherwise—it introduced me at a most impressionable time in my life to a wholly new environment and a very
fresh sense of openness all around. The thing that struck me
most curiously [about] living in Albuquerque, in the town itself,
was that at the end of every street you could see the country,
which was not true of a city like Buffalo or any other metropolitan center in the East from which we came. And that to me was
already a kind of an establishment of metaphorical horizon, so
that past the dwellings and past streets and houses there was the
great vision of the country, and it's never lost its mystery and
wonder for me.

First of all, there is the desert foreground, and then always
the mountain enclosure way beyond, and what seemed and still
seems the illimitable sky. Light is the poetry of the West, I think,
the desert Southwest, and it was that to which I was uncon-
sciously subjected. Gradually I grew more and more under its
spell. Lately it's interested me that a man who's written a piece
about me, named David McCullough, has lighted upon the idea
that light itself is a great theme recurring through my writing, and I never had been conscious of this. But it [this theme]
reflects my concern for landscape both as an amateur painter and
as an observer and [as] one who likes to translate environment
and surrounding into character—because there is, of course, an
immediate exchange of interest and significance between these
two elements of life. And I thought it attractive and discerning

of him to decide that light was one of the animating elements of my work because it never occurred to me at all.

In the civic sense, Albuquerque was primitive then. One small personal illustration of that: in Buffalo I had been this music student in the way of studying violin in the private school to which I went, and many "oohs" and "ahs" accompanied my student recitals—child recitals, really. But when I got to Albuquerque, there was no violin teacher, and that lapsed. Nothing continued that way for me, so I never became a performer. Now, of course, like everyone who is a victim of this interruption, I bitterly regret it. Nothing would please me more than playing sonatas. But I can listen to them.

JL: Can you describe to me how the concept of *Great River* began to evolve?

PH: That's a large question. It really began in this childhood phase, the twelve years and later, through friendship and companionship with Francis Fergusson of the great Fergusson family of Albuquerque—because his grandfather, Franz Huning, had been a trader or merchant on the Santa Fe Trail, a German immigrant, whom I saw once or twice as a very, very old man crawling around his grape arbors and gardens in Albuquerque. But he built this Rhenish castle, romantic German castle, a *schloss* in its own park with peacocks and willows and acequias [irrigation ditches], cultivated land, and also wild woodland edging the river. So his property took in a great stretch—I don't know how many miles of the banks of the river north and south.

His grandson Francis had the free run of this place. No other boys did except marauders [from] the Mexican colony in Albuquerque, and they were our natural enemies, of course, at childhood age. There were skirmishes and apprehensivenesses and all this kind of brat nonsense that go on in anybody's childhood. But the fact is that the mystery and beauty of the river in which we swam and in which we played and built castles and romanticized in every possible way—he, too, had a very strong literary and intellectual bent early in life—it became a realm of fantasy long before I had any notion of dealing with it in adult life as a writer or even as a painter. So that when my interests grew very serious years and years later, it surely was fed with the spring waters of this early experience, almost into a kind of pygmy ownership of that glorious affair that's known as the river itself. It was the conditioning landscape of those years between, say, the ages of twelve and seventeen or eighteen. A very impressionable time, naturally. And when I came eventually to frame a concept for a book that became *Great River*, all these earliest impressions had a deep emotional attachment [for me], a love and a fondness and a respect, the recollection of which meant everything to, I think, the texture of how I dealt with [the place] later.

JL: It's a magnificent intellectual feat, the writing of this book. You must have done prodigious research.

PH: It took about ten years of work, and it did take a good deal of digging. I think there's a bibliography of twenty-five pages of reading for the historical fabric. Before I got to that, I felt that I had to know it [the river] physically, and the result was that in 1947, after I'd left service in the army and gone back to live in New Mexico, I decided to see the river from top to bottom. The result was that through the next several years I made three complete trips, over two thousand miles, the course as close as I could get to the river itself by road (I did this by car, of course) in order to have immediate physical enclosure for what I would write about historically. It seemed to me that the book had to be as visual as it was factual and to bring these elements together, [so that] the result could have a spark of life. That's the way I pursued it.

Then after I felt fairly secure with the images of the river from the Continental Divide in Colorado to the Gulf of Mexico, I felt that every time I came upon a written reference, a historical study, I could see where the results occurred that I was going to

describe and touch upon, because I think they're inextricable—
they must belong together, these two elements of historical pre-
sentation. And I was merely trying to re-create the narrative of
the past through the many cultures that the river fed.

JL: In your writing, not only do you include the cultures themselves, but you brilliantly bring the entire area together as an
integrated environment. I'd like to ask you how you perceive
that environment in your recollection—the various factors
included in that environment that you feel became the real
coordinates for your thinking.

PH: Perhaps this will get to the answer, maybe roundabout. It seemed
to me that if you look at a map, there is no feature comparable
to the Río Grande from top to bottom, from beginning to end,
which does embrace the heart of the historical and cultural
essence of the Southwest. Certainly the Indian life—both New
Mexican and Texan along the Big Bend, the cave culture of the
Big Bend region and below—all [groups] had to relate to the
river for sustenance. Then certainly the various colonial efforts
of the three nations that followed, the [Spanish] and, shall I say,
[Texas] and the United States, all had to have the same relation
to the river where they built their colonies and their first planta-
tions. It was a natural course for life to take, assuming that people were going to come and stay. Therefore, despite its varieties
of landscape, the river was the one continuum, both culturally
and physically, that seemed to me to justify my attempt to take
it from its physical whole scope through its centuries of succes-
sions culturally and bind them together in terms of what really
happened and where.

One factor that always interested me was the change in the
physical nature of the river course, from the Rocky Mountains
and the eternal winter of the source down through the New
Mexico canyons of the north and then into the benignly beautiful pastoral passages in central New Mexico, which even in
my first glimpses of [them] made me feel that, for instance, the

landscape painting of Poussin and these classical groves that you come upon around Albuquerque and farther along down toward Socorro—all these things are interrelated, I think, to my picture, my concept of the river. And then farther on down toward El Paso and the southeastern course of the Texas [portion of the] river into the true desert and the great vast spaces of the mountainless emptiness, and yet here this constant flow came and made its way to the garden river of the Gulf [of Mexico] and its littoral, which was still another phase—the semitropical airs of the river itself and the towns along the last phase going toward the gulf, a hundred miles inland perhaps.

The old seabed quality of that landscape speaks eloquently to this day, and it united the river to the sea in a marvelously intimate way for me, too. So I had these wonderful successive impressions that I wanted to make into a coherent flow, both physically and historically, as I keep saying.

JL: Could you please describe to me the trip that you took with your good friend Ernst Bacon?

PH: What a delightful summer! Ernst Bacon, the composer, who I think is one of the great voices of music in my lifetime in this country—I think he's due, probably posthumously, for a marvelous recognition that has never come to him in sufficient degree in his lifetime. He's still living; we still are together at times. In Rochester in 1923, I went to the Eastman School of Music and Theater, where I spent three years, first as a singing musical student and then as a factotum of the theater staff under Ruben Mamoulian, the great director of stage and film. And Ernst Bacon came there as sort of a *répétiteur* of the newly formed opera company, the Rochester American Opera Company. We became fast friends there.

As a result, when the time came twenty or thirty years later to get into this book, we were still in close correspondence—[and it] turned out Ernst would like to go with me one summer, must have been the summer of '49 or '50, to look for the northernmost source of the Río Grande. There are three general sources: the northernmost, the west source through Creede and off the Continental Divide, and the third from the southwest of Wolf Creek and Wolf Creek Pass coming out of southwestern Colorado. The latter two were easily accessible to me, but the first one—the northernmost—was not in my grasp.

Luckily, Ernst Bacon was a great mountain climber. He had the aesthetics of the mountain in his spirit, in his whole soul. He joined me in a motor trip through Colorado that summer to look where we wanted to find the first northern waters of the river. We started out from Gunnison, Colorado, itself a magnificent spot with its Black Canyon. I think we came over Clear Creek Pass and started down through high alpine meadows. I remember a heavenly summer day. Ernst had a USGS [U.S. Geological Survey] map with him that he could interpret, which I couldn't. Knowing mountainhood, he could read what I couldn't both in the land features and on the paper of the map. It was a very dramatic instance when as I was driving, he was watching. I remember that he said, "Now take it easy, I think we're coming somewhere. We're getting close to something." So we began peering forward. Within half an hour, we came to a great pile of boulders. I remember it was to my left of the driver's seat from my car. He said, "Slow down." I said, "We're getting there. I think this is it." Adjacent to those boulders, we stopped and got out, and the north side of the boulders was dry, and the south side was wet with a spring that bubbled up from under these rocks into a little trough of streambed. And he said, "This is it." We followed it on foot a ways and saw it grow with little tributaries, tiny tributaries at first. We got back in the car and then paralleled it as closely as we could by driving.

We'd get out every now and then. Within five miles, we had a substantial stream and then a waterfall, considerable waterfall—not a Niagara, of course, but a plunge of water over a rocky thing. From then on it was a lusty stream. There we had the northernmost vein of water that came down and joined the center flow of the river that came from Creede and went through places like Del Norte, Monte Vista, Alamosa, those three towns. And then we came out into the great southern flats of Colorado, and there we were.

I'll tell you about Wolf Creek Pass, too. I saw the wolf of Wolf Creek Pass. I was driving alone on another trip in the wintertime, and I was coming down this time toward Durango over the Wolf Creek Pass, and I was going very slowly because I was watching terrain and so forth, recording optically. All of a sudden I saw this great gray blur rush out of the bushes by the side of the road, begin biting, snapping at my tires. It was a great gray wolf, and I know it was Mr. Wolf of Wolf Creek Pass—it must have been. It was a lovely moment. So I gave him great respect and reverence and slowed down, of course, and watched as long as I could. But I heard his jaws snap—splendid.

JL: You spent a fair amount of time in Roswell.

PH: I returned from Rochester to the New Mexico Military Institute in Roswell in 1926 as librarian with a provision that the job would permit me to write. That's what I came home to do. I did have every morning at my disposal, provided this did not interrupt my duties to the school and to the library itself, which, I'm pleased to say, was built up quite considerably during my tenure [of] sixteen or eighteen years until I went in the army in '42. There were interesting faculty colleagues, but my main concerns and friendships in those days were the Peter Hurds. Peter and I had been cadets together in the school, and then he went to West Point, and I diverged later to Rochester, but we remained great friends. When he married Henriette Wyeth, N. C. Wyeth's daughter, they settled first at Chadds Ford [Pennsylvania] with their family, and I would go there to visit them, and then they moved to New Mexico, and then we were adjacent and incessantly together.

JL: Returning to *Great River*, can you give a sense of your impressions of the antiquity of the Puebloans who settled along the Río Grande?

PH: That's very difficult for me because I have very little competence in anthropology or archaeology.

JL: I'm thinking more of your sensitivities than [of] your intellect.

PH: It's impossible to see, even in the modern context, the Pueblo civilization without feeling the immensity and depth of its roots. Prehistoric, yes, to be sure, but even deeper than we usually mean by that, I think. You have a sense, you know, really of the Asian migration almost just [by] seeing the [Puebloans'] faces and feeling the impassivity that's generally exposed to visitors. I never have had any intimate contact at all with any Indians. I don't know that I'd have the gift for it. But their ordinary dignity and reserve had so evidently a deep inheritance that I always felt, as I encountered them in my travels and my pauses at various pueblos in order to make notes for the river book, really transported in a quite different world—in fact, so alien almost that it was a little unsettling.

I remember very well going up twice to the pueblo of Acoma before it became so easily accessible by motor road, which is an absurd thing. But while I was up on the mesa, I always felt slightly a sense of shivering apprehensiveness to be so removed from my Earth connections way below the cliffs and [of] their occupancy of this flat[ness] in the sky, quite removed from any experience that I could relate to. But [I] also [felt] deeply, deeply impressed by the completeness and the harmony of the village, the great church of San Estevan there—a wholly different kind of life. But I wasn't easy till I got on the ground.

JL: Something I've noted with different Indian peoples in the Southwest is that it becomes apparent after a while in conversation, after a period of time, that the thought processes function apparently differently between people from our [non-Native] continuum and people from the Puebloan continuum or the Athabascan continuum. And I'd like to relate something that was brought out in a conversation with my close friend, historian Alvin Josephy, that when the first migrations came across what was then the Bering landmass, Neanderthal people were still extant in the other hemisphere, which is something I'd never considered.

PH: Amazing. That is an amazing juxtaposition in time. That really explains something of what I was feeling. I don't know—some very dim apprehensiveness.

JL: I've always sensed among the Puebloans and the Navajo people and other Athabascans that there is a different way of perceiving reality. It's more of an integrated thing than the linear way in which we've been taught to perceive, and this is something that I've been curious about for a long, long time.

PH: I have an anecdote of Acoma if I can tell it. One time I was there when the houses were being replastered. I went and made my due to the authority, the governor's house, and the governor himself, a middle-aged Indian, very impressive man, decided to escort me around the place. It wasn't quite cozy, I won't say that, but it was more comfortable than I had been before in my trips there. The place had a great fascination for me always. And at one point we came to the point where one of the trails, the one used by the burros, came up and down to the top of the mesa, and a procession of burros was going by with their basket panniers to go down, the train of them, to pick up more earth for the plastering of the houses or the church, whatever they were doing. And the very last burro, a particularly small one at the end of this line of animals, had on its rump the most enchanting little boy, oh, four or five, six years old, riding the animal. And I exclaimed, I said to the governor, "What a beautiful little fellow that is!" And he said, "Yes, it's my son."

Well, I had known before I came there that day that there was great contention between Acoma and Laguna over a land claim, and it had been, if not resolved, [then] at least [settled in that] the inclination . . . on the part the commissioner, who was Mr. John Collier, [was] to award the rights to Laguna. This bears on the outcome of the anecdote because I said, "And also it's a very fine burro he's riding." And the governor said, "Yes. Do you know what the burro's name is?" I said, "No." He said, "Commissioner. Stubborn animal."

JL: That's wonderful. Have you spent any time at all on the Taos Pueblo?

PH: No, I haven't. I've seen it. I somehow don't have much interest in Taos. I think it's probably a fastidious revulsion on my part to the atmosphere of Mabel Dodge Lujan and all the chi-chi that was connected with that and the false Bohemianism and her tyranny over her particular wing of the intellectual life up there. So I never was drawn there. I've been through it off and on, but that's all.

JL: Who did you regard as your friends among the literary people of New Mexico when you lived there?

PH: Well, certainly Mr. Witter Bynner. To a lesser degree I knew Haniel Long. Phillip Stevenson, a novelist who lived in Santa Fe until he defected to California and the movies and also to the Communists. Winfield Scott, a great friend whom I respected largely. Oliver La Farge I would see occasionally and was very fond of. Very early, one of the first poets I ever knew in my life was a man named Maurice Lieseman, who had a charming talent. It didn't flower very greatly in later years, but he was a protégé of Alice Corbin Henderson, who was extremely generous to me in my formative times. Who else? Names throng and disappear. I never felt identified with the Santa Fe group of literary people in the sense of belonging to a colony. I know there was that assumption that there was a literary and artistic colony there, but I've never been a colonial myself in such an environment. But I did have very fine individual friends who were creative people.

JL: I'd like to ask you to give your sense of Spanish colonization—
        how the Spaniards actually became an isolated cultural milieu
        of their very own in northern New Mexico—and to talk about
        any things of that nature that interest you with regard to
        Great River.

PH: Yes. Well, of course I had to begin with the vestiges that are
        visible in this century, and they're the obvious ones of nomen-
        clatures of natural features, styles of architecture, and habits of
        living—that kind of thing. But that's all superficial. I think I trace
        in the book, at least meant to, the immense powerful stream of
        colonization from Spain into Mexico and, after the tragedy of
        the Aztec Empire, the implantation of the European style and
        culture there, modified by the mestizo thing that came about
        naturally through mingling. Then the northward thrust toward
        New Mexico in exploration and of course of El Dorado. Still,
        the fealty was to the Crown and to the Church, as originally
        postulated by the entire enterprise from the king, the emperor,
        Charles V. Then, as the centuries went by, the diminishing rela-
        tionship not only between Spain and Mexico, but [between]
        Mexico and New Mexico, and therefore the river culture, the
        river being their main highway of communication and suste-
        nance. Until finally the energy began dying at the roots of the
        home empire, and the northernmost tendrils had to be self-suf-
        ficient and live according to what was available in this physically
        bleak, although visually glorious, country.

        Then came the necessary ingenuities of making do. In that
        act, they had to learn a great deal from those who had made do
        for centuries, meaning the Indians. So the intercultural details
        and energies and factors of how the final phase of the colony,
        the colonization, took place were really intercultural—accultur-
        ation both ways, but chiefly I think [with] more influence on
        the Spanish than [from] the Spanish onto the Pueblo, as far as
        I can tell as an amateur observer anthropologically. Much of
        the beauty of Spanish ritual, of course, became simplified and

rusty by distance, by severance of the great source of the original supply of form and style and energy. But what remained then became a native culture by its combination with local elements of the Indians and so forth—quite an original expression, but infinitely reduced in its range from the ideal that brought them there and [that] they brought with them. So what remains [of the Spanish], then, is—I dealt with all this in a chapter of *Great River* about the haciendas—their slow decline and their slow achievement of independence in all expressions, but a life kept alive along the northern river, both by the bounty of the land and [by] the river itself. And the deep reverence in the Hispanic nature for tradition, for ritual—as deep a reverence as the Indians had for the ways of the ancestors, but modified by reduced circumstances.

JL: One of the aspects of that particular chapter is their great distance from Durango, the location of the nearest archbishop.

PH: Yes.

JL: And you also addressed the presence of the Penitentes as the result of this great distance because there were so few padres who lived along the river. What I'm leading up to is to ask you to please describe your sense of Archbishop [Jean-Baptiste] Lamy because you wrote so eloquently about him in a later book.

PH: It's very hard to encapsulate a whole life and the great range of his career in a few statements. The striking aspect that most people light upon, of course, is the imposition of a French culture upon a Hispanic established way of life. It's now very fashionable to present this because there's a great cult, and a respectable one, for the native Mexican American tradition, and people felt that he corrupted that by his importations of his own culture, which was the most natural thing for him to do. All governing powers always bring with them their styles, and, of course, he did so, too, in the best of faith. He found, as we all know, a church corrupt in its local applications, which offended his deep piety and his deep conviction of faith and his also deeply ingrained feeling for discipline, and he set to work to put things right as he saw the right, and I believe succeeded largely.

But I think what really most importantly survives of his time and of his reign as archbishop is the beauty and simplicity and strength of his own nature. He simply happened to be a man of deep quality, deep simplicity, coming from peasant stock in France in the Auvergne. I could find no evidence of pretentiousness about him in any way, nor, hard as I searched in my study of his life and relationships, could I find anything adverse about him. I thought that no biography could possibly be respectable unless you had lights and darks about the central figure, and I searched and searched for darks—couldn't find any. How to make a book of any interest about what would seem, then, a one-dimensional person was difficult. But his sheer accomplishments spoke so truly of his nature to me that all the personal evidences of his life and his performance supported my impression of his great goodness, his selflessness, his infinite courage in dealing with a frail physical body in the most merciless hardship in performance of his duties over this immense tract where he presided. His diocese was bigger than all of France.

So I came out with a sense that his very being there was a blessing for the whole area. He brought the benefits of the best parts of civilization, I think, to a world that was trapped in isolation and primitiveness in cultural ways. These he opened up with institutions of charity and of learning and of spiritual solace through the church. I don't mean to make him a paragon, but I [found] almost a faultless performance of duty all through his life. My book ends with a quotation I found in the little parish from which he sprang in the peasant district of France where he came from, which said that his death was the end of a fine day, and that's just how I felt about him.

JL: His apparent difficulties with Padre [Antonio José] Martínez of Taos set a true historic system of parameters that are still felt in northern New Mexico. Is there any aspect of that particular difficulty that you would feel comfortable addressing?

PH: Well, I think he did to Martínez what had to be done in the way of discipline, and Martínez openly defied him, vilified him, mocked him. The documents that I got in Rome clearly indicate it, and they're all noted and cited in my book. I know that there's now a modern movement to rehabilitate Martínez at the expense of Lamy. I don't deny the gifts that Martínez had. He was before his time, a pioneer in learning and in social enlightenment, to a degree. A very original character. But he clearly went beyond the bounds of permissible behavior in his defiance of the archbishop and his attempt to create an offshoot, an independent church of his own in Taos—which I don't think that Lamy could be expected to accept.

JL: Do you feel there was much jealousy there?

PH: I never thought of it as such. It may have been. He was a man, obviously, of immense ego, Martínez. But he probably was jealous of his independence, which was invaded by the arrival of the bishop. Nobody ever thought to discipline him before or thought any reason for it. But there was a cabal against Lamy by certain clergy of the time, and it was probably a very natural antagonism. But I think the modern attempt to build up Martínez as a hero of independence, [of] integrity, is misbegotten.

JL: This is a bit of an aside, but it certainly relates to this particular situation. Do you think that history is sometimes modified within the present to accommodate people who may have been villainous at one time?

PH: Yes, definitely. It's a very sound observation, I think. It's very, very often the case, I think, in history and its branch, biography, that the past is judged and seen in terms of current values, contemporary values of the historian, whereas it seems that the only way to revive the past is to give it in the context of its own time.

Let the judgment come from the reader—that's how I proceeded always. I've been greatly criticized at times for my seeming championing of the greater power, as Indian against Spaniard, so and so. It isn't lack of sympathy. It's simply how things happened. I could be among the first to champion civil liberties of anyone oppressed, but that wasn't the feeling at the time, and the feeling at the time was what I was trying to capture. That's my whole purpose as a narrator, both in history and in fiction. So I think your remark is well taken, that the shibboleths of our intellectual climate are often applied to and in judgment of periods and events that could possibly have no relation to [those shibboleths] in the past.

There's now a resurgence of feeling of the Hispanic community in New Mexico, as far as I can tell from here, toward a renewal of their identity and their self-feeling and their self-respect, all of which is perfectly worthy.

JL: Please talk about the coming of the Anglo and the array of relationships that existed or came to exist between the Anglo and the Indian and [between] the Anglo and the Hispano, and how all cultures finally resulted in a meld in juxtaposition, so to speak.

PH: Yes, that's an enormously rich thing. Of course, the very first motive was commercial, the coming of the Anglos. And though a not wholly ignoble motive, it certainly was a selfish one. Therefore, something of that emotional commitment to a purpose had enduring effect on all relationships that resulted between the occupants—namely, the Indians and the Hispanos and the incoming Yankees, Anglos. I know that superior judgments were almost invariably rendered upon the inhabitants by those who came—for instance, Josiah Gregg, of whom I've written and who was himself a very interesting and useful, admirable person. Still, [he] and others who came to Santa Fe early saw what they [considered] a squalid society. Well, [that other society] was different and it was simple and it was primitive, but it had its qualities of goodness and integrity, but it was alien.

But it was the enormous power of the commercial interests—the mercantile interests that were the first to invade New Mexico and get established—that got the upper hand very fast because of their superior economic weight. And that endured—I suppose it still does—in numbers.

I know that when we moved to Albuquerque and we had our first encounters with the local Mexican American population, [this attitude] was always given to us among acquaintances of our kind, always given to us as a comic superiority that we had over the Natives. And I wasn't exactly a crusader, but I felt at the time that I had a curious, subcutaneous almost, sense that this was unjust and not very nice. It wasn't till later that I consciously saw that it was a very poor relationship and that there was one section of the population subjugated by the other on economic terms and denial of opportunity within that framework of economy. And I'm sure that that survives today, and it's one of the reasons, probably, why the present upsurge of the Hispanic identity has such energy, such vitality, trying to adjust this imbalance.

JL: Right now as we speak, in 1987, the human situation in New Mexico goes through permutation after permutation. Many more people are going there to live. I would like to ask you your thoughts with regard to the preservation of the environment of the Southwest, bearing in mind that we live in a time when the human species is overpopulating enormously.

PH: I'm sorry to say I'm a little pessimistic because the vast Sunbelt, as it's called, of which New Mexico and the Southwest are a great part, has such attractions that you can't conceive of denying them to anyone who really wants to reach for them. But in reaching for them in vast numbers and in ruthless conversions ecologically, to the expense of the natural environment, [the newcomers] wreak more harm than they derive pleasure—I think, I don't know, not having been there in many years, eight or nine years, I think, now. But I deeply regret that there's not much to be done about it because the huge multitude that is invading these areas, all in search of the same thing—a better life, a more comfortable life, a more aesthetically rewarding life in the countryside—these things have their merit, have their virtue, and yet the result, if you look at it dispassionately, is almost always ugly in a vast array of expressions: in modes of living, in architecture, in technological invasion of privacy, in conversion of deserts into profitable industry.

All these forces are so huge and they're so generally prevalent around the world—not just in the Sunbelt, but everywhere—that it seems to me that they're irresistible in the end. And I think we must address the immense danger of depletion of available water at the eventual expense of entire areas of civil living. This is going to be a major environmental tragedy, and nobody's paying sufficient attention. A few devoted people are; maybe a few bureaucrats and bureaucratic institutions are aware. But the problem is as huge as that of a world war, almost, in terms of survival, and nobody's meeting it in those dimensions, just as nobody is meeting the seem-to-be self-evident necessity of repealing nuclear power in every form lest it do us in forever. These are such vast considerations that when I think of the changes of the Southwest, which is a beloved area in my life for me, they seem relatively minor, but I think they're subject to the same disinclination to look to tomorrow and tomorrow and tomorrow.

And what can be done about it? Only an enlightened civil message coming from what quarter I couldn't possibly predict. I don't know. If there were no foreign crisis and if the economy were in retrieval, I would think that a man of the caliber and character of Franklin Roosevelt perceiving the problem could take immense action and start things rolling. I think it has to come from the very top, and I fail to see any candidate for this beautiful mission anywhere now. There may be one lurking somewhere beyond my ken, but it is that nature of political responsibility combined with cosmic imagination that's got to act and do something on a scale that will meet head on these most threatening forces. This is in the large and general way the picture of what I think is happening in lesser scale to the Sunbelt and the Southwest itself.

Keith Basso, photo by author

Keith Basso

Introduction

Keith Basso studied anthropology with Clyde Kluckhohn at Harvard University, graduating in 1962. He received his Ph.D. from Stanford University and has served on the faculty of the anthropology departments at the University of Arizona, Yale University, and the University of New Mexico.

Basso began his work with the Western Apaches around Cibecue, Arizona, when he was a Harvard undergraduate. He learned their language and over the course of many years came to understand many aspects of their culture.

Keith Basso is the author of many books and articles. One of his best-known books, *Wisdom Sits in Places*, published in 1996 by the University of New Mexico Press, won the Western States Book Award for Creative Nonfiction that year. Basso is also a rancher whose "spread" is located near the homelands of the Western Apaches in Arizona.

In this interview conducted in 2006, Basso reveals a great deal about the relationship of the Western Apaches to their home habitat and the importance of language to cultural continuity.

Keith Basso

JL: I'd like to ask you to talk about where you where born and what wove the tapestry that underlies you in your career.

KB: I was born in rural North Carolina. My father was an author. I moved from North Carolina to Massachusetts and then, after a short time, from there to Connecticut, which is where I went to school. My undergraduate degree is from Harvard, and it was a course with a Harvard professor named Clyde Kluckhohn, an anthropologist who'd spent a lot of time working with the Navajo, that really interested me in anthropology and indigenous peoples of the Southwest. It was also Kluckhohn who arranged for me, as a sophomore, to go to Arizona on my own and spend a summer in what was then a very isolated Western Apache community called Cibecue, where practically everyone spoke Apache [and] where I understood very little but had an absolutely marvelous time. And it was that experience that persuaded me to continue, as an undergraduate, studying anthropology. I then got a fellowship and spent a kind of insignificant year at the Institute for Aboriginal Studies in Australia, came back to this country, went to Stanford for a Ph.D.—all the while spending as much time as possible on the White Mountain Apache reservation and slowly picking up more and more of the language.

As you can tell from *Wisdom Sits in Places*, mine is a very language-oriented conception of ethnography and cultural description. I bend over backwards to try not to impose my own ideas or models upon indigenous people, simply because they're irrelevant, basically, and don't apply. And I think the best way to overcome that is through a careful study of the language because it embodies the conceptual apparatus that they draw upon to make sense of what happens in the world.

JL: Your book reflects how you've let the Apache people speak for themselves, but you do offer some really interesting wonderful narrative that helps put things into a bigger perspective.

Early on in the book I really got involved in thinking about the way you perceive their sense of place making. Could you talk about that, please?

KB: Sure. I draw a distinction between *site* and *place*—site being the physical thing itself. You can photograph a site, you can walk on a site. Sometimes a site will have a distinctive smell. Sites are material. Sites are substantial. In contrast, places are sites that have been invested with meaning. You can't photograph meaning. You can't taste it or touch it. It's immaterial. But it is the source from which the significance of places necessarily comes. So the ethnographer's task is to try to discover what sorts of meanings people attach to different sites in their landscape. What this does, of course, is throw the whole exercise into the area or areas of how meanings get expressed.

Language is a primary vehicle for that [expression]. But it's perfectly clear that the meanings that inform and animate places can be expressed in musical form, in ritual form, in a variety of forms. So whereas I tend to stay fairly closely, at least in *Wisdom Sits in Places*, to what Apaches actually have to say, I wouldn't for a minute preclude or underestimate the way in which they invest places with meaning in songs, in ceremonial performances, and the like. But for me that site/place distinction is conceptually necessary and very basic.

JL: It might be a good idea to try to characterize the habitat of the White Mountain Apache, what it looks like as far as the geophysical and biological characteristics are concerned.

KB: As you know, I've spent most of my time working in a small community in the rugged western region of the White Mountain Apache reservation called Cibecue. In Apache, that's *deschibi-koh* [approx. sp.]. It means "long red bluffs as seen from above." The reason for that [description] is [that] the stream flows through the long red bluffs that lie parallel on both sides of the stream, and many of the dwellings that Apaches have constructed are on top of the bluffs, so you see them best [by] looking down from that elevation. The general environment is wooded. It's at approximately fifty-five hundred feet. There's lots of piñon. In the higher elevations, there's ponderosa pine. It's broken country in the sense that there are lots of draws and washes and box canyons. It's quite impressive—not only visually, but because the population of Apache at Cibecue is only about twelve hundred people. The country surrounding the village, which goes on for miles, is absolutely uninhabited. So there's plenty of wildlife, and it hasn't been messed with much. They've cut some logging roads to some of the timber in the higher elevations, but that's about all.

JL: Can you talk about how the White Mountain Apaches are differentiated from the rest of the Athabascans who came there? Do you have any sense of that?

KB: Well, nobody's quite sure. The standard theory is that the proto-Athabascans, or the ancestral group from which all of the differentiated Athabascans that we know today came from, crossed the Bering [landmass] and trickled down from the northwest coast along the Rockies until they finally make it to the Southwest. All of the Athabascan speakers—which include Navajo, Western Apache, Chiricahua Apache, Mescalero Apache, Jicarilla Apache, and Kiowa Apache—speak deep dialects of the same language. The adjective [*deep*] is useful because some of these dialects are not readily intelligible to those who speak another dialect. But linguists can show with no difficulty whatsoever that, both with respect to the sound system of these languages and the grammatical structure of the languages, there are a host of similarities. So we know or hypothesize that [these groups] had to have at one point split off from an original group of Athabascan speakers, and as they became geographically separated, [they] developed the differences in speech that distinguish them today.

JL: Is there any sense of when they did finally land in the Southwest?

KB: Well, it's controversial. And to tell you the truth, this is an issue that's almost constantly being debated. I can consult my archaeological colleagues for the very latest on this, but I really couldn't tell you. Probably five thousand years ago—maybe less. Maybe a lot less. One of the things that makes it difficult in the Athabascan case to reconstruct their prehistory is that these people always treaded lightly on the land. They left very few prehistoric remains. They didn't build pueblos. They didn't farm extensively. They lived in relatively small groups that were apparently almost constantly on the move, and they made very little pottery. So all of those wonderful things that have allowed archaeologists to reconstruct with some precision the prehistory of the Puebloan groups, let's say, are not available where the Athabascans are concerned. So a lot of guesswork is involved.

JL: Is there any place that you can talk about where they might have begun to culturally differentiate?

KB: No. It's impossible to do. It's highly unlikely that a group of Athabascan speakers made it to the Southwest and from a single spot split into groups. It's more likely that small groups over a period of years, perhaps as long as a century, came successively down from the north, found places that were already occupied by Athabascan speakers, decided not to live with them, and struck out on their own. For reasons I've tried to suggest, it's extremely difficult to gauge when those waves of people might have come into what is now Arizona and New Mexico.

JL: You talk about how the Apaches conceive of their past, and the phrase *well-worn trail* comes in. Could you talk a little about that?

KB: "Tracks" is the metaphor they use primarily. In its fullest sense, anything that seems to have something to say about former times can be described as a "track," for the obvious reason that whatever made it is gone. They refer to places where they know particular events have occurred as a kind of track. They speak of traditional narratives that describe the origin of the world and what took place after Apache people had established themselves within it as "tracks." A letter you got a month ago from a child, let's say, who's off at boarding school can be referred to as a track. "Trail" also is one of those metaphors that gets frequent use to describe the history of the people. They don't have a word for history. They do have a word for the past, and I think that's significant because for us, you and me, [the word] *history* conjures up an academic discipline governed by particular kinds of procedures and located largely in documentary archives—at least that's where the basic material is that historians work on.

Apaches, when they speak of the past, don't have that sort of thing in mind. So "trails," one could say, in their terms, represent ways of understanding the past and ways of representing it, which is somewhat different from our own academized notion of history.

JL: Can you describe what you would imagine as to how the Western Apache conceive of their landscape?

KB: Yeah, I think I can do that. Probably the best place to begin is to note that unlike other indigenous tribes, most Western Apache people continue to occupy lands that were theirs from the very beginning. They have not been displaced. They have not been relocated. So there is this profoundly deep tie that they feel between the landscape today and the landscape as it likely was at the beginning of their life as a group. They don't pay much attention [to] this migration from the north business. As far as most Apaches are concerned, they originated on portions of what are today the White Mountain and San Carlos Apache reservations. They have great respect for the land and everything upon it, ranging from the smallest insects to the winds that come and go. And at different places in this landscape, there are sacred sites, at which particularly important events are understood to have taken place in the past. I'm not at liberty to mention either the names of those sites or to describe what took place at them.

Wisdom Sits in Places contains a number of place-names, and, to be sure, the places to which those names refer are important in the minds of these people. But none of those are sacred sites.

During the map work that produced or led to *Wisdom Sits in Places*, we visited a number of sacred sites. But their location was not pinpointed on the maps. Their names, though recorded, have been kept in a single file that is the property of the White Mountain Apache tribe, and the narratives that were told about the sacred events that took place at these locations—those, too, are under restricted lock and key, as [they] should be.

The chairman of the tribe, Ronnie Lupe, decided along with the tribal council that they should not identify the location of sacred sites because non-Indians and, interestingly, some Indians themselves would not know how to behave at these places. And at certain times of the year, the reservation is open to fishermen and hikers and tourists, basically. It was feared that if these people ever got copies of maps that showed the location of sacred sites, they would, by the very way in which they acted, fail to display the respect required of these places. That's one of the reasons—a very practical one—why [the chairman and the council] didn't want this information made public.

JL: That brings up something that's of great interest to me. I made up a term, *geomythic mapping*. Having worked with so many different tribes—not nearly as deeply as you have with the Apaches— but having worked as much as seven or eight months at a crack with different groups of people throughout the American West and Mexico, [I noticed that] one of the things that's quite apparent is that these sacred sites exist within every cultural perspective. And that to me is the definition of the difference between the way traditional people, indigenous people, see themselves in relation to landscape and the way, say, American or global culture is presently perceiving itself.

For example, there's a site up in Nez Percé country that the Indians wanted me to mention on the radio, so I did—to try to convey the sense of the sacred quality of it. But it's that intuitive difference between perspectives. That's maybe the wrong term, but I try to think of it as the mythic lens that lends itself to a different kind of perspective than we currently have and that leads to a different kind of respect for landscape than we currently have. Does this make any sense to you at all?

KB: Yeah. I think in broad strokes I would agree with that. It's arguable, I think, that perhaps what you've said is a bit too general because I can imagine Israelis having sacred sites, Palestinian Arabs having sacred sites. So I think the idea that all forms of global culture lack sacred sites—maybe you weren't implying that, but I thought you were—I think that's a little premature and hasty. One could even stretch the notion of sacred site, for example, and say that for people living in the United States, where Washington crossed the Delaware [is] some kind of near-sacred site. It's been preserved. There are monuments there. What about the battlefields at Shiloh and Gettysburg? They're not mythic in the sense of being ancient, but they are mythic in having become focal points for turning points of American history.

So like all of these terms, *sacred* can be a slippery adjective, and the ethnographic trick is to try to determine what "they" take sacred to mean. Would a dyed-in-the-wool Confederate-oriented southerner consider the battlefields at Shiloh and Gettysburg sacred sites? That would require some work to find out. Lincoln said they were hallowed ground. That's pretty close. The Apache term [for "sacred"] is *di-YIH* or *godi-YIH* [approx. sp.]. And what's required is nothing more or less than serious work at what linguists call lexical semantics. I mean, I can't determine on the basis of my knowledge or on the basis of English what *godi-YIH* means to these people when they use that term. I've got to sit down with them and discover what they mean when they use that term.

So I guess I'm sounding a quiet note of caution, which I think is useful.

JL: I concur. I was at a western history conference recently and read a paper called "In Celebration of Land Forms," and I tried to point out that within the context of Hebraic tradition, a volcano that is located in eastern Turkey known as Mount Ararat is a sacred site. But that's in the mythic context of *sacred*, whereas the stories in *Wisdom Sits in Places* basically deal with things that could be thought of as historically relevant within the context of Apache historic recollection.

KB: Yeah. There's also a sense, though, in which I think those stories that appear in *Wisdom Sits in Places* and others that might have been included in that book are timeless. They're understood to have taken place in the past, but they're used to address fully contemporary issues and problems. They're kept alive by their relevance, their continuing relevance, to contemporary lives. So in a sense, though ostensibly rooted in the past, they're very modern and in that sense timeless.

JL: What I was trying to convey earlier—and this has been my experience with a lot of especially more traditional indigenous people—is that they don't perceive time in quite the same way as people who are trained in our [non-Indian] culture perceive. To me, they have within their realm a sort of a spirit reference that is pretty timeless. In other words, recording geomythic mapping songs—as I recently did down in Seri Indian country—[shows that] these songs are "now," but they've also been "now forever."

KB: That's a good phrase: "now forever."

JL: I want to allude now to an essay by Garrett Hardin.

KB: He's a good author.

JL: He was. At one point, he wrote an essay entitled "An Ecolate View of the Human Predicament." In that essay, he talked about a way of thinking from within a sphere of reference and [about] how by looking at various relationships between associated notions and clusters of data, one may attempt to extrapolate future possibilities and probabilities. I was thinking about how many of my Native American friends really do that naturally, seeing themselves as part of their traditional homeland and bringing their cultural and individual points of view to bear on problems.

KB: Hm. This is part of the deep tie that I was talking about earlier. Extracting future probabilities is trickier, it seems to me, at least in the Apache case, because there are only a few individuals—so-called medicine men or medicine women—they're called *diyin* or *diyinneh* [approx. sp.], from the term I mentioned before for "holy" or "sacred," *godi-YIH*. These people are trained or at least have cultivated the skills necessary to anticipate future events, but the vast majority of Apaches would not lay claim to those kinds of skills and abilities. So to characterize an entire point of view or an entire worldview as somehow containing what's necessary to anticipate future events, it seems to me again, is a little broad and misleading. Certain individuals can certainly do this and have done it and are teaching younger people to do it, but [they're] a small, small portion of the population.

JL: What I'm trying to get to is that it's sort of a combination of the intuitive realm and the intellectual realm struggling with the overlay of Western culture. Let me try to think of an example here. Many years ago, in 1970, a group of Hopi people asked me if I'd help them to try to stop what was happening up on Black Mesa—the extraction of coal. They took me into the kiva, and they told me all of these stories. They really tried to allow me into their sense of cultural perspective. Then they asked me to take that sense of perspective and from within my own totally different perspective try to get across to the powers that be—

KB: Translate one perspective into another.

JL: And that's where I thought about the whole notion of extrapo-lating future probabilities with regard to the fate or destiny of Black Mesa. So, [what was happening there] to me represented a complete and total model of what NOT to do because not only did the strip-mining of Black Mesa affect the aquifer below, [but] it marred their sacred landscape as a result of what my wife calls the march of the electric kachinas and the coal-bearing railroad. It resulted in major air pollution from the new massive electrical generation station constructed near Lake Powell, and it also had a huge effect on both Hopi and Navajo cultures all at the same time.

KB: Yeah, I'm aware.

JL: So it affected culture and place as well as the landscape itself, and all of those things were borne out over the past thirty-five years. The name of your book, *Wisdom Sits in Places*, is brilliant because, indeed, the sense of wisdom sitting in places conveys a point of view that is not complete within, say, the economics-dominated paradigm that currently prevails in America.

KB: I would agree a hundred percent with that, yeah. I don't think the vast majority of people in this country use places as moral reference points, [whereas] certainly that is true among the Apache and, I have very good reason to believe as you do, among other tribes as well. It's as if major moral tenets—perhaps one would want to say "major moral themes" that undergird these cultures and sustain them—are actually embedded, physically embedded, in these places. So if you're driving along or more likely riding a horse and see that mesa over there and begin to remember or recall what actually took place over there, that informs your whole view or can inform your whole view of how to deal with people, how to deal with animals, how to think about water, how to think about the heavens, et cetera. And that kind of moral embeddedness is not, I think, an attribute of most landscapes as perceived by non-Indian American people.

JL: That's well put. Could you talk about how landscape and language coalesce in Apache culture there?

KB: That's sort of how I began. I don't think you can grasp even provisionally, even roughly, how they perceive and understand the natural environment unless you make a serious effort to acquire the vocabulary to talk about it. I'll give you one singular example of this. I knew a man who's no longer with us, an Apache man, who in his vocabulary had thirty-eight terms for categories of clouds. He was one of the last people—and I'll just translate into English—who could, as we might say, "read the heavens in order to ascertain the likelihood of future events." But compare this with your own cloud vocabulary. You may have *cumulus*, you may have *cirrus*, or like most of us you'll fall back on complete sentences like "That big black one over there over the eastern ridge." The point I'm trying to make is our conceptual resources for distinguishing between different kinds of clouds is radically impoverished compared to what this fellow understood.

The distinctions he drew were based on the intersection of a variety of features, like how fast a cloud formation might be moving, how high or close to the horizon it was, its color (basically very white, white, gray, dark gray, and black), whether or not the clouds were accompanied by other meteorological phenomena such as rain, lightning, thunder. All of these dimensions intersected to define thirty-eight separate categories of clouds. It stands to reason to me, as I think it would to anyone who'd like to exercise common sense, that if you wanted to understand or try to understand, even provisionally, even roughly, how Apache people understand the heavens, how they see the sky, the only reasonable way to go about that is to find out what all of these terms mean. What sorts of categories do they define? Then you're on your way because you've left your own cumuluses and cirruses behind, and you've made a serious effort to conduct whatever further inquiry you might wish to conduct on their own terms.

Now to your general point. You can do this with land forms. There are vocabularies for land forms. You can do it with rocks, rock formations. You can do it with different forms of water sources. Sometimes the English categories seem to me to be virtually identical with the Apache categories. They have a term *tundli,* which means "spring" [source of water]. Their notions of "spring" or "springs" correspond, as far as I can tell, exactly to our own, but that's not the case with rock formations, for example, in which once again the distinctions they make are based upon different attributes of the rock than those that you and I might use. At the most rudimentary level, I find it impossible to imagine any other way of trying to grasp indigenous conceptions of the natural environment except through studying the language resources with which they not only talk about it, but begin teaching the kids as soon as they're able to begin to understand spoken language. It's not just the indigenous environment that these kids grow up with—it's a language for describing and understanding what happens in that environment that they grow up with as well. So the two are, if you will, conjoined or intimately related from the time of linguistic awareness to the end of life itself.

JL: That just sums it up beautifully. Is there anything that you would like to talk about that we haven't addressed that you think would be relevant to this particular conversation?

KB: Oh, I don't know. This is one of those topics that reaches out in all directions at once, and we could sit here for another two hours and probably not bore each other. But given the questions that you've posed, they've all been very interesting because each can be answered in fairly specific terms, but at the same time has general implications. I like questions that work in those two directions at once. [I'm] a rancher and former cowboy, [so] fences interest me a lot, and at some point it would be interesting, given the title of your project [Between Fences], to try to imagine—which I'm not prepared to do at the moment—how very few fences there are in Apache country, and I'm quite sure that with a little bit of ethnography we could begin to understand that they think about fences in ways at least different from ranchers and cowboys. Other than that, I can't think of anything that we've radically missed.

Enrique Lamadrid, photo by author

Enrique Lamadrid

Introduction

In 1983, I was invited to show a film that my friend Jack Parsons and I had produced about Hispano folk music and musicians of el Río Grande del Norte. I reseated myself after the showing. On the other side of the table sat a curly-headed gent with the kindest countenance imaginable. He introduced himself as Enrique Lamadrid, and thus began a deep and abiding friendship that has resulted in many collaborative efforts and myriad hardcore adventures down wilderness rivers. In those early days, Enrique was a professor at Northern New Mexico Community College. Today he is the chairman of the Chicano-Mexicano-Hispano Studies Program at the University of New Mexico and one of America's top folk-lorists. He is also the greatest camp chef I have ever known.

Enrique and I have traveled most of the Camino Real de Tierra Adentro, the Royal Road to the Interior, which is probably the oldest road of European provenance in North America. It follows along the base of the eastern aspect of the Continental Divide from Mexico City to the San Juan Pueblo thirty miles north of Santa Fe, New Mexico. It was in 1598 that Juan de Oñate either forged or followed trails that wound into the Camino Real and, in April of that year, claimed the country along the Río Grande north of present-day El Paso, Texas, in the name of the Spanish monarch. For centuries, New Mexico was a Spanish colony and for a brief period in the nineteenth century was part of Mexico. The boundaries of New Mexico originally included most of the Southwest. Today, though greatly reduced from its original size, New Mexico is still the fifth-largest state in the United States of America.

Enrique Lamadrid is one of the foremost scholars of both the history and lore of the entire region. His knowledge concerning encounters between Spanish colonists and indigenous peoples is enormous, and he has documented much of this history and lore through music. His book *Hermanitos Comanchitos: Indo-Hispano Rituals of Captivity and Redemption* (2003) is a modern classic.

In the interview, Enrique conveys a powerful sense of *encuentro* and *mestizaje* through the centuries of human history of the southern regions near the Continental Divide.

Enrique Lamadrid

JL: I'd like to ask you to give an historic sketch of your perceptions of el Camino Real de Tierra Adentro, the Royal Road to the Interior.

EL: Considering the Camino Real, one of the great thoughts is that here is a route that no one has the right to block. In being a royal road, it is a road that is protected by the king of Spain. The king makes a commitment to free commerce, to free travel, to unimpeded flow of culture. Of course, that is not exactly accurate either, because you had to have permission to travel. But the idea of the Camino Real is that there is a route that the Crown has promised to protect to keep open. It is not like someone can come and start charging a toll. It is not like someone can block it in any way. You had to have permission to travel, but the fact that it was a Camino Real guaranteed this rite of passage, guaranteed this flow of commerce, of culture, of travelers, of government, of everything that is involved with culture in a civilization.

In the *coloquios* and the gatherings of academic scholars and community scholars over the past few years, there is a lot of discussion of, What is officially "el Camino Real"? And the answer is basically that it goes from regional center to regional center. From capital to capital, if you will. Say, from Chihuahua to Santa Fe. And there is a debate. Is it a *camino real* in the part that goes to Taos? Well, Taos isn't the capital. There is certainly a route. There is certainly a road. But the king's resources were limited. And he couldn't guarantee every road. The Camino Real itself was certainly guaranteed and that there would be military protection, even though budgets were tight—this is one of the expectations of the Camino Real itself. So scholars will quibble about, "Is this section in it? Is that section in it?" And of course what we are talking about is a braid of routes. It is not one single road. It is a true braid of roads, of alternate routes, depending on what is going on in the valley that you are going through. If there is a river there, if one route is muddy, you go around it.

Some of the major destinations on the route have to do with things like where the salt is. If you are moving large quantities of animals, it is not just water. People think of water first. And of course that is the obvious. But one of the factors that maybe is not so obvious is the need of salt for the animals and the people. And so you will see the road taking swings in certain directions for reasons besides water. And one of those big reasons is of course salt.

JL: Could you talk about the significance of the Mexican town of Valle de Allende in Chihuahua, Mexico?

EL: Valle de Allende is an amazing little community. I learned recently that it was pretty well razed by one of the divisions of the French army of Napoleon III that went through there. They got mad at the people in Valle de Allende, and they pretty much burned down the town. But one of the surviving buildings there is quite interesting. It is the old *aduana*, the old customs house. Valle de Allende was the port of entry for New Mexico. To come to New Mexico, you had to have permission to come to New Mexico. Not everybody could come up the Camino from central Chihuahua. If you were going to come up, you had to be married. If you weren't bringing your family, you still had to be married. They didn't want certain kinds of disturbances to take place. If you let a bunch of unmarried men in an area, they are going to have a good time. And who are the women in New Mexico? There are Indian women here, and they were thinking of all of those things. And so, not only did they check your civil status and your traveling papers, they actually did a health check as well. They didn't want any sick people traveling, obviously. So a lot of things happened at that aduana. That is where you would check in the livestock that you were bringing down from the north or the livestock that you were taking up to the north. It is a very interesting little building right there on the Camino Real near the plaza in the beautiful town of Valle de Allende.

JL: Can you also address the notion of mestizaje?

EL: Sure. We recently looked at the very first founding documents of the Villa de Santa Cruz de la Cañada. On those documents, when people identify themselves, they say, "Nosotros los Mexicanos de la Villa Real de Santa Cruz de la Cañada." As the community gets established, about ten years later, you start seeing the term "Españoles Mexicanos." Mexico was still under the caste system until after the War of Independence with Spain. There are the famous paintings in Mexico City of all the dozens of possible combinations of different racial mixes. What happens if you have an Español and an Indian in a marriage? You get a mestizo. There are dozens of these caste terms. Some of them are quite humorous. There is a term for a really low caste called *salta patras*, which means "a big step backward." What that would mean is a person of color marrying a person of darker color, and their kids are headed down on the caste scale. So old caste terms include terms like *coyote*, which is still used in New Mexico. There are caste terms passed into English, terms like *octoroon*, or especially [the terms for] the different gradations of African European mixture, including *mulatto*, [which] actually comes from the word *mula*, or mule, the cross of a mare and a donkey. Clear through the nineteenth century, people believed that miscegenation would lead to a degeneration of the human being. And say, the mix of a white European and a black African was thought to be a highly degenerate human being, kind of like a mule. They might be useful for work, but they might not even be able to reproduce. Any geneticist can tell you that these kinds of mixtures are actually very positive. That mixing up of the gene pool actually results in some fine robust examples of humanity.

So people all along the Camino Real in colonial times were very aware of their civil status, and they tried to improve it any time they could. When a child was born, they would try to convince the priest writing down the race of the child in the record books to maybe put the word *mestizo* there. Maybe put a higher-caste term than the child really was. So these documents are very wishful in a lot of ways. You will see terms like *naturales* for the Indians or *vecinos*, kind of a code term for Spanish Mexicans. And of course, what complicates it even further is the fact that a lot of Tlascalan Indians came to New Mexico. By the eighteenth century, the Tlascaltecos, since they were allied with the Spanish in the conquest of Mexico, had a very privileged status after that. They could get land grants. They had the same rights as *conquistadores*. They had rights of conquest. And so, over the centuries, people would marry in there, and by the eighteenth century, you get some very mestizo Tlascalecans. They were much more than servants. They were colonizers just like the other colonizers. In fact, some of them were agricultural specialists, horticulturists. That was just one of their big trades. And in a lot of the colonizing expeditions, there were *maestros* Tlascaltecos sent along, just the way there would be a carpenter sent along, or a weaver. You want to get these horticulturists and these specialists along for the ride because they are going to improve the overall enterprise. So mestizaje . . . there is a great mixing of races and cultures in

Mexico. After the revolution, that is seen as a positive value. But when it comes down to state policy, there is really so little support for indigenous cultural programs in Mexico that mestizaje as a government policy works quite to the opposite. It works toward the oppression of indigenous culture and indigenous communities. So, in one sense, it is a very proud expression of the fact that Mexico is indeed a mixed-race nation, with strong Indian roots. But the governments haven't supported indigenous people very well over the years.

JL: What about the mestizaje along the Río Grande?

EL: The Españoles Mexicanos, as they call themselves, lived alongside the Indian pueblos, and the government encouraged the separation of the pueblos from the *placitas*—the placitas being the Spanish Mexican communities and the pueblos being the Indian communities. The courts really did support the land rights of the pueblos. There were special lawyers that protected the rights of Indian people. The Pueblo people used the courts frequently for things like encroachment upon their land, and the courts ruled in their favor all the time in comparison to the American [U.S.] period, in which Indians didn't really come into full citizenship rights until 1948, well into the twentieth century. Back in colonial times, Indian people were actually well provided for on paper, in the law. And, of course, in practice is always what you have to compare that to.

    There were close relations between the pueblos and the Spanish Mexicans after a lot of the basic differences were resolved in the post–Pueblo Revolt era. After the reconquest, these communities came together. They came together for mutual defense. They came to respect each other and build what we know as New Mexico. Now, I am not trying to gloss over the differences of the past. There were big differences. But people basically struggled to maintain the integrity of their communities, to maintain the autonomy of their communities. And they were largely successful. So you get some mestizaje, of course, between Pueblo Indians and Spanish Mexicans. But there were wars with other Indians, including the Comanches and the Utes and the Athabascan groups, such as the Navajos and the Apaches. Those wars were not resolved until well into the American period. [For] the victims of that warfare, children who were taken as captives, there is a greater admixture, you could say, demographically speaking, with these other people, with these *genízaros*, as they have been come to be called. In the census roles and popular usage, a genízaro is one of these other people who was incorporated into Hispanic New Mexican society and who becomes assimilated and acculturated into the ways of the Hispanic majority. By 1776, according to some historians, this accounts for fully one-third of the Spanish Mexican population. So there is quite a bit of mestizaje. You could say there is probably more in the category of the genízaros, the previous Navajos, Apaches, Comanches, Utes. There is more mixture with those groups than with Pueblos. The Pueblos are neighbors. Of course, there is intermarriage there [too].

JL: The history of el Camino Real de Tierra Adentro is an unfolding of one human adventure after the other. To me, one of the most interesting is how Benito Juárez escaped from Emperor Maximilian in the 1860s.

EL: The history of northern Mexico is very dynamic. There are tons of rebellions and popular and military uprisings. There are just endless wars with the Apaches. The Apaches are really scapegoated in a lot of instances. One of the great images for me comes during what we call the "Intervención Francesa de Reforma" period, when Napoleon III sent his armies into Mexico. Benito Juárez was in his early days as president of Mexico. There was nothing in the national treasury. It was all mortgaged to the hilt. And for the government to do anything, they asked for postponement or cancellation of these debts. That led to military invasion. The biggest army was France's army under Napoleon III, who brought his cousin Maximiliano in to become the emperor of Mexico. Here is a country that struggled to get rid of Spanish monarchy, and here is another monarchist coming in. The legitimate government was the Republic of Mexico under President Juárez. Early on, you get the defeat of the French army, or at least a major battle won, by the Mexican resistance at the battle of Puebla in May 1862. But French troops kept flowing into Veracruz, and a year later Puebla fell, and Benito Juárez fled the capital north on the Camino Real. That is one of the great images when we think of the history of the trail. Benito Juárez in his little black coach, a very distinctive, very sturdy, and very stylish black coach, traveling north, literally ahead of the imperial army of France.

When he left Mexico City, Juarez had in tow the entire national archive in wagons behind him. And of course that was kind of unwieldy. So they found a good place to hide those in haciendas and places where the French would not find them. But Benito Juárez began his journey north, to Chihuahua. In the fall of 1864, he reached Valle de Allende. He came into Chihuahua. He was in the state for a couple of years. And what we must realize is that this was the future of Mexico traveling in this little black coach. This was the future of democratic government, of the Republic of Mexico, in the person of Benito Juárez. If they had captured him, it could have all come crashing down. But he was very astute, and the republican and liberal cause in those days was accompanied by a whole lot of socializing. When Benito Juárez arrived in Chihuahua, there was a constant series of celebrations and parties. And people were celebrating the great ideas of nineteenth-century liberalism, the idea of freedom, the idea of freedom of religion, the idea of a democratically elected government, the idea of a government whose purpose is to serve its people. And these liberal causes, of course, were invested in Juárez's government, in his person, and at his parties. He gave great parties. There was music. There was dancing. Interestingly enough, a lot of the music that Maximiliano probably brought in with those Austrian bands and the new dances like the waltz and the polka were so popular that I believe Benito Juárez probably had a role in bringing them north as well. Because he was such a party guy.

Anyway, by August 1865, the French army showed up, and Napoleon III's army occupied Chihuahua. A lot of people don't realize that European imperial armies actually got so close to us here in New Mexico. It is important to remember that and to honor the memory of this great Zapotec Indian politician and leader, don Benito Juárez. So he fled from Chihuahua up to El Paso del Norte. The capital of the Republic of Mexico moved again with the person of Benito Juárez in his little black coach. They came rolling into El Paso del Norte. He was there maybe three or four months before the French army retreated. He was able to go back down to Chihuahua. We remember that El Paso was indeed the capital of Mexico, even though it was [just] for a couple of months. And that is of course why Ciudad Juárez is named after Benito Juárez. So it is one of the great images in my mind of history, literally rolling down the Camino Real, but not just history, not just revolts and uprisings, but literally the future of a republic, the future of liberalism, and these modern ideas of government actually prevailing in these journeys of don Benito up and down the Camino Real.

JL: Can you talk about other revolts that took place?

EL: There were the great Indian revolts of the second half of the seventeenth century. Of course, [they] affected New Mexico. [The area involved in the revolts] was really all of northern Mexico, or Nueva Viscaya, as the Chihuahua-Durango area was called back then. The Tepejuanes revolted. The Tarajumaras revolted. The Pueblo Indians of New Mexico revolted. And the Spanish Conquest was very much hanging in the balance at that point. Of course, the Pueblo Revolt in New Mexico was successful and really changed the cultural landscape of New Mexico as a result. But there were other revolts, farther to the south. Since there were mines there, the Spanish government and army were much more persistent in pursuing and snuffing out these revolts because there was so much silver at stake.

One of the great Tarajumara leaders of the seventeenth century was a fellow by the name of Teporaca, which means "Battle Axe" or "Battle Hammer." And he was active along that whole Papiochic Valley; that was his homeland area. Also the city of Guerrero. And he led a very successful uprising. He proved himself as someone who galvanized the leadership of a very dispersed and very microregionally autonomous people. Tarajumaras live all over the place. And anybody who could galvanize them and lead them the way the Teporaca did is deserving of historical note and credit. There are statues of Teporaca in this area. There is a statue of him in downtown Chihuahua. He was finally caught and hung in the village of Tomochic. And there is also a statue of him there because the Mexican government of today of course honors rebels of the past because [it is] a revolutionary government.

JL: I think it would be good to address the fact that New Mexico was at one time part of Mexico. Could you talk about the international boundary between Mexico and the United States as it is now?

EL: One of the great things to realize about these routes of trade and commerce, such as the Camino Real, is how extensive they were. We talk about the Camino Real de Tierra Adentro and celebrate its history. But we have got to realize that we are also talking about the Santa Fe Trail. A lot of the American merchants whose destination was Santa Fe were also very interested in Chihuahua. And they didn't just stop in Santa Fe. As soon as they crossed the border, they were in Mexico, and the border was the Arkansas River. The Arkansas River runs out of the Rocky Mountains in the general area of Pueblo, Colorado, and flows into the whole Missouri-Mississippi watershed. Earlier on, [then,] the Arkansas River was the northern boundary of Mexico. Borders really complicate our lives.

In the El Paso area, the state of Chihuahua, the state of Texas, and the state of New Mexico come together. It makes people's lives really complicated. The whole concept of a border doesn't even come along until the nineteenth century—the border as we know it, as the line of demarcation, of a republic, of a nation. Before that, people didn't worry about it too much. If you lived in a monarchy, monarchies had very fuzzy borders. And what counted was your loyalty to the Crown, the religion of the Crown, to the government. It didn't matter where you went. You would always be a Spaniard or a Frenchman or an Englishman. But now that we have these borders, now that they are defended, they have complicated our lives immeasurably. You may say that the border west of El Paso is an imaginary line crossing the desert, but let me tell you, it is a well-patrolled imaginary line that has disrupted the lives of thousands and thousands of people. And it also disrupts our historical consciousness. New Mexico and Chihuahua, the two northern regions united by the Camino Real de Tierra Adentro, are one cultural historical unit. They are not a single geopolitical unit anymore because they now belong to two republics. But the culture and the history certainly unite the two regions that are so separated by this border. So when we consider the Camino Real, we have really got to think beyond that border.

One of the most amusing parts of our border here is the Río Grande. El Río del Norte, el Río Bravo. Before the dams were put in, this border was constantly shifting. A lot of the towns that used to be on the southern part, the current Mexican part of the border, are now on the northern part of the border. And this created great confusion to nationalists trying to work out their interests. Some of these areas became political footballs in the twentieth century. You get case studies like the Chamisal area, the area that became part of the United States because of the whims of the Río Grande in flood. Lyndon Johnson returned it to Mexico back in the 1960s. All the people that lived there had to move away. Their property was condemned, and they lost their houses, and they got pennies on the dollar. It [was] another displaced community. What we must remember is that this border moved more than five hundred miles.

The border used to be along the Arkansas River, which flows east from Pueblo, Colorado. And so [at the time] when the Santa Fe Trail and Chihuahua Trail and those Camino Real de Tierra Adentro traders, those American and New Mexican businessmen, crossed the Arkansas River traveling from the north through the area of Bent's Fort, Mexico began up there. We have to set aside our modern notions about the border with Mexico when we are talking about the past, especially the past [before] the nineteenth century. Nowadays the border is a concept that goes well beyond geography into the geography of the soul, into psychology. We carry these borders inside our psyches. Every time we open our mouths as border people, we think, "Are we going to speak in Spanish? Are we going to speak in English? ¿Que vamos a decir? What are we going to say? And who are we going to say it to?" We are always negotiating that border that is inside of us. Here in New Mexico, we didn't cross the border—the border crossed us as New Mexicans.

Estevan Rael-Galvez,
photo by author

Estevan Rael-Galvez

Introduction

Estevan Rael-Galvez is the New Mexico State Historian, administrator of the state archives, and a man of profound insight into the ever-shifting cultural mosaic that distinguishes the southern region of the Continental Divide in the United States. He was born in the San Luis Valley of southern Colorado in that span of landscape that separates the Sangre de Cristo Mountains to the east from the San Juan Mountains to the west. Two major rivers spring from the San Juan Mountains: the Río Grande, which empties into the Gulf of Mexico, and the San Juan River, which once joined the Colorado River before the damming of Glen Canyon that resulted in Lake Powell. The headwaters of these rivers are separated by only a few miles—and the Continental Divide.

Rael-Galvez grew up as the son of a *borreguero*, or sheep rancher, and was grounded in the traditions of his family by listening to stories that revealed the comingled bloodlines of his ancestors. Gifted with a fine intellect, he attended the University of California at Berkeley as an undergraduate and earned both a master's degree and a Ph.D. at the University of Michigan.

Rael-Galvez is deeply aware of the cultural boundaries that separate the indigenous peoples of the region and how the mestizaje resulted not only in the mixture of bloodlines, but also in the cultural characteristics now shared by many traditional Hispanos in the Southwest. He has done a great amount of research in the archives over which he now presides and has delved into many oral histories compiled during the 1930s by New Mexican writers funded by Franklin D. Roosevelt's New Deal Works Progress Administration [WPA] Writers' Project. I interviewed my friend Estevan in Santa Fe during the autumn of 2003.

Estevan Rael-Galvez

JL: May I ask you a bit about yourself? Where you were born and raised?

ERG: I was born in La Jara, Colorado, a place named for the abundance of willows that once grew along the rivers of the upper Río Grande, but I was raised in two places. The first [was] with my parents on their farm at the base of the Costilla River, named for the bend in the river and within the shadow of Ute Mountain, which stands as a vigilant reminder of both an absence as well as the inherited presence of a people now displaced. I was also raised up along the Kiowa Trail, now mapped only by memory, in the century-old home of my grandparents in Cuesta, a village formerly named and remembered still as San Antonio del Río Colorado.

        I was also born into stories that not only place me, but also tell me about my place. "I was there," my tío Arcenio said of my father's birth; "he was born with irrigation boots on," he said playfully, referring to the fact that my father had spent all his life with his shovel in hand, moving waters. My dad always encouraged me to find words and stories as a way *out*. And as a complement, my mother, who spent decades schooling children in her own village, taught me how to use words and stories as a way *in*. Yet it was my grandmother who most inspired my imagination and learning. Once, while holding my hand in hers, she ran it gently against her village walls, revealing that I was also born into generations of people that belonged to those walls, to that mountain, and to that river that ran right through it. She taught me that stories are gifts, but gifts always carry a great responsibility, especially those stories that were not meant to be passed on—stories that are silenced.

JL: I understand that your ancestral family member was a captive.

ERG: As is true of many families in New Mexico, there were several individuals in my own family who were Indian captives and slaves. These are the stories that raised me up. Even as a young child, I began to understand how the stories of Indian servitude positioned me in a number of ways—that is, they told me where I stood and who I am. I wish there were enough time and space today to unfold the extent of those stories, but let me share just one. My great-grandmother Dulcinea Arellano always told me the same story. "La India Panana," she began, her back stiffening as she told the story that had also raised her up. I didn't know what "Panana" meant then, but would learn that it was Spanish for "Pawnee." La India Panana didn't have a name in those stories, and in telling the story Mamá Nea would purse her lips and point southward, noting that [this woman] had been captured by another Indian clan in the south. They also captured one of Dulcinea's great-great-grandfathers, whose name was Miguel Arellano. Evidently, this Pawnee woman asked Miguel to help her escape and if he was brave enough to run away with her. They escaped and eventually came to the wide stream, Arroyo Hondo, and from there their family's lives would descend. This woman was baptized Rosa, the Rose that is that Arellano family's matriarch. It was her singular life that perhaps changed the course of who that family would be, who I would be.

    And so, as I was trying to think about identity, a profound identity in northern New Mexico, I tried to reach deep into these stories, into a consciousness and a memory that had been passed down to me. The more I started to dig into the records, the more I realized there was not a single family, not a single individual living in northern New Mexico that had not inherited this legacy at some level. I started to find these stories everywhere, in different interviews and documents. All equally worth telling.

JL: Where were the Pawnees located?

ERG: The Pawnee homeland evidently once encompassed an area that is now Texas and then extended to the area of the Platte River valley in south-central Nebraska and northern Kansas. This ancestor's captivity may have moved her from tribe to tribe across the vast landscape. Her story survived only with a memory of my own great-grandmother being able to point south. Her origins were obscured, as is the case with many slave experiences.

JL: Years ago I interviewed Mr. Edwin Berry, the late, great lore master from Tomé, New Mexico. He described his family history and said that he and most of the other traditional residents of Tomé were part Comanche. He said that there were twenty-eight families that settled after the Pueblo Revolt of 1680, and only one family was pure Spanish. He talked about *cautivos* and genízaros. Could you define the differences between the cautivo and the genízaro?

ERG: Literally, [the word] *cautivo* means "captive," and the difference between the terms is really one of timing. [Cautivo] refers to individuals who were captured and brought into New Mexican households. But that is only part of the story, and what they become is the other part. The reality was that thousands of indigenous women and children were captured and held in households throughout New Mexico as slaves. What these dispossessed peoples were called once they were baptized and entered into the families changes through the centuries, but in colonial New Mexico they were known as genízaros. In time, it even became an ethnic category. [The word] *genízaro* derives from the Turkish word *yeniçeri*, or [in English] *janissary*, terms used to describe Christian captives who as children had been forcibly abducted, traded, and trained as the nucleus of the Ottoman Empire's standing army. In New Mexico after

1821, the term is no longer being used officially, but the system of capturing and enslaving Indian people continues, and with it other euphemisms begin to be used, terms like *criado* and *famula.*

JL: Is it true the genízaro was largely of Indian origin, whereas a cautivo was an Hispano who had been captured?

ERG: This was not a one-way trade to be sure, and people from various indigenous communities as well as Spanish Mexican communities all fell victim to those captivities. Really, the term cautivo could be used for anyone who was captured.

JL: Please talk about the different tribes during the colonial, Mexican, and territorial periods when capturing and enslavement took place.

ERG: There were so many different tribes that were affected by warfare, capture, and enslavement. In the colonial period, [they] included Apaches, Navajos, Pawnees, Aas, Jumanos, and Comanches. By the 1800s, attention shifted to Shoshone speakers to the north, which included Paiutes and Utes. [From] the 1820s through [the] 1870s, the Navajos became the chief victims of this trade. In fact, the 1860s is the zenith of the slave trade. It is when the most captives, in any time period in New Mexico, were being brought into the colony. And that was because there were different Indian wars going on, and the Bosque Redondo Long Walk had taken place, which made the Navajo and Apache increasingly vulnerable at that point for captivity.

JL: Where did the Bosque Redondo Long Walk intersect with the Camino Real?

ERG: There were as many points of intersection as there were occurrences of removal. However, one of the main points was in Albuquerque.

I just looked through a couple of documents yesterday, and I recall two documents that I would like to reference. One is a 1714 document by Governor [Juan Ignacio Flores] Mogollon, who insisted that too many captives were being taken down the *camino*, and I am sure he meant the Camino Real. Too many were taken south down the camino that were dying without having received the sacraments of baptism. He likens those captives to black slaves being brought into the ports of New Spain without having received the sacraments. And then he decrees that all captive Apaches leaving the province of New Mexico must be baptized. It is a great document in full. It makes reference to the comparison, but also to what is happening. If they are too young, they fall off the horse and are killed. In some cases, they were very young; infants to two, three, four, five years old were the most common ages of captives. Those that are older, he says, often are killed in raids. So even in the trading parties that were going down south to trade some of these captives in places like Parral or even in Mexico City, they must have also had to deal with raiding parties coming in to take those captives.

JL: So there were a fair number of Indians enslaved and taken south?

ERG: There were more than a fair number, and thousands of lives changed as a result of these displacements. And for each individual, there are at least that many stories. It is daunting to know even where to begin. I think of the moment when, following the defeat of Acoma, there were sixty to seventy girls under the age of twelve reportedly taken down the Camino Real, apportioned out to various convents in Mexico. In 1612, it was reported that the girls had become nuns. How do we account for little girls who one day are watching their grandmother grind corn, sitting on top of a beautiful mesa, and the next [are] cloaked in a nunnery, worshipping in ways that would never recall where they came from, who they were, and to whom they might worship?

JL: When did slavery become illegal?

ERG: It was illegal even before New Mexico was colonized. In 1542, Indian slavery was banned. However, the "just war" doctrine was at the core of Indian captivity in the Americas, including New Mexico. That clause held that when "hostile Indians" were "captured" in times of conflict, the Spanish citizenry were encouraged to "redeem" their Indian captives from their captors, baptize them into the Catholic faith, and acculturate them as new "detribalized" colonial subjects. Hence, this legal doctrine both justified the captivity and enslavement and obscured [them]. I am convinced that officials used that theory to justify the enslavement and the captivity, and while there were "legal raids" based on retribution with different tribes, there were also many unsanctioned raids. One of the most notorious of the governors who sanctioned illegal raids was Governor [Luis de] Rosas in the eighteenth century. It was under his administration that many, many slaves were taken down south. Some of these governors were actually tried for slaving, but the punishment was not that severe. In some cases, they were fined, and [in] some cases they were told that the slaves had to [be] return[ed] back to their homeland, back in New Mexico. But most of the slaves ended up dying en route.

JL: Would you talk about Hispanos who might have been captured by Native Americans?

ERG: These stories intersect just like the people who are affected by them. Certainly, there are many stories of Hispanos being taken. I think of one story in particular that was written down some years ago by Moises Rael of Cuesta. His story, entitled "Pablito Martínez," reveals how three different children were taken by the Navajos. This must have been in the nineteenth-century San Antonio del Río Colorado, present-day Cuesta. The mothers were left heartbroken, yet determined to take some sort of action. Accordingly, they decided to bury the plaster replica of San Antonio, the patron saint of the village, until their captive children returned to them. The next summer, the Navajo returned. As the story goes, they were negotiating a trade for their own captives by bringing these three children that had been taken the summer before. And so that is how they end up. The mothers attribute it to the patron saint, San Antonio. There is another interesting point of intersection in that story, though. The Navajo in the story refer to the Cuesteños as "Nocayeces." When I started investigating the term, it comes from the Navajo term for Mexicans, "Nakai." "Nakai" means "Those Who Walk upon the Land Too Much" or "Those Who Are Defined by Metal." We know that there is a Nakai clan. So when the Navajos defined the people from along the Río Grande, including San Antonio del Río Colorado, they called them Nacaieses—Mexicans, essentially. This being said, it is critical to note that based on my research I have [found] that for each Hispano taken, there [were] at least twenty American Indians brought in.

JL: The term *mestizaje* is associated with intermingling blood-lines. Doesn't this go far beyond the Spanish Mexicanos and the Puebloan Indians?

ERG: It does. Mestizaje—generations of racial and cultural mixture, defined as much by amicable unions as by coercive relations— also emerged as a direct consequence of these enslavements. In spite of stories of purity told time and time again, a large extent of New Mexico's complexity emerges precisely out of the pres-ence of Indian captives living inside these Hispano communities and households. Baptismal records reveal thousands of children of Indian slaves, many of course with a "father unknown." While most remained unmarried, some did marry, mostly [the] men. Recently, I was visiting with the Mares family from Black Lake, extending a story from the archive. In 1938, Mr. [Simeón] Tejada arrived in Black Lake, a settlement located thirty-five miles southeast of Cuesta, and at the home of eighty-four-year-old José María Mares. In that WPA interview [conducted by Tejada], Mares indicated that shortly after his marriage in 1882, he, his wife, Jenara, and their son, Amadeo, had moved from Taos to Black Lake, becoming its founding family. Mares complicates the story of settlement by noting simply that his parents were

Navajo and that he only came to be a Mares through captivity. "When he was about 9 years old," writes Tejada, "a party that was hunting Indians captured him, his brother, and three Indian girls in 1857."

JL: Could you address the meaning of *querencia*?

ERG: I will try to tell it in terms of this mestizo context because I think that you very much have these different peoples, different communities, who are brought together for any number of reasons, violent or otherwise, who end up connecting to the land. Whether it is el Camino Real de Tierra Adentro that brought them there, el Río Grande that brought them there, or the landscape that surrounded them. Most of these people who have been captured were captured as children. And so when the federal government is trying to release them, they oftentimes turn to the army or the federal courts and say, "We are from here. This is our family." There are subtle differences that I try to point out that they were treated differently than family. But essentially this is what they had come to know. And in time and through different generations, those families would become part of that landscape that would be inseparable from who they are and how they define themselves and their love for the landscape. Because of the landscape, they came to be defined there.

JL: It's interesting that there is no English equivalent for the word querencia.

ERG: No, we can try and define it in different ways, but you are right. There is no single word that really and fully defines how the people of northern New Mexico think of querencia. In this way, it may be important to think that, rather than a word, it is a story, which includes landscape, identity, consciousness, memory, and, finally . . . spirit.

JL: It is the spirit of place for me. In every sense, Hispano culture in northern New Mexico must be regarded as indigenous to this landscape. Back in the 1960s and early 1970s, the concept of la

Raza was generated. It's a very important concept. Would you talk about that a little bit?

ERG: I think of how it was used back then, particularly as José Vasconcelos conceptualized "la Raza Cósmica" and how the Chicano movement would wrestle with and even extend that meaning. I also think of how some of the elders were struggling with these definitions, not wanting to define themselves either as Españoles or Mexicanos, but perhaps that struggle came from the desire, the memory of identity here being something larger, something deeper. To this day, some of my relatives will still refer to themselves as "Nuestra Raza," simply as who they are. And even though you can translate the term *raza* to "race," I hesitate because raza, the way it is used, has a deeper meaning than simply "the race."

JL: The concepts of "la querencia" and "la Raza" intermingle. That implies the spirit as well.

ERG: Absolutely. It is the people and the places that are coming together, and as Keith Basso writes, "Wisdom does sit in places." And so, too, do people sit in places. People hold that wisdom as much as the mountains and the rivers and the streams [do], even through the generations, passing them down from one generation to the next.

JL: How long has your own family lived in this part of the world?

ERG: Grandmothers of mine would have said since time immemorial. I can choose any part of my family and trace it back through time as easily as I can across the landscape from Cuesta to Arroyo Seco to Taos, from Costilla to Abiquiu to Santa Fe to Mexico, up and down the Camino Real and in every direction around it. One thing that pains me in New Mexico is the forgetting and the denial. Thinking of the Camino Real, I think that in New Mexico, tragically, we disclaim where this road begins and where it once ended. Until we understand this, we will never be able to fully understand the significance of el Camino Real de

Tierra Adentro; neither will we be able to see either what underlies it or the arteries that extend from it. It will remain like a museum piece stock, still under a piece of glass, a static relic. That is not what identity is, here or perhaps anywhere.

JL: The Camino Real gradually edged its way northward.

ERG: Absolutely. Indeed, it edges northward, southward, eastward, westward, and for every direction there centers and margins a struggle between competing homelands and empires. The mestizaje was born of it and because of it came from communities that were shifted in the colonial world, where Pueblo people were relocated to the south and indigenous Mexicanos relocated to the north. Just as the Long Walk intersected with the Camino Real, so too did the Santa Fe Trail converge. Ideas and knowledge also came with each of these shifts. So when I speak of mestizaje, it is not just the people—it is ideology, consciousness. It is a reflection of what happened in this place, a reflection of the tragedy and beauty.

Roy Kady, photo by author

Roy Kady

Introduction

My friend Roy Kady is a traditional Navajo weaver who lives in the community of Teec Nos Pos near the northern aspect of the Carrizo Mountains south of the San Juan River in the Navajo Nation. Roy grew up in a traditional *hooghan*, or Navajo home structure, on a mesa top, the northern aspect of which falls off into the San Juan River valley. The hooghan is round, constructed of rough timbers like a log cabin, and plastered on the outside with a thick layer of mud. It was in this setting that Roy learned the ways of his people, the Dineh, the way of beauty.

Roy has become both one of the most respected Navajo weavers of his time and a lore master who records and documents the stories, songs, and lifeways of his people. He is on intimate terms with the landscape of Dinetah, or Navajo homeland, and recognizes the extreme value of the biomythic and geomythic perspective that is vital to the alignment of his people to their homeland.

One day in the midautumn of 2004, I climbed into the passenger seat of Roy's four-wheel-drive pickup truck, and he drove us over a hard-core jeep trail for twenty-five miles or so to the family hooghan where he grew up. He pointed out various aspects of the landscape, and when we arrived, he invited me to enter the hooghan, where I set up my recorder and microphones. Roy pulled a tobacco pouch out of his medicine bag and filled a pipe with Indian tobacco. Using sacred smoke, he blessed the hooghan, me, my recording equipment, and himself. It was only then that we were free to begin our conversation.

Roy Kady

RK: I was born on March 16, 1965, at the old hospital in Shiprock, New Mexico, when it was still PHS, which stood for Public Health Service. Now they have this big modern facility and also a new name that goes with it, which is Northern Navajo Medical Center. It's a beautiful structure. But just right behind the new hospital is where I was born, and then growing up was basically here. My mom brought me back here to the family, which consists of her and my siblings and also my grandfather and my grandmother. We all lived here, believe it or not, in this structure right here that we're sitting in. So this is where I grew up until I was about ten or eleven years old, and that's when we made the homestead there at the farm location where you came by, and [we've] been living there since.

JL: So you actually spent the first ten or eleven years of your life right here.

RK: Mm-hmm, right here. And I can remember a lot of the things that went on, just recall it just sitting here. The sheep in the corral and the little lambs and the goats we used to feed, and the shepherding places up and around the canyons here, playing up on the mesas, and then going to the river, of course, to go swimming and put our feet in the river. Yeah, this is where it all happened for those ten years.

JL: Were there many stories told in the winter?

RK: Oh, my grandfather was an apprentice from what I hear from my mother, at that time, learning the Blessingway and the Beautyway—the Hozhonji, the ways of walking in beauty. And he knew a lot of the songs and also the chants, the prayers that tied in with that. So every winter he told us the creation stories and stories about sheep and horses and everything, here in this hooghan—because it's reserved only for winter months. A lot of the animals that are told about in the creation stories are in hibernation, so in retrospect you have that respect for them so that you can talk about them at that time.

JL: I know that it's against the cultural practice to tell the stories in the warmer months. When does it shift from the warmer months to the winter?

RK: When the lightnings cease. Right now you still see lightnings. So once the lightnings stop is when you usually can start telling. Some people say, well, it all varies; when the lightning does cease, you'll know. And when it snows. And so that's usually when a lot of the emergence stories are usually told; a lot of the traditional stories are told then.

JL: Are there many people left who remember all of those stories?

RK: I don't think there is. I think a lot of the stories are still with the elderlies that are still around; and even with my mother, she doesn't remember all of the stories. She's only able to tell me some. But I continually visit a lot of the elderlies that I know or who are akin to me and can retrieve some of those stories for my documentation, and I share it with all the youth and whoever's interested. Just in my community here in Teec Nos Pos, two most important figures for the stories and some of the ceremonies have passed on just most recently. So they would have been the ones. But fortunately with one of them, the son took up the practice of the ceremonies. From my mom telling me these stories, [I know that] he has a lot of my grandfather's *jish*, which is the paraphernalia used, that was given to them when my grandfather died. So he's continually my resource when it comes to questions or things needing answers. And even [for] the stories, I go to him, and he tells me the stories, the traditional stories.

JL: Do you feel in yourself the right things to be an *hataali* [medicine man]?

RK: I think I'm still in the stage where there's a lot that's still out there for me to learn. I'm not rushing into it. I feel that it'll come to me when the time is ready, and that's what I've always been told, anyways—that one should never rush into that sort of practice, that things will just come to you. I think [that] rushing into it, the way I understand, could also mean you're rushing life along. So I feel that I have a lot more years to live, a lot more years to learn and to finally acquire the abilities to be one. But it's interesting that you ask because there are people that show up at my house, and since my grandfather was a known person in the community and him knowing a lot of the Hozhonji ways, the Beautyway, people kind of automatically think that maybe I'm the one that's the hataali now and actually inquire and say, "We would like for him to do a prayer for us or to do a sing for us."

But my mom—she teases me and she says, "You don't know it, but you're already a medicine man because you have people at your doorstep asking for these [prayers]." But she tells them, "He's not ready for it yet. He still has got a lot more things to learn." That's where I'm at.

JL: Is there a way that you could characterize the system of attitudes, the wonderful point of view, that's shared by all Dineh? I know that unless one is born into a culture, one can never get more than an inch or two deep. It would be wonderful if people from the bigger Western-dominant culture could have a clue as to what it means to be in that beautiful place that really does characterize Dineh.

RK: From what my grandfather has taught me and what my mom continues to share with me to this day, [in] a lot of my offerings in the morning I include everyone. My people, the whole world, the whole universe are mentioned in my offerings and in my prayers—even down to the insects that we share this Earth with.

So unless one knows where you stand on this Earth, I think only then you're able to identify yourself as to actually what it is in life that you're placed here for. I think being a Dineh, we're very peaceful people. We're very with the Earth, and that's what "Dineh" means—People of the Earth, the Earth People, the Five-Fingered People.

My grandfather had this teaching that my mom always reminds us [about] a lot, and not so often with me, but with a lot of my sisters and my nieces and my nephews. She says, "Your grandfather always said that you should always help one another, that you should not overlook a person or individual who is in need of your help. When you go by there and you see that the person is in need of some sort of a hand, you should always offer that. And even if the person has given you a negative attitude or for some reason has talked to you harshly, that didn't matter. You should always lend a hand to that person and help that individual." He said that "because you, at one point in life, will also need that. You will also need a hand to grasp to help you out."

So that was his teaching, and that's basically what he did with the community. A lot of places where I go, just with my last name people are able to identify who my grandfather is, my last name being Kady—because that was his first name. So when I say who I am, my clan and my name, they say, "Ah. We know who you are, and we know where you're coming from, the family that you're coming from. We hold your grandfather in a special place in our life because this is how he helped us. This is what he did for us." They always share that with me. That continues—it helps me to realize where I fit in my culture and in my community and in the world where I stand. I think that answered what you're asking me. That's where the teaching comes from. I think a lot of the elderlies hold that. But I think they don't share it as much because a lot of them—it's hard for them to share it.

For instance, with my family, a lot of my nephews and my nieces don't talk the language or understand the language, so my mother is unable to communicate with them. There's usually a lot of interpreting going on when I'm there when we have our family gatherings because they're always saying, "What did Grandma say?" when my mom is correcting them and telling them, "This is how it's done, and don't have this attitude, and this is how you carry yourself in public, and this is the gratifications of being this kind of an individual." So I do a lot of interpretations for them when that comes about.

JL: Can you talk a little bit about the importance of remembering language and how it helps to sustain culture? Because there's such a huge difference between languages. I would think that there must be a hugely different way of thinking in Navajo, in Dineh, than there is in any of the European languages.

RK: In a lot of the stories that my grandfather used to tell us in this hooghan that we're sitting in, he said, "You were given this beautiful language, the beautiful language that you were given when you were born from the east, which is a purity, peace. And then as you grow, the beautiful language that is given to you from the south, the Turquoise language, which is at the age where you're learning a lot of new words and a lot of good words." He summed it up to where, "You're given this beautiful language to talk to people, to be kind in your words, in the way you sound your words, because this is a beautiful language that is given to all of us, and we should never talk harshly among each other, with everything, with our livestocks and whatever work we do, [with] the people that we meet. Because this language is so powerful in that way that it's also a healing language. It is a gift that is just given to you and can be taken from you if you don't use it the way you're supposed to."

That's the language that he talked about, which I totally understand. And . . . some people, when they do interviews with me, they would always say, "That's how your words are. You're calm, and your words are very peaceful." But that's how my grandfather [was], and that's how his teachings were, and that's just the way my mother is also, with whoever she meets. She's very kind word. And those were the only words that were given to us. There were no other words of harshness. So that's the language that was given to us. It's just really sad to see that [for] a lot of the youth, it's not important to them. They don't see the importance of this beautiful language that is given to us. I've heard them say, "I don't want to talk Navajo. I don't want to sound"—they call [it] a "john accent," kind of like an accent that they don't want to carry for some reason. And there's nothing wrong with it. To me, it's very beautiful to know your language because you have that powerful tongue that you can talk and cure people with. It's a healing word, and it's really holistic, and everything about our language is very beautiful.

JL: I love to hear it. Unless one's born into it, there's no way to really understand it.

RK: Yeah. So in our offerings, in our prayers, we always start with the beautiful language, which is *A dé kwiszho to*, "From here on, may it always be beautiful." And that's why you name the four mountains, the four directional mountains, because that's where we acquired the language. And [the offerings and prayers are] placed in the mountains. That's why we go to these mountains and we make offerings to them on a yearly basis—to continue that.

JL: Is it appropriate to name the four mountains?

RK: Mm-hmm. To the east we have Tsisnaasjini', and when you say the mountains and your offerings [in the] early morning, when you say "Tsisnaasjini'," you're saying, "In beauty may you surround me with a protection of a rainbow belt to protect me on my track, my daily track or in life." When you say "Tsoodzil," which is the south mountain, Mount Taylor, you're saying, "Also give me the beautiful language of turquoise to give me the ability to communicate what I have to communicate today. May my words be all beautiful." And then our west mountain is Dookʼoʼoosliid, and when you say "Dookʼoʼoosliid," you say, "From the tip of the peak of San Francisco, may I always have this beam of light to light where I'm going, whether it be day or night. May that beam always be bright for me so that I know my path, where I'm headed." And then when you say "Dibe Nitsaa," which is the northern mountain, Mount Hesperus, you're talking about the sacred sheep that we all know is the backbone of the Navajo society. That is a very sacred animal, and that's why our fourth sacred mountain is named Dibe Nitsaa. With that we're strong, and the reason why [the] sheep is so important—in a lot of our traditional stories that are told with all the monsters, it was the sheep, the bighorn sheep, that was the sole survivor of all poverty. Everything that has to do with poverty, the bighorn sheep withstood every test, even with the lightning gods. They tried to strike him down, to cease him. But the bighorn sheep always survived and was the only animal to do that. And that's why the northern mountain stands for that. It's the mountain that gives us strength. It's the mountain that is our protecting mountain. It has a lot of strength, and then that's why it's called Bighorn Sheep Mountain.

JL: I think that in my experience with the Dineh, just about every place has a sacred story that goes with it. Not to get into those stories, but that's what makes it so important that the Dineh live on the land that they understand the stories within.

RK: Yes.

JL: Could you talk about that a little bit?

RK: There are very significant sites just all over, everywhere, where there's a reminder left imprinted or there's a reminder in the shape of the hill or a rock or maybe even a grain of sand—where once an important event took place in the creation stories. And that ties into a lot of these sites everywhere. It's all over the Dinetah, which is in between the boundaries of the four sacred mountains. So they're important sites because those sites draw out the stories of teaching. They're the sites where we're able to find comfort if we need comfort. Those are the places where we go to give offerings for a certain ceremony or to grab a handful of sand for its healing properties or a pebble to take back to a ceremony to be part of an offering so that you can get reconnected to these sites. They're like beams of positive energy. If it's cut off, that Beautyway, [then] that beauty balanced-ness that you need to be on this Earth is cut short. So you're able to make that reconnection at these sacred sites, and that's why these sites are very important to us and the stories that are rooted there. And that's how we value the sites.

In every area, in every community, there are places where there are sites that are named after some event that happened in the creation story—some important event that took place.

JL: I've never gone on top of it because I didn't think it was appropriate, and I probably won't say this right, but one of the most beautiful of the sacred sites to me is Ch'oolii.

RK: Mm-hmm. That's where our emergence took place, around that area. Yeah, it's a very sacred and very spiritual place to be. There's a lot to that place that's tied in.

JL: I've always hoped that somehow, because that's either Forest Service or BLM [Bureau of Land Management] land right now, I've always tried to figure out how one could go about maybe incorporating it into—

RK: Back into, part of, the Dineh land. I've often thought about these sites the same way you're thinking about it, and I've always wondered how that could be possible. I think one of the ways is just with a lot more education about these places because not all Navajo know about these places. I think one of the things that every Navajo should do is probably visit that place and feel the energy there, because it's there. It's very powerful. I think that's one of the things that needs to happen. Maybe then they can realize how important the area is there. That's where our place of emergence took place. Kind of like [what] some people refer to [as] the Navajo Holy Land is around that area.

JL: One of the things that I think would be really fine to do would be—in Bilaagane [non-Indian] words, the geomythic mapping of the whole region. That would be so important to do.

RK: I've heard from my elders if you look at our land from up above, you'll be able to see two individuals lying side by side, and the head and the foot and all these areas are outlined by the mountains. In each hand, they're holding a mountain. That I would like to see because I've only heard about it. I'd love to see it from up above, if possible, because some of the medicine men that I know say that it was amazing when they saw it. I'm not sure as to how exactly they were able to see it. Maybe there was a photograph from NASA; I don't know. I haven't really researched that yet. But that is the one thing I think would be in the map and to do that map.

And then there's a male and a female counterpart just lying right next to each other. Right now, from my understanding, they're mining the female counterpart in the Peabody coal mine. And the coal that they're digging is actually the liver that they're digging from this [woman], and that's why we have the drought, that's why we have fires, that's why we probably have global warming. That's basically what they're saying. But who's listening to them? I don't think anybody is.

JL: Am I correct in thinking or hearing that Black Mesa is the body of the female mountain, and the head of the mountain is Navajo Mountain?

RK: Mm-hmm. That's correct.

JL: And the male mountain is—where's that?

RK: The male mountain, I think, is over here. Mount Hesperus, the northern mountain. With the female mountain, I think, she has a bag that we call the mountains over here by Bear's Ears—we call that Medicine Mountain, *jishhezeh* [or] *hezeh* meaning "medicine," where you can find almost any cure if you knew what you were looking for, and that's in the pouch that she has. Either she has it in the pouch, or she has it in her hands—I don't remember. I wish I could see that from up top.

JL: You were talking about how the bighorn sheep survives everything. I think it's important for people who don't know to understand that sheep have been part of the Dineh mind-set long before the churro sheep even came into this country.

RK: Exactly. In the stories, of course, coming from our elders again, they talk about when the animals were created. When it came to creating the sheep, I think it was Talking God who created the sheep. He took down some clouds and shaped the body of the sheep, and then he took some twigs, some willows, and stuck them in as the leg of the sheep. And then of course he put rainbows as its hooves. And so he took some plants and placed them in the head of the sheep for the ears, and then he found some rock crystal and placed them in the eyes. Then after that he blew breath into the sheep. He said, "The sheep will come to you at a later time. There's one already that is among you, which is the bighorn sheep, that was created earlier. This sheep will be provided, will be given to you by a holy person who will bring you this sheep, and when you get that sheep you will always forever prosper as a group, as a people, as a nation. So you must never forget and extinguish, or not ever let the sheep die, because with the sheep you will always prosper in life. It's your protector. It will provide you with everything in life that you will ever need." That's why we call our celebration the "Sheep Is Life Celebration," because to us sheep is life in every way, even down to the dung. We use it to protect ourselves, like when we go on travels. When I went to D.C.—get some sheep dung, bless yourself with it. You say, "I'll always come back here safe and sound." That's how we protect ourselves with the sheep.

That's why when I bring the youth to the sheep corral, and they say, "Oh, it stinks," and they close their nose, I tell them the story. Then I tell them the story about how the bighorn sheep survived all destructions, and that's how [the] sheep is valued. That's how we look at sheep. And then when you get to show them everything that is made with sheep, they finally get a general understanding. Because a lot of them don't know that, before, we made everything from sheep. Not only just the clothing and the shoes, [but] bedrolls—everything. Sinews: certain parts of the body you can get sinews to sew clothing. Everything was eaten; even inside the hooves, there was something edible in there. The hooves were made into rattles for different ceremonies.

The churro sheep, when that came to us, I guess the person who brought the churro sheep to us was the holy individual who was supposed to bring it to us. That's how we acquired the sheep. I have [my sheep horn] at home, but I have it in the sheep corral for that protection. But the bighorn sheep horns are very valuable. People used to wear them around their neck as a necklace for protection from lightning, protection from any type of influenza, whatever. I don't wear mine as often. I just keep [it] mainly there for the sheep. I also have heard stories to where kids, when it hung around their neck, a lot of times they nibble in the sheep.

The whole importance of carrying on the sheep tradition— it has powerful teachings, because [it means] you're strong-minded. You're strong-willed with sheep because you get up early and you're out with them. [They have] provided you with sanity, peaceful thoughts, and just being out with the land you were able to appreciate the Earth and the mother, which is the Earth. You knew everything that was out there—not only the geological formations, but all the impurities, all the plants that grow for different healing properties. You knew that. That's what sheep provided you with—intelligence. That's how powerful the sheep is to us. We want to continue to teach that because I feel, and then some of the elders I talk to, they feel that the sheep tradition must continue because it would be total devastation if we were ever to let that go.

JL: One of the things I've noticed [is] that there are fewer people with sheep than there used to be when I was at Navajo Mountain more than forty years ago. That's where I learned how to herd sheep. I didn't realize it at the time, but I was herding churro sheep. I thought they were goats because of—

RK: The long hair.

JL: Yeah.

RK: When people see my sheep, they initially say, "Oh, the goats look different." I do have goats in there. I think, "How different do my goats look?" "Are they all goats?" I go, "Oh no, they're the churro sheep." They're like, "Wow. We've never seen a churro sheep." They do look like goats to somebody who's never seen them. And what's powerful, too, is I've seen a lot of elderlies who have gone. I visit them when I have the time, when I'm in town, because a lot of them are in the nursing home. A lot of them don't get frequent visits from their family. And so I go there, and I take some wool with me and some of my weaving instruments, even just to hold. I guess it gives them a peaceful mind. It takes them back, and it gives them strength again to live on. I've heard a lot of my elders, including my grandfather, asking for the sheep on his deathbed. It was like him telling me, "Don't let go of the sheep. Always take care of and always have sheep," because that's how he referred to the sheep, like, "Where are the sheep? Are they taken care of? Are the sheep grazing? Do they have water? Are the sheep OK? Did you corral them back in?" And they could hear it. I think for my grandfather, it really gave him that last peaceful departure from here with the sheep. Then I still see that, I still sense that, when I go to visit a lot of these elders who are now in nursing homes. There're great stories that you hear from everybody with sheep tying into them. They're very ill and sick and old, of course, and they have to sell their sheep off because there's nobody else who's interested in them. The grandmother or the mother just becomes even more ill after that happens.

JL: You're a fine weaver, and if it were possible and appropriate, could you describe the state of mind that you go into when you're weaving? That would be a really nice thing to hear.

RK: A lot of times when I start to weave, it takes me back to my sheepherding—some of my favorite spots where I can take the sheep, and I know the sheep are very happy there because I can feel that. They spend a lot of time there, and you try to move them along because you don't want them to eat all the grass—to save some so it can be replenished. So with my weaving, that's what it does. It puts me into a trance state to where I think about a lot of the stories that my grandfather has told me—my grandfather and my grandmother—about their sheepherding. How it had made them feel, how it had made them a stronger person, and how they've learned through the sheep what life is all about. So it takes me to these places. It refreshes my memory with all these stories, these beautiful stories that were told. Next thing you know I'm done with the weaving, but that's where my weaving takes me. It's very meditative to me, very soothing. When you hear that pounding noise, it reminds me of the Earth's heartbeat, because when the looms were structured, they took the horizons, and they took the sky cord and the Earth cord and fastened the loom together. They took the rain streams and then did the warp strings, and then they took the lightning and fastened the top beams for tension. The comb, when the comb was made, it was white shell that made the comb.

I think a lot about how the stories are told in the traditional way—how weaving was given to us, also as a protector, also as a way of life for us. So in that sense we're enduring people with it. And so that's what I think about when I weave. I think a lot about that. Some of the songs that are tied into the weaving songs, are appropriate only at a ceremony when the tools are here in front of you. That's when the weaving songs are recited. A lot of the songs are that way. They're reserved for those special times. So you've gotta have that connection, that respect for the loom and for the tools. That's when you would sing the song—whether it's [with]in you or whether it's out loud, that's all up to you.

Some people think, when you tell them "you must know the songs," [that] you must know the spinning songs, the weaving songs, the tool songs—you must know these songs in order to weave. It doesn't mean that you know the songs word for word to where you can sing them. It means you're able to identify them. When the songs were given to me initially, my brother by clan— his name was . . . Willy Weaver—his father was a weaver, so that's why his last name is Weaver. His father's name was At'oha, which means "Weaver." And Willy Weaver, which is my brother by clan, his name was At'o-oyabeyeh. Since his dad was deceased, that's why they say at'l-o-oyeh, meaning "deceased"; beyeh, meaning "the son of." And that was him. He's the one that gave me the weaving songs.

I didn't request them. He knew I wove because he did a lot of my Blessingway ceremonies, my Beautyway ceremonies for me, my Protectionway. I've taken weavings to him for consultation because I do some pictorials, and I say, "I don't know if I offended anyone in my repertoire here. And if so, can we correct that?" So he did all that for me. He finally had been doing it full time again for at least ten years. The ten years after I picked up weaving again, I went and took a piece that I had woven that had 102 birds, and all the birds and all the colors in there were natural and vegetal dye. The vegetal dyes I've learned from my mother, my grandmother, two of my grandaunts, and some other people in my community, because not all of them knew all the colors. Some knew a certain shade and a certain color that I've learned from them, they taught me. So when he saw that piece, when I laid it out for him to do a sing over, he was awestruck, and that's when he says, "Well, little brother, you're now a master. Here are the songs for you. I will sing these songs for you, and you will always identify them. Later you'll learn because in your Blessingway, your Beautyway ceremonies that I've conducted, they were always a part of it. But I've never pointed them out. I don't know if you've ever noticed that they were the songs and that's where you can recite them, when the piece is there and the tools are here, because you're singing for them. They're happy that way. Their spirit is alive, and you've got to think of them as living beings. That's how you'll treat them." So that's how I acquired those songs. Then every time I have my Blessingway, the songs are recited on my tools.

There's not just one song—there are some twelve different songs. Not all the songs I know, but the basic one I've learned, and that's the same way with the sheep song and the horse song. I think I would ask Willy's son—his name is Herman Weaver. He's the one that took all the jish and the paraphernalia, and he's the one that conducts my Blessingways. So you hear a lot of the sacred, beautiful songs of just everything—horse riding, sheep, everything. The spindle. I think one of the things I can share with you here [is] when Spider Man, Nasjehiestih, taught his counterpart, which is Spider Woman, and how he used, like I was saying earlier, the sky cords and the Earth cords to build the loom and how he constructed the whole thing for her, taught her. He gave the names to all the tools, and he gave them all the names, and he says, "The tools will be called *yodeh'yanehdishishih.*" But she says, "No, we'll call it"—she changed the names.

For a male weaver, for me being a male weaver, I use the word *yodeh'yanehdishishih.* For a female weaver, she'll call it *yodeh'athkaseh yanehdishishih,* which means "mixed stones." For me, it's mainly white shell. All my tools are made with the stories. When you listen to the stories of Spider Man and Spider Woman, all my tools were initially made out of white shell. When she picked up the tools, she named them all of "mixed stones," which was even more beautiful, too. Here again, a lot of these stories don't get shared, so people just—a lot of even our own people—think that only women weave. That's not true. And that's why we have that wonderful exhibit up in Window Rock [Arizona] trying to educate our own people about it.

JL: That's wonderful. I was going to ask you if you could talk a little bit about the tradition of weaving horse blankets.

RK: My grandmother always wove horse blankets. She used to weave them for my grandfather. She took a lot of pride and joy into these pieces. I could just see it. She was not only happy to weave a new saddle blanket for him, but she always said that she left [in it] either a pollen knot, a strand of her hair, and also sometimes some hummingbird feathers, which is for safe travel, so that the horse [could] also be as swift as the hummingbird and "that he will always come back to me," she said. And that's why she did that.

The saddle blankets, a lot of them were just in bands, just corner designs at that initial time because a lot of our weavings back then were coming from, again, from the creation stories of the four blankets that were woven initially when Spider Man taught Spider Woman how to weave. She wove four blankets of the four directions, and each one was a directional color, and [in] each one the design had a different meaning. So that's how a lot of the saddle blankets were woven. Some of them had just a plain field in the middle. It was a tool for the horse and the rider. It was a protection for them so that they [could] always come home safe, and that the horse and the rider [would] always be healthy and strong and endure wherever they [went].

One of the songs that my grandfather used to always sing right before he rode off kind of went, "Shileyeh aneyeh, aneneyeh, aneneyeh. Shileyeh aneyeh, aney-yay-yay. Shileyey aneyey, aneyey, aneyeh, aneyeh. Shileyeh aneyeh, aney-yay-yay." What that means is, "My beautiful horse, I hear his beautiful neigh." In the same way, this song is carried kind of like a neighing sound. So when you say *aneh*, meaning, "I can hear my beautiful horse neighing for me," when the horse neighs, you know the horse is happy, content, and is a healthy horse. So it just ties into the songs. A lot of the horse songs are very beautiful because [they] talk about the horse. There're about twelve of the horse songs, and [a song] talks about the horse greeting you, meeting you. It talks about the horse standing on buckskin of mixed stone. It talks about the horse nibbling on the most precious flowers that only is reserved for the horse. It talks about the horse drinking of the mists that are on these petals that are reserved only for the horse.

It's the same way with the sheep. The sheep and the horse, they share so much together. When he [my grandfather] went to do the offering to the horse, he always greeted him—from the east he came to him and gave him an offering. The hooves, throughout the backbone, all the way down to the tip of the tail. What that represents is rainbows. Rainbows are a very important traveling instrument. Only the gods travel on rainbows. They're able to place a rainbow to their distance, and they travel on that. That's why we never point at rainbows. We can use our thumb, or we can just use our lip and say, "The gods are there." You know the gods are around traveling within, around you, when you see the rainbows. That's how the horses are blessed, just with rainbows, around the hooves and everywhere. Just like Tsisnaasjini' is a belt of rainbow.

The chief blankets, the band patterns—a lot of the band patterns are very traditional. It's just like you're in a blanket of rainbow for protection. That's what the chief blanket represents. All that band stripe, that's the rainbow that we refer to that you see in the sand paintings that guard the main curing motifs in the middle. They're guardians—the rainbows are guardians.

Rina Swentzell, photo by author

Rina Swentzell

Introduction

Rina Swentzell was born into the heart of the Tewa world in the Santa Clara Pueblo. She grew up within brief walking distance of the Río Grande. She is a daughter, sister, mother, and grandmother in the venerated Naranjo family of Puebloan people whose ancestry in this watershed extends deep into antiquity.

Rina successfully maintained the system of attitudes intrinsic to Puebloan culture while earning a master's degree in architecture and a Ph.D. in American studies. Today, she is venerated as a scholar, as a spokesperson on behalf of Native American perspectives, and as a truly great fellow human by all who know her.

In 1988, I had the great honor and privilege to go with Rina to the home of her mother, Rose Naranjo, in the Santa Clara Pueblo. There I recorded her mother singing childhood songs. For several hours, I sat in the shade of the great cottonwood tree outside the family kitchen door absorbing some of the evolved consciousness and great beauty exuded by that remarkable family.

In 1996, I recorded a conversation with my dear friend Rina Swentzell as she reflected on the human pageant within the flow of Nature.

Rina Swentzell

JL: Would you just give your thoughts with regard to community and its importance?

RS: What I have been thinking is that we have too small a definition of community. I go back to the pueblo thinking because their [Puebloans'] community was not just the human community. It included the place within which we lived, so that the mountains were part of community. The water was part of community. Trees, rock, plants, animals. You couldn't have moved through any day in that Old World, even when I was growing up, without knowing that you were part of that whole community of trees, rocks, people. Today, what we do is just talk about human community. It gets to be such a small thing within the larger scope of things. And I think that that is the demise of our modern lives today. We keep making the world smaller and smaller until it is nothing but us, just human beings out of our natural context, out of our cosmological context. We have become so small in our view of the world as simply us human beings, and it is crucial that we get beyond that and move back again to seeing ourselves within context.

JL: Within the context of Santa Clara and Puebloan culture, is the tradition of perceiving that way still relatively strong?

RS: It is fading very fast, and that is frightening for me. I think of community as all of us together, because trees are living beings. Rocks are living beings. Water. The spirit moves through the water. An incredible word that we have for the source of life is *on-oh-huh*: water-wind-breath. It is there in the water and in the wind that we can see the spirit, that we can see life moving, where the life-force is visible—as well as in the clouds, of course. We don't take the life-force and put it in a superhuman being, as Christians do with God. That already begins to show the focus on human beings, when you put the life-force in a superhuman creature. God in superhuman form. We keep it within the trees. Within the water. Within the wind. Within the clouds. And we move through that context, with the water, the wind, and breathe the same breath. To say, "We are breathing the same breath that the rocks do, that the wind does." And that gives you a totally different feeling. This is it. There is no other reality. We don't go to heaven. We don't leave this dirty world to go to a golden, clean heaven. We are here. This is it. This is the world. It doesn't get any better than this. And if we don't honor it in the sense that this is as beautiful as it is ever going to be, then we can't take care of it if we think that it is a place to be shunned. If we think we have better things to look forward to, then we can't walk respectfully where we are at this moment and take care of things and touch things with honor. And breathe each breath. That is what that water-wind-breath is about because every second I can breathe it in and become a part of this world and know I am a part of this world that I live in every second, because I believe it every second.

JL: A few years ago I realized that the largest ecosystem that I could comfortably conceive of was our solar system. That relationship between the sun and our planet is truly a vibrant interrelationship that resulted in the ability for us to be here. Metaphorically, it is a marriage between the sun and the Earth that results in life. I tried to imagine the universe as being the biggest ecosystem, but my brain could not possibly do that.

RS: I think it is beyond us to really see it in that scale of things. But that scale of seeing in the way of the old Pueblo people—they were trying to make sense of what was around them. You know here, especially in the Southwest, you look around you, and you see that horizon, that 360-degree horizon around you. And then you see that blue with the clouds going over you, and the sense they made of it. You are the center. At any point that you stand in the Southwest, you are the center, and you are in containment. That is you at the center. The Pueblo people really picked up on that and said, "Look, we live within the Earth bowl. This is where we dwell. And wherever we are, we are at the center." Which is literally true. That is what we experience every day. We don't experience abstract planets out there. We experience this in a very central way, every day. And being at the center, seeing that far horizon, with the mountains that contain us in this Earth bowl, and all of the symbolic kiva bowls that the Pueblo people make, with the mountains along the rim, that is all about that. And the Earth is covered by the sky basket.

You were talking about the marriage between the Earth and sky. That is exactly what they were talking about. The father and the mother. But it was not in terms so much of male and female as it was [in terms of] father and mother, which is a very different concept. Male and female then become included within father and mother. That is a very different meaning than saying the "male sky" and the "female earth," which brings in real explicit sexuality, which the Pueblo people weren't so much interested in as in the parental nature within which creation happens. Because it is only when the male and female come together as father and mother, and [when] children are produced that creation really happens. And in that sense, Pueblo people talk about community as having mothers and fathers and children. The oldest people are usually talked about as fathers and then [as] the mothers in that community, whether they are your mothers or not. Everybody else is children. Those people are also children. There is the flexibility of roles in that way. The notion of having people who are responsible and nurturing and caring about the entire context that one lives in is that kind of model that was taken from the way they saw the cosmos as being structured and ordered.

JL: One of the things that I wanted to bring up to ask you about is the importance of ceremony, or the ceremonial, in keeping this concept intact—how that might become increasingly important as time goes on.

RS: There are a couple of things that I think happen with ceremony. I'm afraid that there is a negative aspect when it becomes ritual for ritual's sake. But I think that ceremony, if we take the time to be extremely thoughtful about where we are, what we are doing, and how we are doing things, then ceremony in that sense becomes very embracing of many ways to do things. This is the appropriate way to do it. The appropriate way to do anything is thoughtfully and graciously—and with as much soul as you can pull around you. I think that in that definition of ceremony, then yes, we all absolutely need that.

JL: Are the young people still involved in doing ceremonials?

RS: I think more as a thing that is supposed to be done and more for identification with the human community than for the larger community. I think that the Pueblo world is moving toward the separation of the human from the natural world. In my understanding of what is going on, that is the real critical move that is happening today within the Pueblo world—the move toward isolated human communities.

JL: In trying to imagine how to forestall that or how to reroute back into a realistic system of attitudes inherent in traditional Puebloan culture, can you conceive of anything that you would invoke?

RS: I think that there are always people in any social or cultural context that remember. The transformation that is happening in the Pueblo world right now is so dramatic. The rate is so fast. Running after what the Western world has is happening at such a speed that that act of thoughtful remembering is difficult to hold onto. I don't know that we as human beings have anything except for what comes internally out of us. Whether we consciously acknowledge that we are a part of this natural world that we live in or not, we *are* part of the natural world. We cannot live, any of us, without acknowledging that. It always has to happen from the inside. Sometimes all I have to do is take a walk and have the world come back down around me again. And it is mostly that feeling of, "Oh, it is around me again. I am a part of it." I forget so easily.

JL: Thinking about the upper Río Grande, which is central to Puebloan thought, could you describe the way that it is traditionally perceived by the Puebloan people?

RS: The old ancestral people moved through this region for thousands of years, and the intimacy that they developed with the land is what I think has kept them going for so long in such a place. Even today, I think that what helped our people survive for so long is that intimacy that we have with the land. With the place. With the rocks, the mountains. Part of that intimacy, of course, especially in this region, is to know where the water areas are. And the water is seen as being absolutely important for life. Without it, creation doesn't happen. It is the semen of the father that keeps creation going. But the snaking water through this region, the Río Grande, the lakes, and, of course, throughout all of Pueblo mythology, all water places are extremely important. Without water, we don't survive here. Water is so sparse. The lakes are very important. They are also places where the energy of the world is very strong because they are places to go into the underworlds, into other levels of existence. The Río Grande is a place that is also frightening to the Pueblo people. It is frightening because it comes with incredible power. And that is why I think that we talk about the water-wind-breath—because the power of all of creation is there. It can be in the wind, and it is certainly in the water, especially in that strong flowing water. Tewa for "Río Grande" is *O-son-ge*, the "Large Water Place." It is actually seen as a place. It is not just there. It is a place.

JL: What you said earlier about water, wind, and breath is very critical. I think that one of the things that everybody has to do in order to remain at all affiliated is to be outside in it. If we look at ourselves as a group of decentralized communities that are related by the land in which we live and also [by] the water that sustains us, and if we maintain a mutually acceptable perception of the sacred quality of habitat and within the terms of modern Western culture accept the biological necessity of habitat remaining unencumbered, perhaps we'll finally understand that some habitat must remain unencumbered in order to sustain us all. Whether we be humans or trees or coyotes or whatever we happen to be. That is a major factor that needs to be expressed. Within the context of many mythologies, there was a time when other creatures of the animal kingdom and humans could all intercommunicate. That is metaphoric. And that metaphor is disappearing rapidly. I wonder if you could address the importance of that.

RS: You know, communication is felt to be very different in Pueblo communities. I think that to some degree we are actually communicating with the clouds as a way of moving our bodies, so that the energy communication is where you take from it as you give to it. It is the same thing that happens with the races that still happen at Taos Pueblo annually, when the sun is starting to go down in its journey across the sky. Its starts going lower and lower. The people come out in order to get movement going, to give it energy. That always just astonishes me . . . that idea that it is possible to give and take with the sun, to give and take with the clouds. I always think about it as communication, and not just verbal communication. It was possible to begin to know something so well. We had a Santa Clara man—he is dead now, but in the evenings he would hear the coyotes on the hill. And then after a while, you would hear this other sound coming from the end of the village. There would be this conversation that would happen between our uncle and the coyotes on the hill. Then sometimes you would see him walking up into the hills, and everybody said, "There he goes again. He is going to go be with the coyotes." He was always capable of being with them in the way that other people couldn't do.

I think one of the reasons that Pueblo people chose to remain at a spiritual place was that they wanted that sense of communication with creatures other than human beings. We talked earlier about community, our notion of community shrinking so much that it's just [the] human [element]. I think part of what has happened also is that spoken language has become so important. We think that spoken language is the only possible means of communication. I think that what the Pueblo people were doing was saying, "Be quiet. Listen." For healthy survival, you need to be quiet and not talk so much. We are always told, "Don't talk so much. How can you be responsible if you don't know what is going on around you?" Then communication really has to extend beyond spoken language.

JL: Within most wholesome and healthy communities, elders are highly venerated, and their points of view are very much listened to by all of the people in the community. The relationship between elders and youngsters is extremely important. Could you talk about that for a little bit?

RS: I think elders in those communities were much more connected to the Earth, not just to people, but to place and all of the creatures. Elders in those communities play[ed] a very important part because they felt themselves to be connected. I think that things work in union. If older people don't have a sense of their own meaning and their own sense of place within community, which I think a lot of people have lost in all communities, then other people can't relate to them that way. You know, in any culture we can't just honor someone because they are sixty-eight years old or whatever, but [because] that sixty-eight- or eighty-eight-year-old person has something that flows out of [him or her] anyway. That means that they have had a lifetime in which they have thought about things and that they have been careful about things, and then they really can be people who can begin to put their arms around other people. If they don't have that capability within themselves, then we are really all lost because we need those older people to be coming around us and telling us, "Now, stop. Listen. Look around. You are acting too fast. This is appropriate for where everybody else is, including where the clouds are. This is what we should be doing." It seems right for old people to be taking on that role. But what happens to people who don't grow up ever experiencing that for themselves? Then how can they do that for other people? I think that's a real dilemma we have got. We are having generations of people who don't know how to behave like that, so then how can there be older people whom other people can respect? It is a real loss.

JL: I'm trying to identify the things that could be addressed if we as a culture at large were expansive enough. Humans have inhabited this region for a very long time. Our human population, demographically, has shifted enormously in the 450 years since the Spaniards first arrived. Which is not to say that it is wrong for people to move in, because people have been moving into the area for somewhere between 12,000 and 30,000 years, depending on how you interpret the evidence.

RS: But they didn't come in cars. They didn't arrive with the kinds of demands that we have. Look at us sitting in this house, the amount of space that I demand for myself, as each of us does. We can't seem to move on the land with our feet very far. We have to get in the car. Those are incredible factors. Population is one thing, but the way we choose to live is a really big thing.

JL: Well, invoking a basic minimum technology, once again . . . three generations ago, our grandparents and great-grandparents still lived in a way that was more or less commensurate with our habitat. What I am getting to is that I think of community in a more or less decentralized fashion, not seeing it as utterly separate from other communities, but as a place where there is a population of people who exist, who have a sense of themselves in relation to place, and have a sense of place as the predominant characteristic of their thinking. Determining how they can occur with other communities throughout the region, in a successful eco-systemic fashion, seems to me to be imperative now. Looking for ways through that labyrinth is the tricky part. Do you have any thoughts you might share as to how to get young people aware of these things? What is it about a community that works?

RS: Children so desperately need a sense of belonging more than anything. I don't think that they need all the distractions that they now have. They don't even need their biological mother and father as much as they need a sense of belonging in a place with a group of people. We have gone to the nuclear family to such an extent that it is another way of pulling apart the whole notion of community. The nuclear family becomes such an isolated unit, and that is not what kids need. Kids need a real rootedness in a place that means a lot more than just a mother and father. They need grandparents around them. They need aunts and uncles around them. They need to know that whatever they are doing at any time in the day, they are being watched by people who care about them. Not just mother and father. I think we always worry about the nuclear family. We need to open it up again . . . having extended groupings of people who really care about each other. Community can come in many sizes. They can be cities. A small group of people located in a corner or a cul-de-sac can be a community of people. And if that community of people really cares, that care is going to show itself throughout that whole. Of course, the larger the scale, the less likely that that is going to happen because then you don't know each other. Care can't happen if you don't know people. I don't think it is possible in large communities. Even in a city the size of Santa Fe, I think what we need to look toward are neighborhoods, places where that kind of care and consideration and sense of responsibility can happen. Where you can look into other people's eyes and say, "I care about you. What you are doing? Do you have enough to eat? Can I do something for you?" And [where I] know that when I don't feel well, someone will be concerned about me.

But, you know, I think we get blown up to thinking that the cities that we have are what we are supposed to care about. That is where all the political decision making is going on, and that is because we keep giving all of our politicians power. We keep giving the U.S. government power. Just think that if we all stopped and returned to healthy small units all over the country that we can really deal with, what an incredible country we would be! We wouldn't need somebody else to be telling us what to do with our water systems or whatever. We would be taking care of it ourselves. I do know that Pueblo people felt that way. That is why they always knew that whatever they could see out there, they were responsible for.

JL: Did you ever read any of the work of Peter Kropotkin? He was a turn-of-the-twentieth-century anarchist thinker in the deepest sense, contending that people had to assume responsibility for themselves within the context of their communities, and that communities evolved by consensus and also in reaction to their habitats. He was born in 1842. It was during [Kropotkin's] teenage years that Darwin started publishing his own work, which greatly affected Kropotkin, who then became a geographer. He went off into Siberia and mapped mountain ranges, but also observed natural history and concluded that evolution of species owes more to mutual cooperation than to mutual antagonism. Which is a great thought. Subsequently, he wrote several books, the most important of which is *Mutual Aid*. Terrific book. He lived in exile in Britain for many years, but returned to Russia shortly before his death in 1921. He was pessimistic about the way things were going under Lenin's highly centralized Bolshevism. And he saw bureaucracy as a major enemy.

RS: I do, too. I think that it is really doing us in. We talk about children today. The bureaucracy of education I think is one of the biggest things happening to our Pueblo world right now. We are being done in by the way our kids are being educated. They are not in that caring environment that I was talking about earlier, with grandparents and really feeling a sense of connection. Being taken out of community and put in a boarding school context, out of contact with people who might give them a sense of belonging somewhere, what are they going to do? They are not going to care about anybody. They are not going to care about what happens to the plant that grows out there or the animals out there. They care for themselves. And then they are going to move through the world in that way. What do they have to do with community? What does that have to do with community anywhere? It doesn't. And then more bureaucracy. I see them [i.e., bureaucrats] more as agents to take us out of community.

JL: Back in the 1960s, when I was working with Lee Udall, I visited all of the BIA [Bureau of Indian Affairs] schools on the Navajo reservation. In those days, each of the schools had a little placard posted that stated, "Tradition is the enemy of progress." I took down as many of those as I could. I have always thought that tradition is one of the truly great vehicles through which we can maintain our sense of relationship to our bigger community of life. Is there anything that you have to say about the role of tradition like that?

RS: I think that tradition and community go hand in hand. In a way, you really can't have one without the other because tradition is really about rootedness. It is about a group of people having been alive within a place for a long period of time and having set up certain ways of behaving, certain ways of doing things. It takes a long time for people to feel comfortable with being in a certain place. I have to wake up every single morning, be aware of where the sun comes up over those mountains, and be careful about watching. And what does that mean? It means every morning I am in connection with that sun out there in the sense that "here is my world right here." And depending on where that sun comes up this morning, I know whether I am going to have to build a fire or not. It's not much more than just really seeing those elements come to create a place for you, within which you feel comfortable and safe. What if that sun doesn't come out where it is supposed to come out? I mean, the place would fall apart. Literally. There would be no more place. If those rhythms that we take for granted, those traditional rhythms or whatever they are . . . if [as a child] I don't know that my grandmother is going to be there and have a pot of beans going, . . . then it does start falling apart. And there aren't rhythms. Having a grandmother is as natural a rhythm as having the sun come up every day.

JL: Beautiful. That is absolutely correct. One of the things about mainstream culture, as I think of it, is that we have largely stopped being able to see in terms of the interrelationships of things because of the very linear way that we have been taught to intellectualize.

RS: And what that linear way does is isolate us. You know, the linear way of doing things, getting up, going to school every day, is a continual process of being pulled away from natural patterns and natural rhythms. How can we even relate to the natural things around us? The mountains and the trees? We are continuously being pulled out of relationship with them and not feeling the rhythms that come with them.

JL: If one can think in terms of a sphere of reference, rather than a frame of reference, and put one's head in the middle of that, then see how all things interconnect and how ramifications of different acts occur, that to me is something that traditional Pueblo people have mastered.

RS: One of the points is thinking that whatever you do affects everything else in the world, which is part of that new physics sort of thinking, where a butterfly flaps its wings, and we are in some way affected by that flapping. I mean, the Pueblo people [have] always [known] that whenever I moved my hand or said a word . . . that is why they are always saying, "Don't talk. Or if you are going to talk, say it carefully, or say it as well as you can say it."

Because it does go out there. It does ripple out there. And when I move my hand in a certain way, it creates an effect on you somehow, both physically and psychically. Any move that I make affects your inner self somewhere, and we affect the system.

JL: Now that brings up something else, and that is the importance of art within a culture. Art reflects the relationship between the human aspect of the community and the rest of the community. That is something that Puebloan culture has done really well within the arts.

RS: And you know, there is no word for "art" there. I think that there was no word for "art" because there wasn't a need for people to make an object and say, "Look how great I am." So that it wasn't using creation to show one's superior capability. Again, the focus is a sense of bringing power into individual self. I think again how you could touch the clay and move with it so that you felt an incredible oneness with it. And then you knew that that [object] was going to go into everyday living, so that you were going to drink out of it, eat out of it, not that you were going to make this thing so you could get six hundred dollars for it. It is a matter of seeing that I am a creative alive being, and when I see the world out there, my eyes, my ears, my nose, my fingers, everything reacts to it. And this is what it looks like to me. This is the sense I make of it, and leaving it at that. Not using that incredible creative power in order to bring in money. Money alienates so much. Not that I don't use it. I certainly do use it. But how do we move from that world of money, which is an abstraction, and deal with that abstraction when we are trying to find connection?

JL: Ed Abbey extended the concept of money being the root of all evil to excessive money buying excessive power, and that, indeed, the quest for power is the true root of all evil.

RS: Now that's what I keep trying to get at when it turns into an individual thing and not an internal search for connection. It turns into that grabbing for power. Somehow that is an incredible difference that happens.

JL: One can just extrapolate from there. I look at the whole political world and realize that most politicians are in quest of power. So if we empower a politician, we have to be mighty careful how much empowerment we pass along. I do believe that the community itself has to retain responsibility. And so there is a differentiation there between the maintenance of responsibility and the relinquishing of power.

Changing focus here, I've done a fair amount of field recording of traditional music, and I believe that the songs carry the message about the relationship of culture to habitat. Could you talk about that a little bit?

RS: I have always been struck that during dances that happen publicly at Santa Clara, most of the songs talk about movement through land, through the geographical space. You talk about all the young women, young men, as clouds. There they are now. They are on top of that peak. During the goat dance, the old goat woman is coming over this peak and now is over this valley. Now is over on those hills. Now it is there. And now finally it has come to our place. It has come to the center. And it is usually about how different kinds of different beings, on whom we are dependent as a community, are moving through the landscape and are bringing in the energies that are located in those different places to this center place that we dwell in. And now they are here. Beautiful. It is a rhythmical movement through the landscape and finally to the center where we dwell. And it is always in thankfulness, for their [the beings'] moving and bringing in the very kind of energies from the land to this human center place. They are really beautiful songs that way.

JL: That was beautifully stated. Could you name the Tewa-speaking Pueblos?

RS: There are San Juan, Santa Clara, Tesuque, Nambe, San Ildefonso, and then one in Hopi.

JL: Now those are different specific communities, but they all follow the Tewa community of practice based on language and traditions that have worked for an awfully long time.

RS: The amazing thing is that the basic Pueblo beliefs aren't language specific. The Hopis and Zunis, for instance, speak totally different languages from us, and yet the major ideals of what we call the Pueblo world are the same in spite of very different languages. So it really makes me feel that that relationship to land, relationship to place, which all of us experience together—we all have that basic relationship. And we talk about it in essentially the same way . . . Father Sky, Mother Earth, Children, the need for connection, relationship, but yet the languages are very, very different. They are not even related languages. And yet the ideas that grew out of the land are very much the same.

It was the land that dictated what we were to believe and how we were to behave. And now language is being made a big thing of because it is the one thing that people can hold on to. They say, "That will take us back into our traditions." Yes, it is an avenue. It is a way to do it. But the more basic thing is thought. What is the relationship to place? That is what brought up the traditions in the first place, and that is what brought up the language anyway. And the language expresses it. But it is not a dependency on language. It is something more basic.

JL: Is it possible, do you think, to maintain that sense even if language changes or goes away?

RS: I think that it is the universal human need that the Pueblo people were responding to. And I think that that is what we need to return back to. It is a need that you have as an Anglo person and [that] I have as an Indian person. And I can speak Tewa, but I have no doubt that your need to feel connected with and be a careful considerate person in [a] community is a need that I can recognize in myself as well.

Greg Cajete is an environmental educator, and he wrote this book. He looks at all Native traditions across the country, and it is amazing how different groups across the country really do operate off of that notion of relatedness. What he is doing is determining that for Native peoples across the country, their primary thing was, "How do we live in this place? How do we relate to these specific things?" That the definition of us as a group of people is really dependent on the plants that we eat, is really nurtured by the water we drink. And that the water we drink actually determines our character as a group of people.

JL: Everywhere I have gone during the forty-some years that I've been wandering in this landscape and talking to people from every conceivable culture, all of the traditional Indian people that I have ever met have maintained that very notion as the central theme of existence. And I have discovered that in several places the sense of culture and community is strengthening rather than continuing to deteriorate. Can you imagine any scenarios whereby the young people can have the traditional sense of place be the primary motivating factor, yet can use available educational systems to bring it together to forestall future disasters?

RS: I think that one thing that education does is to make people feel more confident in dealing with that large monoculture—call it Western culture, that thing that we all live in anymore, the ocean that we swim around in. As Indian people, we didn't know what that world was about, and it is a very intimidating world. It is such a fast-moving, aggressive kind of world. I find it, sometimes, very difficult. There are good people out there, I know that. But there are also people who are seeing that the more education you get, the more money you can earn. It is a way to get out of community, and that certainly is something that is happening. It is almost like trying to keep this overwhelming culture around us.

Western culture really does feel like swimming in an ocean. It is everywhere. It is sleeping in every corner. It's coming in. And there is no way to make that ocean around us go away. Look at Albuquerque. The only free lands that Albuquerque can't develop now are the Indian reservations that surround it. What happens almost on a daily basis is the encroachment of that insidious value system that is there. Even if we were successful in keeping Albuquerque at bay with Indian reservations, what is happening internally, I feel, is wrong. Granted, the land does give [a] reprieve when we go take a walk in a beautiful place that has not been touched by development. But what do we carry to that place? I still think it comes down to each one of us as individual people and what we decide to do with what we have to do with. I feel like the best survival for me is to take a deep breath and take care of the small world that I can take care of. And that doesn't help anybody anywhere, but it helps me and those people that are close to me.

All I can do is look at the sun and the shadows and really be happy that I am here at this moment and act accordingly. If I am thankful, then I better act accordingly.

Warner Glenn, photo
by Kelly Glenn-Kimbro

Warner Glenn

Introduction

In the autumn of 2004, my late friend the historian Alvin Josephy and I were visiting poet and rancher Drummond Hadley on his ranch in the bootheel of southwestern New Mexico. The ranch is bordered on the south by the international boundary with Mexico. Drum had been instrumental in rallying a coterie of fellow ranchers into forming the Malpai Border Group, which is committed to the pursuit of environmentally sound ranching practices and the preservation of rangeland habitat. Many times Drum had spoken to me of his great friend and fellow rancher Warner Glenn, who has a spread somewhat west of Drum's ranch. Drum took Alvin and me to Warner and Wendy Glenn's home, where I interviewed Warner about his life.

Warner was born in 1936 in the heart of the Great Depression. He has devoted his entire life to ranching and hunting and is part of a cultural milieu that is itself endangered. His Malpai Ranch provides headquarters for the Malpai Border Group, where the Glenns and fellow ranchers wage a vigorous campaign to protect their homeland from development that threatens not only their way of life, but their habitat, which comprises some of the most remote and wild landscape in the American Southwest.

This tall and rangy rancher has spent much of his long life out of doors. In every way, he embodies all that is good about life on the range. The heritage he preserves reveals the spirit of individualism, integrity, and honor that epitomizes the way most of us wish we were.

Warner Glenn

JL: This close to the Mexican border; one of the things that's really interesting is the interplay between what we think of as American culture and Mexican culture.

WG: I have neighbors on the south down in Mexico, and we neighbor back and forth. If our cattle get down there, I go get those cowboys to help me bring them back, and vice versa. If they have cattle get up here, they come up and help me. We've maintained the fence together. Believe it or not, that border fence, you'd think it'd be maintained by the U.S. government or one of its agencies, but any work done on that fence we have to do it. It's a big problem, that border fence.

But as far as the ranching industry [goes], we do things just about the same as they do things down there. Now, the farther you go south, it goes to different quite a bit, but right here along the border it's just about the same.

JL: Is there much of a difference in style between the Mexican vaqueros and the gringo cowboys?

WG: You know, there's a little bit. Jack, most of those cowboys down there still carry those long, either the rawhide riatas [lariats] or the long, like, forty-five, fifty foot of small-diameter nylon ropes. Up here they carry the short rope, usually about thirty feet. Saddles—most of the people up here ride the low-cantle saddles with very little swells and [the] kind of big-type horn down there. Most of those Mexican cowboys still ride the large swells and the high cantles and those typical Mexican saddles with taps on the stirrups. Up here, now I've used taps on all our stirrups because we hunt in those mountains a lot, and I use that as a safety factor as far as keeping a limb from running through your stirrup or somebody getting a foot caught. Down there in Mexico, all the Mexican cowboys wear those taps on their stirrups. Same purpose, really, but they go in for a lot of the looks on their taps. They have the shoulders or the fenders on their taps, you know, and they wear a lot larger spur. They use that for a purpose, but there's a lot of show in their equipment down there, maybe a little more than there is up here with the cowboys on this side.

JL: Warner, I would like to ask you to talk about how ranching might have changed in your way of seeing it over the past forty-odd years, say, compared to when you started out, the way you learned from your family, and the way it's taken into account right now.

WG: Jack, actually in the past forty years it hasn't changed that much. Here in Arizona you have to manage these ranches for the drought years that we have rather than the good years, and they were doing that back in those days, too. Now at the turn of the [twentieth] century, they brought all kinds of cattle in here, and they kind of overloaded this country with cattle numbers just for the simple reason [that] they didn't realize what the country could stand. There was a sea of grass, and it was raining pretty good during those periods, and they thought they could harvest that grass via the cow, and it'd all come back. That happens when it rains, when you get the moisture. But I tell you, in this country we don't always get that moisture. So the difference now would be fewer cattle numbers on the same amount of land and also the building of pasture fences so you can rotate your grazing. I would say the ranch management has changed more in the way we manage the individual ranch than it has generally speaking. The event of plastic pipelines has come in, so we can use that plastic pipe to distribute that water all over the ranch at a fairly reasonable cost, and that's a big thing. Those cattle in the old days were concentrated around the permanent waters, wherever that may have been. That led to the overgrazing of certain portions of the range. In a way, that was all right because there was always some good feed left in places, but now we have fences—we've built fences in different pastures so we can rotate, and we try to have water in every pasture and different places to distribute that grazing.

As far as the markets go, we do have a local livestock auction in Wilcox, Arizona, now that we can market cattle any time of year, and the old-timers did not have that. They usually sold their cattle in the fall and a few in the spring, but mostly in the fall of the year. Now we can market those cattle any time whenever they reach a certain weight; or if drought conditions tell us we'd better sell off some, there's always an available market. The price is still determined by the different things that we don't have control of, or we don't think we do, so you're still tied to whatever price at that time. But we are able to market cattle year-around now. So that would be one thing that's changed a little bit.

Of course, in the real early days, up until the '20s and early '30s, they drove cattle to market, and we had a railroad through here at that time. There's no longer a railroad furnishing this part of the state now. Most of the cattle were driven to railroad heads and loaded on the trains. Now they're trucked. Now we have a truck to come out to the ranch and pick them up and either take them to Wilcox or take them to a feedlot somewhere, wherever you decide to go with them.

As far as supplemental feeding goes, there's systems of feeding your cattle now that are a little easier—supplement feeding when you have to. Hay is available. You can get hay trucked in now if you have to have hay. But most of us use some kind of a protein and vitamin-and-mineral supplement, and we leave it out there most of the year, especially when your feed conditions are dry. [In] the dry feed conditions, we put a supplement out there just to keep those cows, keep their body in a little bit of an even healthy state year-around.

JL: One of the things I'd like to ask you to talk about is drought. We've had a heck of a drought up north.

WG: We have here, too, Jack. This country's terrible, looking at it right now. I think just about every rancher in this part of the area has gotten rid of probably half of their cattle. I think probably a third of the ranchers have gotten rid of just about all of their cattle in this whole area, and I'm saying all of them. I'd say a ranch that would run maybe three to four hundred head are down to a hundred head. Some of them are down to thirty or forty head. They just try to keep a little bit of the original stock for when it does rain and our pastures come back, [so] we'll have a little bit of that breed of cattle that we raised here that's used to the country and know the feed conditions and know the conditions of the ground. And I'm talking about rocks. You've got to have rock-footed cattle in this country. If you bring a bunch of new cattle in here, once it does rain—if you go out and buy a bunch of cows and bring them in, they'll get so doggone sore-footed for the first year, they're not going to do you any good. You're better off buying young heifers and letting them get used to it and just sacrifice raising that calf for a while. You're going to be waiting two years, anyway. So it's hard to build back. That drought really affects things in this country.

Right here on the Malpais Ranch, we haven't had a good year for the past six years. And it wasn't even very good for the past ten. So we're ready for a change.

JL: Something I'd like you to talk about, could you describe the annual cycle of your work here on the ranch?

WG: Why don't we start at the first of January? January and February, you're usually putting supplement feed out for those cows and taking care of them, and you're supplementing those bulls and getting them in good shape. Those cows, in this area here we start calving, the perfect time usually is about the first of March, and [we] try to get those calves on the ground, all of them, by the end of April. So you're talking about March and April for calving. We put the bulls out about the fifteenth of March to the first of April. And then I leave those bulls out clear into the fall. Usually we start branding our calves in April and May. In the summer, hopefully our summer rains will be starting about the fourth to the tenth of July, the monsoon season. July and August is our big growing season here for our perennial grasses. That's what we really depend on, for the year's feed is those perennial grasses. So that's a big thing in the summertime.

In the fall, we start thinking about gathering those cattle and getting them into your shipping pasture about the first of October. Those calves usually go out of here weighing about 480 to 500 pounds about the middle to the last of October. We ship those calves, and of course the cows, they do a little bawling around for a few days, and then we scatter those cattle back out in the pastures on fresh feed, hopefully. We usually take those bulls up about the middle of October. I leave my bulls out longer than some people do because I like those cows to have every chance in the world to breed back if they're going to. And then in November and December, those cows are just trying to build back. Hopefully you've got them on good feed so they can build back. They don't have that calf draining on them right now. Supposedly they have a calf in them. You sure want them bred well before that. They'll build back their strength and everything going into the first of January and February again, so they'll be ready to start calving.

JL: What's the gestation period for cattle?

WG: Gestation period is nine months, just about like a human.

JL: In a normal year, how many inches of rain do you get?

WG: Our normal year would be twelve to fourteen inches on the Malpai. In the mountains at a little higher elevation, I would say sixteen to eighteen inches a year. We'll usually get about eight inches of that during the monsoon season and about four inches during the winter. That's here in the valley. Up in the mountains, we do get some snow, and not snow like you folks know it, like up to two or three feet. We get like six or eight inches to a foot. In the higher mountains, it can get two to three feet, like in the nine-, ten-thousand-foot elevation. But we haven't had those type of winters for quite a while. But that does recharge our groundwater. In the past two or three years here, we've had a little under three inches in the Malpai. So you're looking at country that's looking pretty hammered at this time, just barely holding on.

JL: I'd like to ask you to talk about the Malpai Border Group if you could and how you got into it.

WG: I know you talked to Drum Hadley. I give him a lot of credit. But things that were decided in our agencies like your BLM [Bureau of Land Management] or your Forest Service or your state Land Department concerning grazing, concerning fires, concerning even wildlife activity on the land—we thought maybe if we got together and started working with these people and threw together our own scientific research, then maybe we could influence these agencies in the way they did some of their planning [of these things].

     Surprisingly, when we started this, it was so rare, I think, to have cattle ranchers trying to work with the agency people that they were really receptive to this [idea] and really did get in and cooperate and listen to what we had to say. And we've come a long way as far as trying to establish certain criteria, especially with fires, being healthy for our rangeland. Periodically, whether it was once every ten years or once every five years—it varied a lot—but the whole country would probably burn. It kept a lot of the woody species that have taken over our pasturelands and grazing land nowadays at a kind of a minimum because they were burned off—they were pruned by Nature, you might say. And it helped our grasslands, it revitalized the grasslands. A lot of people that fought us on these fires were people concerned about a species of wildlife or insects even or birdlife that they were afraid fires would inhibit their habitat, so to speak, and they weren't looking back that these things all evolved with fire and they continued to be healthy with fire. So bringing fire back into the ecosystem is kind of a normal thing to do, but it was hard to get the different agencies and different groups to agree on this. They kind of agreed, but they didn't quite know how to get it done.

One thing, you have a lot of concern about your air pollution. Nobody wants to build smoke anymore on account of the air, and everybody's afraid of hurting some kind of endangered species or their habitat and that type of thing. That's why our science team plays such a big part to kind of prove that this [fire] doesn't harm those things; it's just kind of a healthy thing for the whole ecosystem.

JL: Ray Turner is one the scientists who works with you, isn't he?

WG: A wonderful man. Ray is invaluable to us. He's done studies with pictures that he's taken and compared to pictures in the past—the whole border area of Mexico and Arizona and New Mexico. He's kept records on rainfall amounts and different things that have affected the rangeland, including grazing. There's a lot of things that affect these rangelands besides grazing. He's brought the whole weather picture into perspective, so we're not blaming it all on the cows anymore. We're kind of sharing the blame with a few other things that can happen. And Ray Turner, we have him to thank for a lot of that. He coordinates a lot of our science program and advises us.

JL: Is there any room for collaboration between the ranching folks that you know and the environmental people?

WG: Oh, yes. Drum Hadley had a lot to do with bringing some of The Nature Conservancy people into this whole group. When we started the Malpai Group, they were right there at the table with us. They were helping us sit down and decide what we wanted, and we owe a lot to them. I tell you what, they're a wonderful group of people, and they're realizing also that maybe ranching is the best way to preserve open space not only for the country as a whole, but for wildlife corridors and the whole picture, the whole ecosystem. Their help has been invaluable. I would just mention Nature Conservancy as one group that has really been helpful to us.

JL: I know the Peloncillo Mountains are a tremendous wildlife corridor. You had a major experience up there with a jaguar. Could you tell that story?

WG: Sure did, Jack. That was in '96. I'm a professional hunter. We do that to supplement our income here because these are small ranches that we have. We were guiding a mountain lion hunt at that time in the Peloncillos and struck a track early one morning and thought it was a large male lion. But it ended up when we got this animal bayed, and I first saw it with my own eyes there. It was in a terrible rough steep country there. I tied my mule to go down to where the dogs had this animal bayed on this big bluff. I started walking down there and saw this cat on the bluff at about a hundred yards and realized it was a jaguar. I saw this big beautiful spotted cat. He had his rump kind of quartered toward me. He couldn't see me at that point, and I was a long ways from him.

Man, when I saw it was a jaguar, I ran back to my mule and grabbed a little camera I had on my saddle horn pouch and slipped around there and took a picture, and I thought that might be the only picture I'd get. That's why I was anxious to get one. It was hard for me to believe, and I didn't figure anybody else would believe me. Then I figured I had to go down and get those dogs. Now, they couldn't reach him at that point. He was up about thirty feet on top of this boulder. So I slipped down there to get close enough to call those dogs back, and I was taking pictures as I got closer and got some wonderful pictures of that cat.

That cat looked at me, and at that time I was probably thirty feet from him. He looked around and saw me standing there snapping pictures. In an instant, he was uneasy. He was a little bit contented there on that rock. The dogs were barking below, but they didn't seem to be bothering him that much. But, boy, when he saw me, a man, standing there, he started looking around, and I knew he was going to leave. He was looking for a place to get out of there, and he went over the rock out of my sight, and I think with the idea of jumping off, and it was a little too high. It was about a forty-foot, straight-down leap at that point for him. So he came back over the rock toward me, and I had changed positions a little bit. So I got some wonderful pictures of him going off that rock, and he made his jump on the uphill side, which was about twenty feet off, and then he took off again. The dogs bayed him again in another canyon, and I had to run up the hill to get my mule. When I caught up to the dogs again, they were baying this jaguar on the ground, but he was in kind of a cove. It wasn't a cave; it was just in a cove there with his back to the rock, and the dogs were kind of above him.

When I rode down to him, I could hear him roar. He wasn't growling or spitting like a big old tom lion would do. He was actually roaring a big guttural throaty roar, and it just was a strange sound to me because I hadn't ever heard anything do that. Again I tied my mule and went in there to try to get the dogs back and took some more pictures. At that point, I was so close, I was like eight or ten feet from him. He actually laid his ears back and locked onto my eyes, and he seemed to forget about the dogs at that point. He made a leap out of there in my direction, and he actually charged me at that point. When he hit right in front of me, about seven feet from me there, those dogs met him head on, and they all went backwards over into that place he had been, and he threw a couple of those dogs completely over him. He bit one dog through the hind leg, broke her leg. She was able to jump clear. I ran in at that time and kicked some dirt. I was hollering at the dogs, of course, to get back, and

I kicked some debris—it had rolled off of that bank about four feet—and hit the jaguar on the rear end, and he turned that one dog loose and whipped around. I think he thought those other dogs were coming in on him.

At that point, the dog jumped off the ledge, and I got the other ones up there back with me. As soon as he felt the pressure ease a little bit, he looked around and he left. He pulled around the ledge there out of my sight. The next time I saw him he was coming out the other side of the canyon probably thirty or forty yards [away], and he was leaving. At that point, I got all the dogs but two stopped. They shortly came back to me. But they were pretty well whipped, and so was I. I was glad to see him leave because I wasn't too sure how I was going to get those dogs away from him at that point. So that was the last I saw of him.

The following summer we saw his sign, just his track. By then we knew what this track was that we had been seeing the previous winter. And then the following fall he came back one more time, and that's the last we saw of his sign in that area. But it was a wonderful experience. Like you said, the Peloncillo Mountains are a wonderful chain of mountains that go right into the Sierra Madres in Mexico. It's a continuous chain to Mexico City. Wonderful wildlife corridor. The valleys on both sides— the Animas Valley to the east and the San Bernardino Valley on the west—are wonderful. Those are the two valleys where we're trying to keep those wildlife corridors open.

JL: What a great story, Warner. That must have been one of the highlights of your life, wasn't it?

WG: You know, Jack, no doubt it was. No doubt it had to be one of the most interesting. Of course, the highlight of my life I'd say was when I married Wendy and of course when we had our children. But as far as outdoor activity, that would have had to be one of the highlights of my life, it certainly was. It was a thrill, and it was a great opportunity for me and a great privilege just to be able to see that cat.

JL: Warner, is there anything that you want to tell me that we haven't really talked about?

WG: Jack, the only thing is a lot of the small ranchers in this country do different things to supplement their income because if you don't have a four-hundred-mother-cow outfit or better, it's hard to make a living for a family on a cattle ranch. And most of us don't. We're running like two to three hundred head of cattle maybe, and some fewer than that. So I would say over half of us have different things. Some of the ranchers' wives are nurses, some of them are teachers. Some of the ranchers work for the county driving a road grader, that type of thing. Some of them work for the agencies. I'm a professional hunting guide, and my daughter helps me with that. We guide from about November through about March—we're usually guiding hunts. Wendy's here taking care of the ranch and the cattle. That's kind of an interesting note. Most of the ranchers here in this area, the small ranches, have to have something going on besides cattle to support their way of life.

JL: I know a rancher up in the Ruby Valley in northern Nevada who was telling me, he says, "A lot of people think that us ranchers go down in the basement and count our money all night long. That isn't the way it is."

WG: If you were counting your money, you would be counting a lot of nothin' because there's not that much to go around. But it's a wonderful way of life, Jack. I don't think any of us would trade it. And that's why we try to stay with it.

PART II

Economic Depression
in the Land of Clear Light

As World War I drew to an end in Europe in 1918, the United States of America emerged as a major world power. The 1920s was a time of unprecedented economic prosperity. Former secretary of commerce Herbert Hoover was elected the thirty-first president of the United States in 1928. Charles Darwin was a pariah, and Thomas Malthus barely lingered in memory's shadowlands. White Americans danced to the Charleston, black Americans sang the blues and jump-started jazz, and Native Americans in the Southwest continued to dance to songs of reverence celebrating Nature's seasonal cycles, while Hispano narrative ballads called corridos recounted significant incidents in their history.

Then the stock market crashed, and America was plunged into the Great Depression, which lasted for more than a decade, from 1929 to 1941 and the outset of World War II. Fortunes disappeared, and one out of four Americans was unemployed. President Hoover, a Republican who had originally gained great respect for his heroic relief efforts during World War I, was criticized for his approach to economic restoration and soundly defeated in his second bid for the presidency by Franklin Delano Roosevelt, governor of New York, in 1932.

Roosevelt focused on a program of economic recovery that came to be known as the New Deal. Three issues of the New Deal were direct relief, economic recovery, and financial reform. Hardest hit by the Depression were the urban populations. Much of rural America took a softer hit because many still practiced subsistence farming, and hunting and fishing contributed to the family larder. The American Southwest was lightly populated, largely with indigenous peoples whose lifeways spared them the need to rely solely on the coin of the realm. Many were poor, even poverty-stricken by the economic standards of the 1920s, but my conversations with elderly Navajos, Puebloans, and Hispanos suggest that their poverty was largely in the eyes of outside beholders.

Al Largo is a Navajo who grew up along the Continental Divide near Thoreau, New Mexico. He recalls his grandmother telling him about the Depression: "My grandmother had over a thousand head of sheep. They were fortunate enough to have these sheep. They were self-reliant throughout the Depression because they would sell their lambs to the trading post. And they had plenty. So that is what was instilled in me at a young age—that if you have sheep, you will never go hungry. The sheep will take care of you. But you are the one that has to take care of them first."

The late Willie Apodaca grew up in San Geronimo, New Mexico, a rural community where subsistence farming had been a way of life for many generations: "In any house you went [to], there was always plenty to eat—plenty of beans, plenty of chile, plenty of potatoes, *biscochitos* [cookies], pumpkin pies. And if you didn't grow no pinto beans and I grow pinto beans, maybe you had a lot of pumpkins, so you give me pumpkins, and I give you pinto beans, or you might have a big patch of blue corn to make blue corn tortillas. So you trade me, and I trade you. The people used to help one another."

It is ironic that New Mexico, which had been a state for less than a quarter century at the time, became a major recipient of New Deal funding. Many who had subsisted satisfactorily within the context of their cultural traditions for hundreds of years were transported almost en masse into the dominant economic paradigm that both prevailed in and threatened much of the rest of America. The lingering presence of the New Deal is still ubiquitous throughout the state.

The interviews in this part give a sense of the New Deal in New Mexico in the 1930s, where echoes of the great Indian wars and the Mexican Revolution still lingered throughout the landscape. The air was pristine, and magic light enchanted artists from beyond the seas. Though money was short, the spirit of the land provided riches beyond measure.

Stewart Udall, photo by author

Stewart Udall

Introduction

Former U.S. secretary of the interior Stewart Udall was a child when the stock market crashed on Black Tuesday in 1929. He lived on the family farm in St. Johns, Arizona, within a hundred miles of the Continental Divide. The family subsisted largely on what they grew, raised, and hunted. Stewart's father became a judge and thus earned a modest income. They survived well enough in a community where neighbor shared with neighbor, and every youth was trained to accept great responsibility as part of life's heritage.

I have been deeply fortunate to know the Udall family for four decades. Lee, Stewart's wife, was my last boss back in the 1960s, when she was the director of the Center for Arts of Indian America and employed me to wander Navajo country as the curator of a traveling exhibition designed to reinvigorate among Navajo youths some interest and pride in their own culture. Lee was indeed one of the greatest friends of my lifetime, and I honor her memory daily.

Over the years, I've had the opportunity to converse with my friend Stewart on countless occasions and even to record him recounting aspects of his amazing life. In the spring of 2006, his daughter Lori and I sat with Stewart in the kitchen of his beautiful home in Santa Fe and urged him to talk about his recollections of the Great Depression.

Stewart Udall

JL: Stewart, I'd like you to characterize your family in St. Johns, Arizona, back when you born and through the 1920s, and what life was like in rural Arizona in that time, because you were nine when the Great Depression hit. You were shaped by that rural atmosphere. So could you talk about that?

SU: Well, Jack, when I was a congressman in the 1950s and then secretary of interior, I was deeply involved in the history of this period. I had to study it for the book I wrote, which is *The Quiet Crisis* [1964]. But my personal memories are on top of that and provide an immediacy that I'm sure you're interested in. I went to school beginning in 1926, and I remember Lindbergh's flight and the impact that had. I remember the first time I listened to the radio. The radio became a very important part of the lives of all Americans, but I first heard radio the night of the 1928 election—Herbert Hoover against Al Smith. Of course, Hoover smashed him. I went with my father to the druggist in town, who had a battery radio system, and that was the first time I heard the radio.

So I have memories of the impact of the Great Depression. We didn't have electricity. In these rural areas, and this is true in the Intermountain West to a large degree, there were a few large cities. I happened to see them while I was a youngster. Salt Lake City. Mormons made pilgrimages there. Phoenix, Albuquerque, Denver—I had brief contacts with all of these different cities. Of course, the main lines of the railroads were in. The Santa Fe line had been there since the 1880s, and there were railroad towns. The culture was different because you did have that contact with the outside world. But you were living in the rural area, which is most of New Mexico and most of Arizona—St. Johns was a farming town, a ranching town. The main economic impacts came from raising cattle, and they'd drive the cattle down to the railroad near Gallup [New Mexico], and the cattle buyers would ship them, I guess, to Kansas City, to Chicago and so on. So that was part of the economic system.

St. Johns had irrigation farming. Our community had what in New Mexico is called an acequia system, and you had your turn for the water, and you had a watermaster, and they'd give you a little slip of paper that said, "You take the water at 2:30 in the morning." Well, if you were a kid ten or eleven or twelve, and you were the oldest boy, you were the one that went to the head gate, took the head gate down, and the water came, and you watered the garden, which you had also helped plant. The children had the responsibility to take care of the garden, to milk the cows—[especially] if you were the oldest boy. My oldest sister milked the cows before I did. You took care of the pigs and the chickens. You were providing a substantial amount of the foodstuffs from either your animals, your garden, or when you slaughtered pigs and cattle.

JL: What watershed is St. Johns in? What river runs nearby?

SU: The Little Colorado. It's part of the Colorado River system. It's west of the Continental Divide. They built dams on the river. You [would] have a spring runoff, and you would build dams with horses, and this was a huge undertaking. The dams that were built in St. Johns were constructed by local people. They built canals, and the water went out into the irrigation system, where you irrigated water on the high ground.

We raised corn and alfalfa hay, and alfalfa was the only money product because we could sell it to dairies in Winslow [Arizona] and Gallup, and I remember going out on the [Navajo] reservation because the trading posts on the reservation would sell hay. Usually it was barter for the products of the Navajo—their sheep and the other things that they produced, like Navajo blankets.

So it was a primitive economy, and it was subsistence. You [were] just doing the best you [could] in terms of getting by.

JL: It was also a character-building way of life.

SU: Well, I think it was character building because work was part of your life. My father had an eighty-acre farm where we raised alfalfa and corn, and as you grew older, that was part of your job. The ambition for a kid like myself when I was sixteen or seventeen was to be the foreman. The foreman meant that your younger brothers were also working there. We baled hay. My father had a hay baler, and I worked first punching wires on the hay baler. I probably was ten or eleven years old. You were farm kids, and during the Depression you were Depression kids. You weren't paid very much, but that helped the whole system work.

JL: When the stock market crashed in 1929, the metropolitan areas in the United States suffered enormously. Could you talk about the impact when the Depression hit in St. Johns? Was it impacted like New York or Los Angeles?

SU: No. There was an enormous difference. In some manufacturing towns, you had 80 percent unemployment. It just sort of shut down. In the big cities, the New Deal programs were focused on public works, finding work that people could do to help restart the economy. The secretary of interior, Harold Ickes, was in charge of not just the Interior Department, but also the Public Works Project. You built post offices, and these provided part-time jobs for people. The New Deal was trying to get the economy started. They never fully succeeded. Until the war came along, it was hard going. The railroads kept running, and that was a success because the railroads connected the cities and people.

        But with us in the rural area in the mountain states like Arizona and New Mexico, that was the one chugging part of the economy that continued to function, although at a lower level. With us in rural areas of the West, we were already depressed in a sense that we were on a subsistence economy that helped the rural areas. What caused hard times, for example, would be a drought when you didn't have the water you needed to make the parts of the economic system work.

JL: How would you say Harold Ickes stacked up as secretary of interior?

SU: He was there for thirteen years. He had this dual responsibility for public works. One public-works project in St. Johns, and I'm sure this is true in other areas, they extended the water service to homes, and they built outhouses. The outhouses were called "Roosevelt Memorials" by some of the critics. But that gave jobs to people. Of course, the other main impact of the New Deal in rural areas like many parts of New Mexico were the CCC [Civilian Conservation Corps] camps. That was a big thing. These were run by the army, incidentally, and they recruited kids in cities. In places like New Mexico, some of the Hispanic kids were enrolled in CCC camps. They were paid twenty-five dollars a month and most of their money went to their parents. It was salvation in places like New Mexico because twenty-five dollars was a lot of money then. They could buy a sack of sugar, flour, beans, and so on from the grocery stores of that time.

I remember the soil conservation program in rural areas in some parts of the Southwest. They would hire people to stop erosion. That was important because it provided a few part-time jobs for people. Everyone needed a schoolteacher in the family because that provided money for the family. Extended families were important because if there were large extended families of brothers and sisters and so on, they shared things. If you killed a deer, if you killed an elk, you brought it home, and you shared it. Not only with your family. You didn't have refrigerators then. You hung it on the north side of the house, and that became an important part of the food. I have talked to people in New Mexico who still have elk, some of them. To kill an elk would provide a lot of the food for the winter period.

JL: You're talking to one of them now. I used to hunt my meat and jerk it. I sliced it into jerky slices, hung it in the top of a tipi, and built an oak fire and let it smoke for a couple of days.

SU: Well, that was common during the Depression. I can tell you, sharing was very important because if the breadwinner was killed, the family rallied around and helped. That wasn't part of the New Deal. It was part of the Depression that you had to work together. The thing that people have a hard time understanding [is that] the Depression lasted eleven years. In contrast to the big cities—in the East, where the Depression hit hard, you had these soup lines providing food for people where some of the families were devastated. You have these old pictures of a man who might have worked for a bank [now] selling apples on the street corners in the cities.

Out here in the West, the projects during the Depression of the 1930s that provided employment were building dams. The interesting thing is [that] the Hoover Dam was built right during the Depression. That was financed. Golden Gate Bridge was financed with bonds, in part. There were big construction projects. The Tennessee Valley Authority, the Columbia River Valley—dams were built there. Those provided employment. They were building transmission lines from hydroelectric plants like Hoover Dam and others, and a lot of that power went to small towns.

JL: I wanted to mention the relationship between the building of dams, the irrigation projects, and the creation of hydroelectricity. That all melded together in these dams, like the Hoover Dam and then subsequently the Glen Canyon Dam. That whole notion really grew to major proportion during the 1930s.

SU: It not only grew, Jack, it turned out to be, just by luck, terribly important. The war came along just at the right time, and the war plants connected with the Manhattan Project [and] Oak Ridge, Tennessee, [and] Hanford in Washington, the aircraft factories in southern California, the Hoover Dam and the power and the water that came to southern California were just in time for the war. So the hydroelectric projects, the big dams, were big projects; they provided work for people, they provided electricity particularly for the small towns that didn't have it, and that was one of the big successes of the New Deal.

The CCC camps, what are they doing? Planting trees in the high country, mostly, where the forest had been stripped or where drought had taken over. So in the western part of the United States, the New Deal was largely a conservation program—building dams, [doing] irrigation projects, providing soil conservation, CCC tree planting. Roosevelt was a great believer. He'd done that in New York as governor, replanting the forests. We moved across this country—that's in my book, *The Quiet Crisis*. The lumber companies had stripped a lot of the forests, in Pennsylvania and eastern states, along through Wisconsin and into the West. There were no rules, and so the need for reforestation was very important. It was needed not just in the West, but in the East. But it was particularly important in the West.

Money was so scarce. Where there were payrolls in these small towns, [it] was for teachers. We kept our commitment to education. Teachers were paid probably seventy-five, one hundred dollars a month, but that was a lot of money in those days, and the other payrolls were for the professional people, the doctors, the lawyers, the merchants in town, the druggist, and so on. This is with a town of thirteen hundred people where I lived. This is cowboy country, too, that I lived in. My father was part owner of a ranch that never made any money in particular. I spent three of my summers [there] when I was about ten, eleven, and twelve—I rode with the cowboys.

With the cattlemen, you sold the cattle in the fall, and you got enough money to last you for the year. But it was hardscrabble times, hard times, particularly if there was a drought. So my father was a judge. From the time he became a judge in 1931 during the Depression until he left the community to go on the Arizona Supreme Court in 1946, his pay never increased. That was true in general. He made four thousand dollars a year. That made him one of the prosperous people in town, and he was able to educate all of his children. There were no pay increases for teachers and other people during that period of time.

In effect, the economy, unless you had a big dam that was being built or something, was just struggling along. The New Deal programs provided part-time employment for people, and that was very important, to have a job that provided any cash. Cash was hard to come by, and that was the reason we needed the produce from a farm, the produce from a garden, what was provided by animals. If you slaughtered a pig, there was a man in town who was the main person that you would hire to come and boil hot water and kill the pig and prepare the meat that you shared with your neighbors or members of your family. You hung it on the north side of the house. You didn't have refrigeration. You had a pantry on the north side of the side where you kept the milk and the vegetables.

If you grew up in a small town, you knew the human comedy, you knew the human tragedy. You might have dug a grave for a relative. That was pick-and-shovel work in those days. Knowing other people and watching the progress of their lives—in a small town, everybody knew everybody's strengths and weaknesses, and you got acquainted. We used to go to trials in the courthouse when we were nine, ten, eleven years old, and then we had a kids' court in my father's garage. We watched the adults. So it was part of your education to understand life. We didn't have banks, so you couldn't have bank robberies. Hard times made for building character, I think. It also enlarged your understanding.

JL: You know, Stewart, a lot of people now don't realize that some programs that evolved during the New Deal are still with us, like Social Security and the FDIC [Federal Deposit Insurance Corporation], which helped ensure that the banks would remain solvent. Those are the enduring things. Would you talk a little bit about that?

SU: Jack, there was no safety net when Social Security came along. It took two years for that to take effect. As far as health care was concerned, it was the business of the family. People got cancer. You didn't have hospitals. You took care of them in your home, and that was the business of people. All these programs that we take for granted now as part of our birthright—health care, Social Security, taking care of older people—this all grew out of the Depression. But the Depression kids, those of us who grew up in the Depression and then fought the war, we were nurtured on this tradition of learning how to subsist on people helping other people in the family, of this tradition of taking care of your own people.

Thirty percent of the workforce in the factories during World War II were women. The famous Rosie the Riveter. They had to develop skills. A private was paid twenty-nine dollars a month. I don't think that changed during the war. If you were in the army or the navy, you were in the service. You didn't need any money, anyway, except if you were going out on a weekend spree, so you sent your paychecks home. You could sign a piece of paper, and your paycheck went home, and your family bought war bonds.

I had sixteen or seventeen hundred dollars at the end of the war that my parents had in war bonds. I bought my first car in 1947 when I cashed in some of my war bonds. It was a little Ford. I think it cost twelve hundred dollars. That was my first big expenditure. I had to buy a car so my wife and I could go on our honeymoon. So the effects of the Depression—the way it developed personal values, the way it influenced your attitude toward money and how important it was to save—[were] built into the system. We're now in 2006. People in this country don't save anymore. They charge. They run their credit cards. The savings rate in 2005 dropped so low that you had to look at 1934–35, the depths of the Depression, for a savings rate that was comparable. Of course, there wasn't much to save then. That shows how thrifty we had to be. Thrift was sort of built into the system. You didn't buy anything you couldn't afford.

JL: That system of attitudes is what shaped you, and basically the Great Depression ended with the beginning of World War II, and you went into the service. In those days, it was known as the Army Air Corps. Could you talk about how your life was affected by going from being a Depression civilian, somebody who lived in rural America, [to being in] the army in those days?

SU: The thing people have to realize about World War II: the New Deal established a lot of very basic important laws. It got parts of the economy going, but we had a recession. The year I graduated from high school in 1937, the economy sagged for a couple of years, and then literally Pearl Harbor transformed the whole country. You had to produce all these weapons of war—bombers and new weapons. The young men became the bulk of the soldiers. Those are the people that fight the wars. So this was an enormous change. But we were going to pay for the war as it went along. We built up a huge debt, but my generation paid for it with balanced budgets in the twenty-five years after the war ended. That's what was extraordinary.

Everybody sacrificed for the country. People not only sacrificed their lives (292,000 Americans died during the four years of that war), but we all sacrificed for the country, and that created the spirit that carried through after the war, I believe, because we had a lot of veterans who went into business, small businesses. We had the GI Bill for people to get an education.

JL: The war ended in 1945. By that time, you were twenty-five years old. At the age of twenty-five, you had experienced not only growing up in a rural neighborhood, but the eleven years of the Great Depression and the entirety of World War II. What were your visions of yourself by the time it got to be 1945?

SU: I was an idealist. I wrote something called "Testament at the Completion of a War." I thought that we owed it to the men who died and who didn't come home to make this a "war to end wars." That was a theme in World War I, you know. It didn't

work out that way because of all the mistakes. So I was an idealist. I belonged to the NAACP [National Association for the
Advancement of Colored People] while I was in the army. I got
involved in veterans' organizations. I got involved in politics. I
helped manage my father's campaign when he ran for office to
win a seat on the [Arizona] Supreme Court. Then later when
I got ambitious and ran for Congress, I was standing on his
shoulders. He was in many ways the most respected judge and
respected human being in a larger circle in Arizona. So I got into
politics in 1954. I was, what, thirty-four.

I later stuck my neck out for Senator [John F.] Kennedy, and
he invited me to be in the cabinet. So all that happened from the
end of the war in 1945 till 1960. I moved up and have had a very
exciting life.

After the war, a year or two afterwards, there was a film,
The Best Years of Our Lives. That [film] expresses this feeling
that all of us developed in this war. We were giving something
to the country, and we had a comradeship, a comradeship that
was important. We weren't out for ourselves during that war. We
were serving the country as best we could.

If you ask, "What was the spirit of [the] people?" I remember the day that I was discharged and I came out, and there was
gasoline rationing. There was a guy who called himself Madman
Muntz. He bought old cars and had mechanics that fixed them
so they'd run, sometimes just down the road a few miles. There's
the commercial side, the advertising side, that took over in our
country, saying, "Buy this, buy this." I just resented it. I walked
out in my uniform, and I hitchhiked home.

The whole debt-is-good, credit-card culture [and] the advertising, which I think has driven so much of this—the economic
concepts changed, and they changed so rapidly. I don't pretend
to be an expert on this, but I think my children grew up with the
attitude that they wanted to succeed, but they weren't greedy.
There's a greediness out there today. It's spawned in the past fifteen, twenty years, I think. Attitudes in corporate America and

the scandals and the corruption and everything else—I'm glad my kids are not involved in any of that. My wife, Lee, and I had the opportunity to do things that we valued and an opportunity for our children to participate in the things that we did and [to] be good parents.

Kathryn Flynn, photo by author

Kathryn Flynn

Introduction

Kathryn Flynn is the executive director of the National New Deal Preservation Association. She is the author of *Treasures on New Mexico Trails* (1995), a book that focuses on the art and architecture that was funded by the New Deal Works Progress Administration (WPA, later the Works Projects Administration) of the 1930s in New Mexico. Her father was a Presbyterian minister, and she was born in Texas. Flynn earned a master's degree in rehabilitation and psychology and has been a resident of New Mexico for many years. It was while working for the New Mexico State Health Department that she visited the Carrie Tingley Hospital, then located in Truth or Consequences, and saw the wonderful murals painted by Gisella Loeffler in the 1930s. Flynn gradually came to discover other murals painted on or in public edifices throughout the state, and her interest in New Deal art projects expanded enormously.

She began working with then secretary of state Stephanie Gonzales in 1991 and produced three New Mexico blue books that focused on murals, art, and courthouse architecture. In 1994, she acquired the necessary nonprofit status to allow her to garner funding to restore New Deal artwork that had been damaged, and thus was born the National New Deal Preservation Association.

Since then, she has become a national authority on the subject. The New Deal WPA funded artists, writers, musicians, and actors to pursue their art forms. In the interview, Kathy Flynn discusses the New Deal, its various components, and its great importance for not only New Mexico, but the entire nation.

Kathryn Flynn

JL: I want to ask you, could you give an overview of Roosevelt's New Deal?

KF: Well, I wouldn't have wanted to be in that man's shoes for any-thing. It was a horrible time in our country. Everybody was in total economic dire straits. He [Franklin D. Roosevelt, FDR] was sworn in on March 4, 1933, the day before nearly all the banks closed, and on March 5, the day after, he did close all the banks, giving them a bank holiday, which was a desperate situation. He looked at it on the basis that he was wanting to maintain, as I understand, a balanced budget, but came to the reality that that wasn't going to work, that they had to take this big leap of faith and take on a variety of things to bring the country back from its economic crisis.

So they looked at, certainly, some forms of relief for the unemployed because a huge of amount of people in this country, the majority of the people in this country, were unemployed. We were just in this terrible depression. So they first tackled the eco-nomics, the bank problems. And in the first hundred days, he passed fifteen bills to deal with this problem. When you think of Congress moving that fast, it's amazing. Among them were the Social Security Act and the Tennessee Valley Authority, dealing with the electrical problems and damming, controlling of the water. There's just practically no aspect of our daily lives that they didn't work toward fixing.

I ran across a quotation that Winston Churchill said that

meeting FDR was like popping a cork on the first bottle of champagne. Another thing that Churchill said was, "A country that forgets its past has no future." And that's the thing I wrap up every speech with about the New Deal because the New Deal saved this country. I just can't even imagine where we would be today because the things that were created as part of those projects, we're still using today.

Now seventy-three years old, those sewer systems and those water systems and our transportation systems—there are so many things that are getting old. But we are still using the courthouses, the city halls, the schools, the museums, the libraries, the parks. The CCC, Civilian Conservation Corps, planted millions of trees. And the forests that we have in this country today in many cases weren't there before. Many buildings in our national parks today were created by the CCC. One of the first things done in that first hundred days was to take advantage of two things that we were wasting, our young men and our land. Roosevelt put the two together with the CCC.

Those guys had to be eighteen to twenty-five years of age, they had to weigh at least 112 pounds, they had to have three natural masticating teeth, and they had to have a family back home that was in dire need. And they got thirty dollars a month, or about a dollar a day, of which they saw five dollars, and the twenty-five went back to the family. And many times those families pushed those boys out the door so they could get that twenty-five dollars because there were so many hungry mouths at home to be fed. And to the man, every CCC fellow that I've ever talked to said it made the biggest difference in their lives. It made them who they were today. It gave them skills. In many cases, they were illiterate. I think I saw one reference to four hundred thousand young boys who were totally illiterate who learned how to read and write in the CCC. Chicago allowed as how their crime rate dropped significantly once the boys got in the CCC.

In New Mexico, we had fifty-six thousand young men involved in conserving this state at forty-two camps, and three-quarters of those were New Mexicans, but the rest were from other parts of the country. And the same thing happened for our guys that went elsewhere. I've heard them say, "I got off that bus, and I looked up, and it was a part of the country I didn't know where I'd gotten dropped off in." So they got exposed to things; they were taught a skill. They learned discipline; they learned how to live with other people that were maybe different and came from different parts of the country. After Pearl Harbor occurred, practically the next day, those CCC boys went right into the army or the navy or the marines, and there were various generals who said, "We were able to win the war because we had a head start because of the CCC guys."

JL: One of the things that I think is kind of great regarding the myriad acronyms that came from all of the programs is the alphabet soup.

KF: Yes. In each one of those—Civilian Works Project, CWA [Civil Works Administration], PWA, Public Works Administration— there was the HABS [Historic American Buildings Survey], where they hired architects to go and survey existing buildings and that I believe are still in use. In terms of the Public Art Project, that started out with Public Works of Art Project, PWAP. It lasted only six months. It hired artists that were already known artists and were professionals, and so they made fairly good money. They made forty-two dollars and fifty cents a week.

Then the Treasury Section Program came in, and it lasted from 1934 to 1938. That was primarily to work with buildings that were being built or public buildings that existed. Then in 1935 was the Treasury Relief Program to finance murals in post offices. There are thousands of murals in post offices in this country.

JL: Let's talk about New Mexico and the artists and the writers.

KF: The art project in New Mexico was run by Russell Vernon Hunter. He had grown up in Texico, New Mexico, over by

Clovis, and he was also down in Roswell. He was, according to his wife, the only Federal Art Project person that stayed throughout the entire time. The Federal Art Project and the others fell under the WPA, and the WPA stood for the Works Progress Administration from 1935 to 1939, and obviously they must have run out of the money, so then they had to go back in and get some more. The second go-round was 1939 to 1942. Then it was called the Works Projects Administration. So when people say, "No, I think it's 'Projects'" or "I think it's 'Progress,'" they're both right. It just was two different times.

Then you also had the Federal Writers' Project, the Music Project, the Art Project, the Theater Project—all of these things—to hire these people also. Now, within the Federal Art Project or any of the WPA projects, you first had to be on relief or on welfare, whereas [with] those previous art projects I mentioned, you did not have to be on welfare. You were a professional artist, and you were either hired based on your capabilities, or you were in competition, and you won a competition to do a post office or something.

So nearly everybody got on the Federal Art Project or music or whatever because everybody was starving or had a family to feed. So you got on the Federal Art Project in New Mexico, and you were either given a specific thing to do or you were given canvases and paints and this sort of thing and told to go paint. You had a supervisor, namely Gustav Baumann, and there's a collection of his critiques on some of those artists that if he'd written today, he'd have been sued up one side and down the other.

The sad thing that every state has found is that there are no complete records on everything. So when you try to go and find out how many people were involved in these projects, you generally have to go and piecemeal it together, and then you don't know whether you've got it all right. But what I have found so far is that we had about 166 people—artists—working in the Federal Art Project here in New Mexico, and that was broken down [into], like, 29 women, 29 or so Native Americans. There was actually a separate Indian project, and John Collier ran that whole Indian project, which was all-encompassing. It included CCC, art projects, building buildings, whatever. I think they had a nineteen-billion-dollar budget. Their total budget for the BIA [Bureau of Indian Affairs] was twenty-one million dollars [at the time], so it was a big project.

We have found 60 murals or mural-size paintings in New Mexico, 657 paintings, 10 sculptures, 43 pieces of Patrocinio Barela's work, and then there were crafts out the *kazak*. The Hispanics really kind of got the short shrift in the sense that bureaucratically, [in] the paperwork, most of the Hispanic artists were just referred to as assistants to whoever they were working with. So for a long time we didn't know who all those people were. And fortunately Tey Marianna Nunn elected to find that out as part of a doctoral program that she completed, and she found, I think, almost all of the Hispanic artists.

JL: Can you name some of them?

KF: Oh, certainly. The only two artists living today in 2006 are Eliseo Rodriguez and Abade Lucero. Of course, now that you ask me . . . Hispanic, and I'm thinking Native American names. Native American: let's see, we've got Maria Martinez and Pablita Velarde and Tonita Peña and Allan Houser and Gerald Nailor. One of the beautiful things for New Mexico, I think, is that [at] the very top portion of the Department of the Interior there are a number of murals, and they all were done by New Mexico Native American artists. So it was Houser, Woody Crumbo, Gerald Nailor, and Velino Shije Herrera. And they've all been restored. I talked to Houser about them before he died, and he was very pleased with the final product. So there were a lot of them.

As far as we know, Harrison Begay is still alive, and we stay in touch with Harrison's family, and he's in his nineties, and he's off again running around—nobody knows where he is, and we're all looking for him. There are three still alive.

JL: Can you talk about some of the Anglo artists a bit?

KF: Let's get my book, *The Treasures on New Mexico Trails*. There's a chapter in that book on who the Hispanic artists were, who the Anglo artists were, who the Native American artists were, and what they did. In fact, we started the book out in the section on the Anglo artists [with]Will Shuster's writing a letter to John Sloan saying, "You know, I don't know what I'm going to do. I've told the utility companies they'll just have to cut it off because I can't pay my utilities. The only place I can get credit is at Kaune's grocery store over there on College Street." And then he writes him a few weeks later and says, "Can you believe it? The federal government is going to pay me to paint, and I have offered them three opportunities that I would do. One would be to redesign the federal currency." The second one was to paint portraits of all the Indian war chiefs in the nation, and the third one is to paint the stalactites and stalagmites in Carlsbad Caverns, "because I've been down there in a bucket and I've seen that." And that's what they let him do. And then of course he did the frescoes in the courtyard of the Museum of Fine Arts [Santa Fe], and those are in great shape. He ground his own paints up and all that. Fremont Ellis, Bill Lumpkins—most people don't know that Bill was [in] on it. William Penhallow Henderson. There are six magnificent, magnificent paintings—mural-size paintings, they are on canvas glued to the wall next to the post office in the federal courthouse [in Santa Fe]. This is one of them on the front of my book. In the coffee table book, all six of them are in there.

Raymond Jonson was also one. The federal government asked artists to depict American realism. So it was the beginning of the American art as we know it today. And for the most part in other states, the artwork was showing the work ethic and giving the sense of hope. In New Mexico, we only have very few of those work ethic pictures. We painted what it looked like back then. We painted ourselves, how we lived, what we did, how our lives were. And we had the whole gamut. I mean, we had Emile Bisttram. Now he's one of the ones that painted also in Washington [D.C.] at the Department of Justice, but in one of the court buildings in Albuquerque there is one of those that looks like what you think the New Deal artwork is. It's *Justice Tempered with Mercy*. Protect the right.

And then there's artwork in the old courthouse in Taos that has a similar feel to the rest of the nation. There're ten murals there. For the most part, we run the gamut. I mean, [there was] Raymond Jonson's modern stuff that was totally different from anybody else's, and then we have Ila McAfee's horses and deer, and Olive Rush's light, lovely frescoes. [The artwork] certainly did portray hope. I think the other thing that came out of it was that it was the first time [that] people—Joe Blow on the street— saw fine art. The only art they'd ever seen before was on calendars. And they also saw artists working, like on the post offices and the courthouses. And they would finally come around just talking to them. They thought that all artists were weirdos. They were strange. And they just discovered they weren't. They sat down and talked with them and watched them work and realized that they were just like them, and they were hungry just the same.

So we had John Jellico, Peter Hurd. The only piece he [Hurd] did in New Mexico is in Alamogordo. It was on the front of the post office there. It's no longer the post office. It's a National Forest Service building, and that's been restored recently. Odon Hullenkremer from Santa Fe did some big pieces and some little ones. Joseph Fleck, another one. Louie Ewing had an assistant named Eliseo Rodriguez, and he and his assistant figured out a way to do serigraphs and silk screening that really worked out well. The other thing about Eliseo's work—and he's such a humble human being, it's wonderful—he said, "You know, I was working on building the rock walls along Water Street, and when we finished that, I didn't really know how I was going to feed my family, and somebody said, 'Don't you like to paint pictures? You ought to go down there and talk to Russell Vernon Hunter and get you a job painting.'" He said, "I did. By gosh, he gave me these canvases and stuff, and then there was somebody that was trying to get some of us to do some different kinds of art, and this woman wanted somebody to do something from Egypt called straw inlay artwork. Nobody wanted to do that." He said a lot of those guys had egos, and he was very careful about saying that. He said, "I figured I'd try anything. I had a family to feed. I tried it, and I kind of liked that." He's famous for it, of course.

He sat there at his kitchen table. His wife, Paula, did it [straw inlay], too. I said, "Eliseo, how many people in your family are making a living doing that now?" He said, "Eleven." He learned it as part of the Federal Art Project.

JF: I wonder if you could talk a little bit about Gisela Loeffler and her work.

KF: She was from Austria and lived in Taos, and she got picked up on the program in Taos. I think Emile Bisttram was the supervisor up in that region. She has a style like nobody else in New Mexico, and here again it's typical of what we were in New Mexico at the time. The two pieces from Carrie Tingley Hospital are untitled.

I have a story about one of them that just brings tears to my eyes every time I tell it. These [pieces] are 72 inches by 120. They're big. Some years later, this man came up to one of the hospital staff and said, "I want to see the painting of the Baby Jesus." And she said, "I don't think we have any paintings of the Baby Jesus. This is a state facility. We don't have any religious paintings." He said, "You better have. You did have, and it saved me during the time I was a little boy with polio down at Hot Springs being treated for polio in this New Deal building." He said, "I would roll my wheelchair up to the Baby Jesus and talk to him every day because I was far away from my mother and daddy, and I was so homesick, and I was in so much pain, and that kept me going."

They walked around and found Gisela's painting with the Baby Jesus—the Nativity scene—right in the foreground.

JL: That painting now is in—

KF: Carrie Tingley Hospital at 1127 University in Albuquerque. It's in the dining-hall area. The story about the building of the hospital down there in Truth or Consequences was told to me by Bill Lumpkins, who was one of the architects. The money came through from Washington and then the state had to put some money in, too. Clyde Tingley was the governor. He decided that the hospital would be named Carrie Tingley Hospital for his wife. Bill said that about two months after they got the money, Carrie came to the architects to see how her hospital plans were coming along, and they all rolled their eyes and looked at one another and said, "I'm sorry, Mrs. Tingley, but we really don't know what a poliomyelitis hospital has to have in it." And she said, "Well, we can take care of that." And she picked up the phone and called Eleanor Roosevelt, who called the architect at Warm Springs, Georgia, where FDR was treated for polio and I understand was referred to as Dr. Roosevelt down there because he also worked with the kids. So that architect flew to Albuquerque, sat down with Bill Lumpkins and Frank Stoddard, and they built the hospital basically along the lines of the one in Warm Springs.

The art project in New Mexico: you had to be on relief. There's art in probably forty-eight towns in public buildings from that period in the state of New Mexico. Let me just say, because you mentioned theater, we did not have a theater project in New Mexico. That's the only one we did not have. It was certainly nationwide.

The Writers' Project in New Mexico was run by Ina Sizer Cassidy. We had forty-eight writers in New Mexico, and they created 780 different pieces of work. Now, every state did what was called the state guidebook, and we did have a state guidebook. Nationwide, when they got started in 1935, they hired sixty-six hundred writers across the nation. So here again the writers were being put to work. They wrote city guides, they wrote state guides, they wrote regional guides, they did children's books. The federal government actually paid for the writers' guide to be done for Washington, D.C., and it's an immense one. It has a big map of Washington in it, and it's 1,141 pages. The smallest guidebook was Idaho with 299 pages. The biggest one was in Pennsylvania.

They also did oral histories on people in every little community and whatnot. In New Mexico, those oral history stories are at the history library downtown [in Santa Fe], the Fray Angelico Chavez Library on Washington [in Santa Fe], and another batch of them is at the state archives. Those are still in those carbon copies on the onionskin paper in file folders. Tey Diana Rebolledo has done a book on collecting the women's stories from those oral histories that were done.

Many of the people that we know today as being the scholars or the artists or whatever were part of that [project]. Ernest Hemingway, John Steinbeck, Saul Bellow. And, of course, the one that's still alive that some people know very well and think highly of still is Studs Terkel in Chicago. He was in the Federal Writers' Project and the Federal Theater Project in Chicago. His book *Hard Times* is about the Depression, and it really is a beautiful book and tells about it.

Going back to Gisella Loeffler, I found a letter that she had written to Eleanor Roosevelt asking her to make sure that she did not get kicked off the Art Project because she needed the money so badly. She was pleading with her because she wanted to do a story of children's folk music and songs and things. She ended up doing that, so it was a combination of the Art Project and the Music Project working together, and she illustrated the books, and the music . . . I don't know who wrote the music part. But it was Spanish American songs and games, and I think there were two separate books, and Gisela illustrated. It was a very special thing to have the two projects working together.

Another thing that came out nationwide musicwise was that they did a whole guide to the study of music in America, and they did an index of American musicians, fourteen thousand names of people who were in music in some form. Here in New Mexico we did a guitar methods book, a volume of children's songs. For professional musicians, the pay range was thirty-nine to ninety-four dollars a month, then the next level was thirty-five to eighty-five dollars a month, then after that I don't have a figure. There were a lot of symphonies that were done, and in Oklahoma I spoke with a conductor. I said that a musician couldn't be playing and performing all the time, so how was it that they were paid the rest of the time when they weren't performing? He said, for example, that reed musicians got paid to make reeds when they weren't performing. Musicians were also copying scores of music.

I heard a horrible story that there were all of these manuscripts that had been hand scored and hand copied, and a museum authority decided that that was against copyright orders and [that] liabilities could come down on them and so threw them all out. Tons and scores of music—threw them out as part of the New Deal. Of course, that's the story in so much of this art and the music. But certainly the art.

So there's a whole chapter in my book [called] "Solve the Unsolved Mysteries of Art." Two little clues you can look for if [a piece was] part of the Federal Art Project. There's generally a brass plaque on the lower portion center of the frame and it says "FAP," or it'll say "Federal Art Project," and it'll give the year. If that little brass plaque isn't there and if it's still the same frame, there are going to be two holes where that brass plaque and the nails were. Sometimes you can turn the painting over, and they'll have written on the back how many hours they worked on that painting and what they got paid for it and what the frame cost.

In New Mexico, the largest collection outside of the Fine Arts Museum in Santa Fe is in Clayton, New Mexico, in the public schools. The home-economics teacher there brought them all together and worked with her students and developed everything that they had in the schools that were involved in the WPA projects because a school superintendent saved the town of Clayton with the WPA. They have thirty-nine paintings in one room. They have colcha-embroidered drapes, they have dishes, they have furniture, they have wrought-iron lamps, and they have copper wastebaskets that came from the copper stills that the ranchers brought in. I figure that was the first recycling in New Mexico—from stills to wastebaskets in the schools.

The other town that has a large collection is Melrose, which is on the east side of the state. I think Melrose probably has a lot because there were so many of these little schools all over eastern New Mexico—WPA built, they all had the same gymnasium, the same buildings. Once they closed, I think Melrose must have gotten a lot of the artwork from those little communities around them. There's a lot of the stuff missing. In one town, there was a large Fremont Ellis painting, and I went in and asked the person who worked in the school system the longest, this person in the cafeteria, who said, "Oh yeah, I remember that painting." I said, "Do you know where it is today?" "Well, no." "Do you remember when you saw it last?" "Yeah." "Where was it?" "In the dumpster." "Why was it in the dumpster?" "Well, the frame broke, so the janitor threw it in the trash."

We as an organization [National New Deal Preservation Association] have spent about four hundred thousand dollars so far. We have just finished a project that Steve Prinz from Santa Fe did at Highlands University in Ilfeld Auditorium. There were eight paintings on canvas glued over the eight doors in the lobby going in and out of the theater at Ilfeld Auditorium. They had five coats of white paint on them. Some of them had six coats of white paint. And all that paint is gone now, and the murals are there, except one. One is not there, and we do not know what ever happened to that one.

Another conservator has started taking a layer of paint off an Olive Rush fresco at New Mexico State, and that was painted over. There was water damage to the painting, and so a couple of the maintenance guys went in with enamel paint and repainted the painting, then signed their names. Now we've hired a conservator to go and take the enamel paint off and have the original fresco come back up. That's a restoration project.

Another project we've got going is a bust of Bronson Cutting [by Bruce Wilder Saville] that is on the west side of the capital [Santa Fe] on the street by the Veteran's Memorial. It's been sitting there on a pedestal for seventy years, and Bronson Cutting was one of the three people who made the decisions where the murals would be done, what buildings would be selected for things. The other two were John Gaw Meem, who designed a lot of the WPA buildings or the PWA buildings, and Mary Austin. So those three people were very prominent here in New Mexico in terms of making decisions [about] what was going to happen and where.

There was a lot of photography done in New Mexico, and there are a number of books [about it]. One has just come out. The Library of Congress has come out with an exhibit called Bound for Glory. The exhibit is an example of how the Farm Security Administration [FSA] photographers were given Kodacolor. Kodak had just come out with Kodacolor, and [the company] wanted to try it out, so they gave the FSA photographers this film, and [the photographers] would take a shot in black and white, and then they would take the shot in color. I've seen the show. There's probably twenty-five photographs in it. I would say more than half of the photographs are [of] New Mexico. The majority of the work that was done was up around Trampas and Truchas and up in there, and then down in Pietown.

A wealth of stuff was done in New Mexico in terms of the FSA, and the Museum of Fine Arts Educational Department [in Santa Fe], I believe, has the majority of the collection of the originals. They depict how we were living. This program [the WPA] not only saved us, but it recorded us ethnically, socially, geographically, environmentally, any numbers of ways. Most people don't have a clue that this all happened. They don't have a clue that they're still using the products of it every day. Not too many are still using the flyproof interior sanitation units, but there are some [units] that are still out there, and if you don't know what a flyproof interior sanitation unit is, I should share with you something that's known probably more naturally as an outhouse. We did hundreds of those, and I have a newspaper clipping that says, "Clyde Tingley, governor, has made good on putting X number of people to work in San Juan County building flyproof interior sanitation units."

I would encourage, enlist, beg everyone [to] do what they can to find the things that were created during the New Deal and to do what they can to preserve or conserve or restore if need be, and that could be writers, music, buildings. Go and sit on the park benches at Bandelier [National Monument], look at the buildings, look at the rock walls around cemeteries, go to the post offices and look over the postmaster's door and see the paintings that you haven't seen. Tap into what your ancestors, your mother, your father, your grandfather, your aunt, your uncle did for you, for the family at the time that you are still enjoying, using, taking advantage of, not taking care of, not seeing, and save them. Make other people aware of them. Tell your local politicians to save these places. Work to make sure the National Park Service doesn't get privatized. This is a legacy that was given to us all that saved our families back then, and it made America, and it made us be who we are. When I got started on this, I kept thinking, "Someday we may come to a time when we'll need something again like this that will give people hope like it gave them hope." I think we're there. We need something to give us hope and believe in ourselves and stand up for what we believe. I think if people realize what was done once, maybe they can do it again. And we must preserve what we can because it's who we are and who we were.

Tey Marianna Nunn,
photo by author

Tey Marianna Nunn

Introduction

Tey Marianna Nunn is a native Nuevo Mexicana, born in Albuquerque into a family of scholars. Dr. Nunn is currently the director of visual arts and chief curator for the National Hispanic Cultural Center in Albuquerque. She was formerly the curator of Hispano and Latino collections at the Museum of International Folk Art in Santa Fe.

Tey Nunn has an abiding interest in New Mexican artists of Hispanic descent. She is the author of *Sin Nombre: Hispana and Hispano Artists of the New Deal Era* that was published by the University of New Mexico Press in 2001. Many of the highly talented native Nuevo Mexicanos of this period were relegated to secondary positions relative to Anglo artists, who received broader attention and higher salaries through the Works Progress Administration (WPA) Art Project. Tey's research for *Sin Nombre* has brought to light the great array of talents and art forms practiced by the large coterie of Nuevo Mexicano artists during the Great Depression.

Nunn has also focused a great deal of attention on the multitalented Santa Fe artist Eliseo Rodriguez, whom she and many others regard as one of the truly great artists of his time and a man who has inspired many younger artists to pursue their art forms.

Nunn shares with her mother, Tey Diana Rebolledo, a passionate interest in the lives of Nuevo Mexicanas whose enormously important roles have been otherwise largely overlooked by most historians. The interview reveals the depth and beauty of Nunn's point of view while providing a glimpse into the influence of the handcrafted life-style on the art of New Mexico.

Tey Marianna Nunn

JL: One of the notions that fascinates me is how the Hispano and Native American cultures were still pretty much subsistence based by the time of the Great Depression. It seems to me that the New Deal basically introduced the prevalent economic paradigm that existed in the rest of the country to the American Southwest. Money was certainly not plentiful, but it wasn't as necessary as it seems to be today. Do you have any thoughts on that at all?

TMN: I think it's really true. The mind-set then among Nuevo Mexicanos and Native peoples and New Mexicans was so much different. One of the things people don't even concentrate on is the fact that there were so many northern Hispanos who traveled, who were actually migrant workers who would travel up to Colorado to pick sugar beets or go to Texas. So there was an agricultural-based existence here. Even sheepherders traveled back and forth seasonally or back and forth across the different states' borders. That's a component that gets left out of histories a lot. So it was very agriculturally based, and people didn't make a lot of money. The WPA came in and introduced this whole other way of looking at things. You didn't need that much then. There were simple pleasures. It was a really wonderful way— sometimes I think we should go back it.

But you're right, and those stories like [the ones] Eliseo Rodriguez tells about Santa Fe in the '20s and the '30s are remarkable.

JL: What I'd like to do is ask you to talk about how the arts actually came to be sort of a flourishing situation in the 1930s during the Great Depression as a result of the WPA.

TMN: One of the reasons I got interested in Hispano artists of the '30s and the '40s was that I figured that because of language and culture, there had to have been a connection between New Mexico in the '30s and the '40s with that flourishing of Mexico art and how Mexican art was becoming so popular with the muralists, with Diego Rivera and [José Clemente] Orozco and [David] Siqueiros. There's a book called *The Enormous Vogue of Things Mexican* where inter-American relations and Pan American relations were all focused on in Mexico. Diego Rivera was creating all the murals here in Chicago and San Francisco and New York.

But I kept on wondering, because of the artists' colonies in Taos and Santa Fe and the artistic legacy in New Mexico, if there was any connection, if any of the Hispano artists had gone down to Mexico or if any of them had come up here, and they just hadn't been recorded. So I started looking around for those names, and there were very few Hispano names, with the exception of the WPA works and the Writers' Project, recorded in New Mexico. So that sort of became my quest. That plays into the flourishing of the arts. The Spanish colonial artistic legacy in New Mexico.

In many ways, the knowledge of it or the recording of it for posterity's sake changed when the railroads came in. It's always easy to blame and say, "Oh, the Hispano population of northern New Mexico and the rest of New Mexico wanted the new things, they wanted the new plaster statues and the mass-produced prints." And there's a number of reasons for that. When you go back and talk about the importance of things, it was just an image. It wasn't necessarily like people didn't appreciate the handmade image, but this was a new image or perhaps a more affordable image, and so that time period with new furniture techniques and Sears catalog and all those sorts of things changed the dynamic and the importance of New Mexican arts.

One of the things that happens, too, is that many of those New Mexican arts were utilitarian. So there's furniture, and there's weaving, and there are santos [saints] and tin *nichos* [niches] or tin mirrors or tin fixtures. They were all utilitarian, so that wasn't something that people normally considered as art. It was something you used every day. So with people like E. Boyd and Frank Applegate and Mary Austin and Anglo artists and writers who come from other places and see this vernacular art form that has really deep-seated roots and has permeated architecture and all sorts of aspects of New Mexico, their way of looking at art from eastern or the midwestern perspective is different. It was a group of Anglo intelligentsia—writers and painters and artists—who recognized the importance of the native Spanish art forms.

JL: Can you name the *cinco pintores* [five painters] who were part of the art colony in Santa Fe at that time?

TMN: Josef Bakos, Fremont Ellis, Walter Mruk, Willard Nash, and Will Shuster.

JL: How did you come to adopt Eliseo Rodriguez as *el sexto pintor*?

TMN: That was kind of revisionist history. The idea of the cinco pintores was that they had kind of a salon, and they hung out together on Canyon Road, and they had parties, and they talked art, and they created art. Artists and writers and journalists who describe the cinco pintores and elevated the cinco pintores to their status left out the fact that there were a whole lot of other people in that group. And one of the people who painted alongside them and who went to the same parties and who went to the same dances and who played off their creativity and who was a member of that group at that time, that creative group in Santa Fe, was Eliseo Rodriguez. He helped Will Shuster create Zozobra [the paper giant burned at fiesta time]. But that's completely left out of the stories. And I think it depends on who's writing those accounts and who's writing those history books and who's writing those art history books and how they categorize different people and different ethnicities as artists.

JL: Could you give your sense of how the WPA Arts Project began?

TMN: It was George Biddle, who was an artist, who suggested to Franklin Delano Roosevelt that perhaps some sort of government federally funded art project along the lines of the Mexican mural project, which was funded by the Mexican government in the '20s and the '30s, take form in the United States to help artists during the Depression. I always see that as a model because there were a lot of ties between the administration of the various WPA programs from Mexico and New Mexico. Some of the same people were involved: John Collier, who started the idea of art centers and vocational schools and helped fuel that idea, was very influenced by the Mexican program.

One of the mottoes of the Federal Art Project for the WPA was "Art for Everyone." So the whole idea was of making art accessible and making it possible for everybody to have that beauty of art and the knowledge of art when the darkest time seemed to have hit the United States with the Depression. When you think of the Depression, you just think gray, and you think it must have been awful, and you think of the Dust Bowl, and those are the images that come to mind because we saw only black-and-white photos of that. So then you realize that these amazing art projects took place in various forms around the United States.

One of the really interesting aspects of it is that New Mexico's art projects were so regional and vernacular. They focused on New Mexico vernacular culture, architecture, colors, and local art materials. One of the other mottoes of the Federal Art Project was "To Depict the American Scene." So in New Mexico you can imagine the administrators coming here, people like Russell Vernon Hunter. New Mexico is so special because of its vernacular architecture and its cultural contributions from Spanish influence, Mexican influence. We can't forget the Mexican influence. And Native influence. One of the other places this happened, for instance, was Minnesota, where that area was very Scandinavian in influence in the WPA projects. And in Oregon, where that influence was very outdoor influenced in the architecture and some of the sculpture that [the] WPA made using local trees and local wood. So that was one of the other components of this.

I think what's so interesting is that Russell Vernon Hunter, who was the director of the Federal Art Project in New Mexico, and other people—including earlier people like Gustave Baumann, who was the head of the Public Works of Art Project, which precedes the Federal Art Project—knew the artists of all the different cultures in New Mexico and recognized them. If they had not been so familiar with New Mexican artists, if they had come from the outside to administer these programs, that might not have happened. So they did have a familiarity. Sometimes the issue is how they treated those artists differently, but at least the artists were included. And they really helped encourage a number of New Mexican artists whose impact on arts is still resounding. The influence and the impact on artists now can be really traced back to a number of these Federal Art Project artists like Eliseo Rodriguez and Paula Rodriguez, his wife, and Patrocinio Barela and José Dolores Lopez and Edward Arsenio Chavez and Juan Sanchez and Pedro Cervantes. The list goes on and on. And the women!

JL: Can you give a list of the arts themselves that the Hispano people actually brought forth during that period?

TMN: I can, and I'll also mention that painting and murals were done, too, because I think we tend to think that the Hispano artists of the WPA just did what were termed handicrafts then, and there's so much more to it. Even though some of the artists perhaps did santos, they were also artists who painted. We tend to recognize them for the santos and forget that they did incredible paintings. So there were paintings and there were murals by Hispano artists in New Mexico. There were santos, or saints, three-dimensional like the statues, the sculptures, and also two-dimensional on retablos, the flat pieces of pine. There was colcha embroidery. There was weaving. And both the colcha embroidery and the weaving utilized native dyes and native techniques or traditional techniques. There was even pottery. There was straw appliqué, tin work, furniture. Those were the basics.

JL: Did the Fred Harvey aspect of things figure largely in this, do you think?

TMN: Well, this is where my old retail background comes in because I was really interested in how these works were sold. There was an interrelationship between some stores and the WPA artists, and it's not that the WPA artists were funded by the government and sold their works, but there were a lot of agreements with the vocational schools and some of the artists on the side to make works to be able to be sold at places like the Fred Harvey hotels and the Native arts store and a number of the stores in Santa Fe and Albuquerque and probably elsewhere in New Mexico. So what happened is that the WPA funding and support elevated those artists to a place where they were known, and there were connections between all the same administrators and people who ran shops—everybody knew each other because everything was still small at the time, and then because the artists were elevated with the WPA support, that helped them make contacts and get recognized by stores. So it was a really great economic development opportunity for the artists who were chosen.

JL: I'd like to ask you, before we get into anything else, if you could talk a bit about Eliseo Rodriguez as a fellow human.

TMN: Well, I am very devoted to Eliseo Rodriguez. I remember the first time I interviewed Eliseo Rodriguez and Paula Rodriguez in their house in Santa Fe. They were very funny because they didn't quite know who I was. So Paula is very good at sort of sussing out whether you're really genuine or you're there for another reason. They invited me over, and what was supposed to be a short interview ended up going more than four hours long, to the point where I was really worried if they were going to be tired. I was the one who was tired in the end because I got so much information from them. The pictures and the old sketch books started coming out, and I was able to run [by them] a whole bunch of archival photos that I had found at the Archives of American Art in Washington, D.C., that I knew were by New Mexican artists, but of course nobody had bothered to put in the artists' names. So even though I knew they weren't things by Eliseo, I showed him the photos. And he was the one who was able to say, "That's by so-and-so, that's by so-and-so, that's by me."

I had known Eliseo as a straw appliqué artist, but what I hadn't realized was that he started off as a painter, and here [in the archive photos] was a reverse painting on glass of a crucifixion in a tin frame by Ildeberto Delgado, who was another WPA artist. And Eliseo pulled out [the] photograph, and it was really a magical moment because I said, "You did this?" It was a beautiful, finely done reverse painting on glass. And Eliseo told me how reverse painting on glass is really, really hard—it was a WPA piece, a Federal Art Project piece. The painting was easy, but writing your name backwards was really, really hard. So we had some good laughs about that, and I asked him if he knew where the piece was, and he said he had no idea where the piece was. He hadn't seen it. But this was a piece that I could tell by the documentation in the National Archives had traveled all around the United States.

One day I was in the Museum of New Mexico central registration office waiting for a registrar to do something, and I looked over my shoulder. There were some documents on top of a file cabinet that said, "Reverse painting on glass of crucifixion in tin frame, artist unknown." I pulled the document out, and it showed that it was in the Palace of the Governors. So that day we went over to the Palace of the Governors, and there in a dark corner was this piece of Eliseo's art. I called the museum photographer, I ran up to get Eliseo, and we have a picture of him holding the piece. And he cried because he hadn't seen it in so long, and it was one of his masterpieces.

What I had learned from all of that experience is that Eliseo isn't just known for doing straw appliqué, but that he was a painter—as he says, he was one of the first Spanish painters in the Santa Fe art school. His impact on contemporary Chicano and Latino and Hispano artists in New Mexico is huge. At that time of the Chicano movement and civil rights movements in the '60s, artists like Luis Tapia, Paula Lopez, and a number of other people—Eliseo was the only person they knew who had painted. So there's actually a poster for which they chose Eliseo's painting for their very pivotal art show. They're known as the La Cofradía de Artesanos and are a group of artists like Frederico Vigil and Luis Tapia and a number of other artists who couldn't find places to hang their art in Santa Fe because museums weren't showing Hispanic and Latino art at the time. So they made their own spaces. This was a nationwide thing.

I think Eliseo's role in the Federal Art Project and the WPA art was huge, as is his impact on New Mexican arts. He was a painter before he took the art of straw appliqué in a whole new way. Before Eliseo's influence, the art of straw appliqué was mostly geometric patterning. Because of Eliseo's painterly painting talents, he paints in straw, and he makes it narrative so that you can tell stories in the straw. So he totally transformed the art form for later artists. So his impact is big.

JL: On a scale of one to ten, how would you rate his impact on Hispano art?

TMN: Ten. And it's been underacknowledged. But Eliseo's impact on art—huge.

JL: Could you talk a bit about how New Mexico art actually rose out of this landscape and reflects the landscape in a way that so-called modern art is reflecting the neurosis that exists in our culture?

TMN: There was a really important vocational school program during the WPA that was funded by the state and also by federal funds. So it's all kind of interwoven and kind of complicated. And the Chupadero school did something that no other school did in New Mexico or the United States, and it became so famous it was mentioned in the *Congressional Record*. It was often cited by Franklin Delano Roosevelt.

Chupadero was so fascinating to me because they had a furniture project there. It was furniture made out of local materials, which were willow and rawhide. And the furniture was sort of ephemeral because it was used for patio furniture, so there aren't many examples around. But they remind you a little bit of Mexican *equipale* furniture, which is the wood slat and leather furniture. [That] may have been what it was modeled after. But it became uniquely New Mexican in that it was willow and rawhide with a different New Mexican aesthetic to it. There are pictures of the artists in the school, in the workshop, creating this work, where you see the bent pieces of willow and the rawhide, and they're all constructing and creating the furniture. Talk about coming directly out of the landscape of what was local material and what was right there around them!

What I think is so interesting is the twist that although [this furniture] was obviously inspired by Mexican furniture, it becomes uniquely New Mexican here in a place like Chupadero. The native art of New Mexico, if you think about it, much of it is from native materials—from materials directly from the land, whether it's straw or natural pigments or handspun wool for doing colcha or the aspen and the different woods for santos, cottonwood. It's all handmade and land made. And I think that's one of the things that makes it so special and unique and easily recognizable.

JL: Please talk about the importance of the Federal Writers' Project in New Mexico.

TMN: Well, I think that what the Federal Writers' Project did for New Mexico is really insert New Mexican culture and history into the greater U.S. culture and history. And one of the ways they did that was with the WPA guide to New Mexico. This is really a bible to not only early-twentieth-century New Mexico, but you can still follow the routes and the roads and everything. It talks about folklore, religion, education, literature, architecture. You know that road culture has taken over because here's this tour guide, and it's probably not the first tour guide of New Mexico. But it was one of the important ones because it was produced with this national initiative so that everybody would have one. Whenever you visited a state on a road trip, you bought the guide. For the basics for tourism and New Mexican history, the Writers' Project was very big.

The Writers' Project had not only Anglo writers from outside the state writing, but they used a lot of New Mexican writers, and they used a lot of Nuevo Mexicano informants to get the stories from. And they recorded at a time when it was really necessary and could have been on the verge of losing folklore and culture. So the New Mexico Writers' Project recorded *dichos* [sayings] and corridos [narrative ballads] and folk stories and local histories, and a reader now can go back and look at those and try to figure out where that story was written. They're so beautifully written that they describe buildings or *camposantos* [graveyards] towns, and you could take the short stories and go into the town and see if you could still find [these things]. The writers were very important, and they were recognized on a national level also. Elba C. De Baca from Las Vegas and Loren Brown and Aurora Lucero White. Reyes Martinez, who not only collected santos and New Mexican arts, but also worked on the Writers' Project. And Arturo Campa at the University of New Mexico helped coordinate all of this. I think one of the amazing things is [that] it was native-born writers who were already cognizant of the importance of their culture. You want to call it an activist movement or a recovery project of the history and the culture.

They also probably put themselves in difficult positions sometimes being the translators of that culture. What they recouped and what they were able to record [are] really extraordinary. And there hasn't been a mass project like that with so many people involved.

One of the other big initiatives during the WPA was the *Coronado quartocentenario* here, celebrating the four hundredth anniversary of Coronado. So that was 1942. And it was a big galvanizing project for the Hispano community around the state to get involved, and also it was another kind of benchmark to finish some of these projects for the WPA because the war had started. The Federal Writers' Project also did all these Spanish song and game books . . . corridos and everything. But they worked with the Federal Music Project and the University of New Mexico to recoup the songs.

JL: Is there is anything that you want to touch on that we haven't touched on, Tey?

TMN: What I found very interesting is that while finding the Hispano artists of New Mexico has been challenging, the men were easier to find than the women. And some of the great photos that I found—the photographs that were taken for the Farm Security Administration, photographs that visually recorded musicians and architecture and art forms and agricultural ways. Some of those photos have become really famous in New Mexico— Pietown, for example. There were photos that were taken for really funny reasons, from really funny agencies like the Office of War Information, because this indicates how inter-American relations were working at that time. The United States was concerned and Latin America was concerned that the bad forces in Europe could come through Latin America and get to the United

States. There was a real fear with the Good Neighbor policy, so the Office of War Information went around New Mexico and took these photos, which was very interesting because there's a Spanish-speaking population here, and so you always wonder why they were recording Hispano culture.

One of the big clues I found [was in] these photos taken up in Taos in the winter in 1941 in a workshop in which women were making furniture. The women were carving the furniture. I don't have those names of the women, but what was really interesting is that I think there's one photo of the workshop in which there's six women, and most of them are wearing skirts and pumps, and it's January 1941 in Taos. They've got their coats kind of thrown over their shoulders so they can carve, but they're carving rosettes, and they're carving the furniture. They're beautiful photos, and in going to talk to the male furniture artists, I would say, "Did women carve furniture?" And they would all say, "No, women never carved furniture." Here I have this photographic proof.

There are so many other layers about this. Just because we have the basic archives and the basic knowledge doesn't mean we have the whole story. That's the interesting part of it. I always like to have a good mystery.

Eliseo Rodriguez, photo by author

Eliseo Rodriguez

Introduction

Eliseo Rodriguez, one of two surviving Hispano Works Progress Administration (WPA) artists from New Mexico, lives with his wife, Paula, herself a noted straw inlay artist, in Santa Fe Canyon near the beautiful adobe Cristo Rey Church. For months, our New Mexico state folklorist Claude Stephenson had been urging me to interview Eliseo Rodriguez for this project. In the late spring of 2006, Claude and I went to the Rodriguez home and conducted a compelling interview.

Señor Rodriguez was born in Santa Fe in 1915 and maintains his roots in the very neighborhood where he grew up. Santa Fe Canyon lies to the east of the plaza, nestled in the foothills of the Sangre de Cristo Mountains. The canyon cradles the Santa Fe River, which provides Santa Fe with much of its water. The community that the *río* nurtures was founded during the first decade of the seventeenth century, and twenty generations of Hispano families have lived here.

In this interview, Señor Rodriguez recounts his own story of his life as an artist. He recalls many of the other artists who lived in Santa Fe Canyon, an enduring art colony still celebrated in galleries that lure collectors from around the world. He speaks of his abiding association with the Anglo artist Louie Ewing. And he recalls his boyhood along the Santa Fe River at a time when most traditional people in the region still practiced handcrafted subsistence life-styles.

Eliseo Rodriguez

ER: I got a scholarship to go to the art school here in Santa Fe. It was a gift by one of the leading writers at the time. His name was Ted Flynn. In memory of his wife, he sent me to art school for three years. Then from there I started doing little carvings and little glass paintings and little gadgets like that, and these wonderful people that owned the Native Market, it was run by a lady named Eleanor Bedell. She was such a wonderful person. Prior to my introducing my work to these people, I used to work digging sewer lines.

But then one day the man said, "Well, we have completed the job, and that's the end of the deal. We have to let everybody go except the ones that are on permanent basis." At the time, Paula and I met, and from the time that we met to the time that we got married—about nine months—that's when I was working digging ditches. But then I didn't have a job, you see. But I had my little artwork that I was doing, and I introduced it to the lady at the Native Market.

JL: Eleanor Bedell?

ER: She was such a wonderful person. She said, "Eliseo, I wish I could help you, but it so happens we're not buying anything. It's a paralyzed situation now." I tell her what I can do. She said, "I'm very well acquainted with Vernon Hunter, who is the state director of the Art Project, the WPA. I'm sure he's seen some of your work. You might have a good chance to get connected and see what you can do." She gave me a piece of paper. From there I went across, and there at the corner of Galisteo Street was a two-story building. It's still there. What happened was, there were a lot of people going upstairs waiting to go talk to this guy Vernon Hunter. "Oh my gosh," I said to myself. "It's going to take a long time before I can get to talk to this guy." It so happened that one fellow who used to deliver telegrams was a friend of mine—Carrillo was his name, from La Cienega. He said, "Hi, how you doing?" We started talking. He said, "I have to deliver this telegram right away to Mr. Vernon Hunter." I said, "Why don't you let me deliver it? It'll be the same." He said, "Sure, why not?"

So I just went. I moved people to one side. "Telegram for Mister—" And I went to his office, and I told him the whole story, see. He was very much impressed how I could have gotten in to talk to him before the other people. He said, "I'll tell you what you do. I think I've seen your work, and I'm very much impressed with what you're doing. A lot of polishing to do, but we can work that out. What you have to do is go to the courthouse and talk to the lady there to see if you can get into the welfare program so that you can be qualified." I say, "OK." So I took off, I went to the courthouse, and, my gosh, again a lot of people there. But finally the lady got to talk to me. They were kind of mean. "At your age you're getting married? You know what you're getting into?" I said, "Yes, I know. I have my wife now, and I'm trying to find a job to keep her going." That was 1936—because we got married on October 21, 1935.

So finally I did get the slip of paper, and they qualified me to be in the welfare department. From there on, I went over to show Mr. Vernon Hunter the paper, and I started working as a painter. He says, "You're going to get your materials, you're going to get your brushes, and you can get started tomorrow." I said, "I'm ready to start right now." And so I started working and doing landscaping and stuff like that. But that was the advantage and the beauty of the whole WPA. People don't realize that. They gave you a chance to experiment, you see. After [I had been] working a while, Vernon Hunter came over to my house one day and said, "Would you be interested in learning how to do some carving?" I said, "Of course I would be, very much." And I started doing little carvings.

Eventually the time came when they asked me if I would be interested in working with Louie Ewing, who was going to start working on silk-screen printing. I said, "Yes, I'd love to do that." So I went and met Louie Ewing on 1006 Canyon Road.

We got together, and we started working and doing all these silk screens. We did posters for the anthropology museum, and it was a pretty good job. Then from there, after working on the silk screen, they asked Louie and me if we would be interested in working with mosaic. We said, "Yes, we'd like to try it." So we started working and keeping going.

Then from there I was sent to work with Paul Lantz, the painter. He was painting murals for the Texas Centennial at the time. So was Howard Schleeter. They loaned us the place at the state capitol so that we could work there in a studio, you see. So we kept on working and working till the job was completed.

Then since I had a little experience as a carver, I applied for a job at the Southwestern Master Craftsmen. Mr. Welton was the owner of the place. He said, "I don't know what I can do, but I can try you." So I started working, and he sent me to the shop down on Agua Fría. The fellow that was running the show was John Stoll. So they said, "Do you know how to use one of these machines?" I said, "No." He [Mr. Stoll] said, "You're going to have to try if you're going to learn this thing." He was kind of mean. He was a very kindhearted man, but kind of [a] nervous type.

So I started cutting a piece of wood, and I did pretty good. Then he said, "I want you to try and see what you can do with the sander." So I said, "That's a lot easier for me than running the machine." When I started working with the sander, I was looking from the side like that and making a groove. He got so mad, he took his cap and stepped on it, he was so mad. He said, "You ruined my wood." I quit then, see. I said, "I'm sorry, but I'm not cut out to do this type of work."

I went back to Palace Avenue. That's where the Southwestern Master Craftsmen store was. I told Mr. Welton, "I can't work. I don't know a darn thing about it, and the man doesn't seem to appreciate what I try to do." He said, "Get your hat, let's go." We went down to the shop, and he told the man off in a big funny way. He said, "He doesn't know. That's why I sent him, so you can teach him. He'll learn. He'll be all right." It was a kind of a rough conversation for a while.

To make the story short, in that particular program I learned how to do the carving. Not only that, but eventually I became foreman of the shop. I was doing a lot of work for Marshall Fields in Chicago and places like that. Not only that, but if Mr. Stoll had to go out and do a job in a certain place, like put in a cupboard or something, the first one that he called is for me to go along with him, you see. So we became good friends, and everything worked out real fine. I kept on going until I went to the army. When I came back from the army, then I got a job teaching for the vocational department, and I was supervisor of classes. I went as far as Santa Cruz and back, and I was in charge of the school over here at St. Michael's College [in Santa Fe]. So things were working out pretty good.

On top of that, then I found another job working for church art. I had a lot of experience in wood things, making altar pieces and screens for the church and all that. That was exciting for me. I loved that. And I worked at Saint Francis on the Mount, Colorado Springs. I did all the interior, the communion rail, the altar, and everything else. From there I went to California, working for the Santa Fe Studio. So I wasn't working at the Southwestern anymore. The Old Mission in Santa Barbara, I did a lot of work for them—all the interior of the back of the church.

JL: Like the reredos [screens behind the altar]?

ER: Yes. And not only that, but I made the pillars where they were going to have the choir. I made the vigas. They were about twelve inches in diameter. But they weren't actually cut up. I built them myself. I made a square first, and then I collared it and then passed it onto the joiner round. They were all equalized all the way through. Pretty nice. That's part of my life.

JL: The Great Depression actually hit in 1929, and it lasted until World War II, until 1941, really. Could you talk about any of the names of any of the other WPA artists that you were in contact with at that time—any of your friends or anybody that you met?

ER: It started down on Canyon Road with Hal West and Jim Morris and Chuck Barrows and Odon Hullenkremer. The whole works. We used to go over to Alfred Morang's place most every weekend, and Paula would cook, for example *chile con frijoles* and tortillas. And then we'd go to this party where Alfred would be playing the violin. He always loved to play the violin. And Dorothy—that was Alfred Morang's wife—she played the piano. And other people were talking about art and designing. Little groups, you see. And then I used to take a bottle of wine. And then somebody else would take something, sandwiches of some kind. Others would take a little beer. It turned out to be everybody. Everybody was just a perfect artist and perfect everything. Will Shuster would be there, and [Josef] Bakos would be there. Only once did I get to see Fremont Ellis. He wasn't very close to them. Another one that we met was also Bill Longley on Camino. We used to get together like that. We used to go out and do our work as a free person, see. We had a nice little car, and we used to go up to Pecos and maybe stay two or three days doing watercolor deals. Paula started working with the straw then.

Vernon Hunter would come here and ask me, Could I be interested in trying that straw business? He said, "Have you seen it?" I said, "No, I've never seen anything like that." He said, "It's supposed to be a little piece of straw," and he'd try to explain everything to me. So I said, "Well, I'm going to try it." He said, "I'll tell you what you do. Try a little bit of that straw and still keep on with your work, but this will be sort of on the side, to see what you can do with it." It was very exciting. Paula started first, and then I started picking it up. I didn't know a thing about it.

The first ones that I was gluing on, instead of splitting in half, I put the whole deal, you see. But then when I'd work it all out, the other half would come out, and the one that was supposed to be the good one was flat and no shine. One night I stayed up all night just trying to figure it out, and it worked, it finally worked. I think that's my first retablo [altarpiece], and that was the head of Christ. I used different shades of the straw, and it looked like a regular mosaic. That man was so excited. He thought that was really something very special. So he ordered about four or five more of the type of design, and he wanted them for Washington, D.C.—What's the name of that?—Smithsonian. So that was how we got started. Then I told Paula, and she just kept on working, working all the time. She was getting to be very good.

JL: I know that Louie Ewing passed away more than twenty years ago now. Could you describe him, kind of characterize him for me?

ER: Yes, of course. I can say that he was a very, very intelligent fellow, and he was kind, easygoing. We always worked together. But then he lived next door to me, and we were all very close. One time things were very rough during the WPA days, and Mary [Louie's wife] had one egg; that's all we had. Paula had some chili powder. She could tell you the story how she worked it, and they made a nice meal with the egg and the cheese and whatever. That's how rough it was to keep it going. He was my next-door neighbor. Then he loved to play sports. He always did that, and I did too. I think that Louie was a very, very excellent artist.

JL: You still see his son and daughter, Mark and Martha?

ER: Yes, yes. His wife, she writes her name Martha Baros Ewing. Baros is her name, see. She learned about straw from Paula. She became very good at it.

CS: One of the times I was here before, we were talking about when you were a boy, before all the artists got here.

ER: Yes. I was the only boy here on the hill. My job was, I was the goatherder and a sheepherder at heart. I used to go there every day—oh, the *corrales* were right about in here, and they covered part of that there on the other side of the wall where the Ewings used to live. Then we used to have a bunch of hogs right on the other side of the road. My father made me a little wagon with little buggy wheels, but they were strong enough that I could bring a tub of garbage from the cemetery, Sun Mount, to feed the animals. Then we raised a lot of corn and all kinds of vegetables right along in here. No money, but the necessities were there, you see. We used to go get wood. That was my way of life in the summertime. Then in the wintertime, that's when I went to school.

JL: Where did you get the wood?

ER: Where did we gather the wood? Right by Arroyo Hondo, right in that section. If you wanted to get fuel wood, we used to go as far as Cañoncito—go down like if you're going to Glorieta. We started real early in the mornings because it's twelve miles. Then cut the wood and everything else. I would go with my father or one of my uncles, and they cut the big tree, and then I hook it with a chain and pull it with a horse by the wagon. Then they have everything ready so that they could come and cut it. You have to haul the little pieces. That's what we used to do.

Oh, another thing that I did was—I take a lot of pride [in it]. We were seven kids in the family, and I was the oldest one. So I was the one that would be helping my mother to cook and do the ironing, and we used to wash clothes in the tub. That was one of my main jobs in the wintertime. So I kept pretty busy. And my mother was a terrific cook. People would hire her in town for special occasions.

PR: The best beans and chile and tacos and tamales. They were the best. They were so good.

ER: In other words, you can very honestly say that I was raised *como solo*—very, very few friends to talk to. When I went to school, I got all excited because I started meeting a lot of the kids. There weren't very many from Cerro Gordo way up Canyon Road.

JL: Do you remember when you were a boy working on the acequias [irrigation ditches]?

ER: We used to work on the acequia that came all the way a little farther down than Flavio [Gonzales's] place. Right about there they started the acequia. It would go all the way down to the *cañada* on the other side of the state penitentiary.

There was Acequia Madre—that's farther down. This one here went by our house, and it went all the way down to Camino del Monte Sol. It crossed Garcia Street and all the way down. We used to do all the cleaning and get it all ready and then start the water going. Oh, there were some pipes over by Apodaca Hill that crosses that arroyo into Camino Cabra. There were big pipes across there, and then it ran all the way down. Oh yeah, I used to do all that. It was nice to get all the people [together], and I used to just love to see the old-timers for a break, and then they rolled their cigarettes. Prince Albert or whatever. It was nice.

JL: Did they ever sing any acequia songs? *Canciones de las acequias*?

ER: *Si! Pero* somebody will be making [up] the verses as he went along. No recording or whatsoever. But nice sound. Like taking the shovel and going and digging. "*Vamos cercando la tierra, vamos [acando] la tierra.*" "All we're doing is pulling the dirt out. What happened to *la yerba*?" And deals like that, you see. And bring our lunch at noon. Nice.

CS: You were telling me you used to take the sheep out here, way off here in the hills?

ER: And that was another beautiful thing, too, because our neighbors—some of the neighbors farther up—they also had goats. So we had a path right along the *cerro* [hill] there so the goats would follow us as far as St. John's more or less. Then they started spreading out, you see. Then they go around on that big hill in between. You come out by El Gancho Inn. By that time, you're coming pretty slow. But when the time comes for the separation here, the goats knew exactly where to go.

What they used to do, my family, they had three or four buckets *grandes* like this one, and they used to boil the water. Then they used the water to wash the wool, you see. They bring in big, white plain bags, and they put them in. All my aunts and my cousins were singing, and they had a *bona fina grande* and were just doing a nice job. Then they had some people right across from Canyon Road. There's a house with a tin roof there—that was my grandfather's house. Some ladies would be cooking, see. So when they had all that wool, they had to wash it and then spread it out to dry it. *Ee,* just as white as could be. And they put it in bags, and they'd take it down to Gormley's Store, and Gormley's Store would deliver them to the depot, you see. That's the way it worked there. So it was nice to see all that.

Oh, and another thing that I used to have fun with was when I was a little boy and they cut the wheat, they put it in as big a pile as this house, for example. Then at night they had lanterns all the way around. Then they had the goats go around and thresh the wheat, you see. I used to like to go as far as I could up there and then slide right down. It would be just like sliding on snow. It was that slippery and beautiful.

JL: There were mills on the Santa Fe River, weren't there?

ER: Yes, there was one here on the Acequia Madre, just a little farther up than the school there. They had so many bags of wheat. They took it to Nambe.

JL: The Santa Fe River—when you were a boy, that ran all the time, didn't it?

ER: Yes. Never stopped. As far back as I can remember, the Santa Fe River always kept on going. And eventually they had this little pond up here, little *tanque*. They had it connected to pipes for the city, see. That's why people did like this part of town better because the water was so fresh. By the time it got through the pipes, it was a little different. To me, it didn't make any difference, but they claimed that it was a difference.

JL: Did you ever catch fish in the Santa Fe River?

ER: Oh yes. It was fun.

JL: What kind?

ER: The rainbow. We'd just get in the river and wait until they get under the rock and then just, choom! You miss it the first time, but then they would go under another one, and before you know it. . . . That was exciting. Oh, and another thing that I used to do—at night when I had to water our cornfield, I had my lantern and everything, and the corn was high. The acequia would be going, and I cut it here to get [it to] this part [of the field], so there's no water here, but there were some fish in there. I'm not lying to you, but sometimes then I could get a big bucket, different sizes. Just a lot of fun doing that.

To me it was a little scary because the corn would be growing. When the corn is growing, I don't know what you would call them—like the leaves—they make a lot of noise. I feel, well, somebody's coming. But just to hear that is kind of scary. It wasn't easy for me. That's why I told my father. He said, "No." He explained to me everything. So he went with me, and he could hear. "Come here, I'll show you." What do you call those? It's not the stem. The leaves on the top. They go "crick!" like that. At first, it's kind of scary, but when my father explained to me everything, no problem.

David Kammer, photo by author

David Kammer

Introduction

David Kammer came to New Mexico from New Jersey more than three decades ago. He earned his Ph.D. in American studies at the University of New Mexico, and finding the sense of place in New Mexico more compelling than the quest for jobs elsewhere, he remained in Albuquerque. He was a lecturer in the English department at the university and gradually began to work surveying historic buildings and writing National Register nominations for the New Mexico Historic Preservation Division back in the mid- and late 1980s. Since 1990, he has worked as a consulting historian doing public-history projects throughout the Southwest.

His 1994 publication *The Historic and Architectural Resources of the New Deal in New Mexico*, written for the New Mexico Historic Preservation Division, provides an in-depth history of the New Deal in New Mexico. The appendices also list Public Works Administration (PWA), Works Progress Administration (WPA), and Civilian Conservation Corps (CCC) projects throughout New Mexico during the Great Depression.

I interviewed Kammer in his home in Albuquerque in mid-2006. He provided compelling insights into the lives of Clyde Tingley, Franklin Delano Roosevelt, and others who sought to restore New Mexico and the rest of America to economic prosperity.

David Kammer

JL: During the Great Depression of the 1930s, there was a sense of a redefinition between what became known as the lifelong conservative and the lifelong liberal. Could you address that subject a little bit before we get into New Mexico history?

DK: I think today when we hear the terms *conservative* and *liberal*, we sometimes get lost in the immediacy of the time, and we don't appreciate that in many ways, many of the things that are castigated today as being liberal in fact came from people who were seeking to conserve the very best things in the American culture. I think of Franklin Roosevelt, for example, [as] not being really a radical, but a pragmatist who saw that there were going to need to be some extreme measures taken to hold onto much of what we saw as American society. In that sense, Roosevelt was a conservative. Much of what became the New Deal, particularly with regard to environmental concerns, came about because of his desire to conserve the historic landscape of the Hudson River Valley, where he got in the habit of planting trees at Hyde Park and in fact even began to have a small model of what would become the Civilian Conservation Corps when he was the governor of New York.

     What's interesting about that period with regard to Albuquerque is a lot of the people who came to Albuquerque in the early part of the twentieth century were tuberculars who had been sent out here as health seekers back in the time of climatological therapy, and although they were here for the dry high climate, their sensibilities forced them to want more greenery than they found in New Mexico. One of those people was Clyde Tingley, who was New Mexico's New Deal governor [and] who, as ex officio mayor of Albuquerque in the mid-1920s, first brought Siberian elms down to Albuquerque, and they became the basis for many of the WPA landscape projects, not just in Albuquerque at Roosevelt Park, but in other communities such as Roswell or Clovis or Estancia that had WPA park projects. So I've often thought that we ought to do a little DNA on those Siberian elms in those parks around the state and see if they don't trace back, in fact, to the Franklin Roosevelt Park here in Albuquerque, which is basically landscaped with Siberian elms.

JL: Are they the same as Chinese elms?

DK: No. As a matter of fact, there's always been that confusion, and some people, maybe taken by the name "Clyde Tingley," assumed that they were Chinese elms because they thought his last name was "Ting Lee."

It's interesting that when you think about the range of plants that were put into Roosevelt Park—it begins as a Civil Works Administration project in late 1933. This is that first year of desperation in the Roosevelt administration, where Harry Hopkins has alerted Roosevelt that this is going to be a very difficult winter for unemployed Americans, and while there is a major moral discussion about having people on the dole, there's nevertheless the recognition that you need to have people earning some wages to get them through the winter. Those first work relief programs resulted in New Mexico in things like the Roosevelt Park here in Albuquerque. Roosevelt Park would actually be completed as a WPA project. In that first year, Tingley was quick to come to the fore and to see the potential. When he went to Washington, D.C., he would wire back to his cadre of young attorneys up in Santa Fe that "we're never going to have another opportunity like this to have this federal money flowing in, and we need to take advantage of it, and let's make sure that we have a long list of projects where we can put people to work."

It's really interesting to think about how much New Mexico—in 1933 a state for only twenty-one years—lacked the infrastructure to be able to receive and deploy the federal monies that were beginning to come out of Washington. There was no state agency here, other than the Child Welfare Bureau and the Highway Department, that had offices in each of the state's counties and was able to coordinate an assessment of what was needed in the counties and then get the money to flow there. So in those early days Tingley goes up to this first organizational meeting and says, "The money's available. I can put twelve hundred people to work tomorrow." He gets the funding to go ahead, and that was in the very, very beginning of the New Deal.

JL: I wanted to ask you if you could give the names of the New Deal [projects] in New Mexico.

DK: There are lots of them. The first of them would have been the Works Projects Administration—the Works Progress Administration, but then in 1941 becomes the Works Projects Administration in its last years.

JL: The WPA.

DK: The WPA, which was generally a labor-intensive set of projects that were proposed and were sponsored by local authorities such as school boards and communities and were designed largely to employ people who [were] designated to be on work relief. Basically, the way that the WPA worked was that the local sponsoring authority would supply necessary building materials or would coordinate the obtaining of those materials. For example, when you go to the old Albuquerque Airport, which was a WPA project, the timbers that were used for the vigas were brought in from the national forest up in the Jemez, and the work crews constructed the adobe bricks on site. Then the money that was used for the wages for the WPA employees from the work relief rolls was what the federal government supplied.

Now, in contrast to that labor-intensive WPA, you had the Public Works Administration, which was directed and supervised and—much to Clyde Tingley's dismay—scrutinized by Harold Ickes, the secretary of the interior, who had some very interesting New Mexico connections. Although he was a Republican attorney from Chicago, his wife had been an asthmatic and was also an anthropologist who published articles. The Ickeses had a great interest in the Native peoples of the Southwest and had come out to New Mexico for health well before Roosevelt was elected president. They actually had a *hooghan* [Navajo living structure] up on the Continental Divide north of Route 66, east of Gallup, and it was in that context of their being out here in the summers that Ickes became involved in the effort of Indians and Indian traders to preserve the integrity of the Indian-made handicrafts as opposed to things that were increasingly knocked off in factories. He wrote the bylaws for the formation of the United Indian Traders in 1929, which became the means of holding onto the integrity of Indian arts for a long time after that.

But with the Public Works Administration, the people who were hired were more people who had the specialization to do dam construction or electrical work, for these were the large capital-intensive projects as opposed to the labor-intensive projects of the WPA. In New Mexico, you had, I believe, ninety-six PWA projects that included the construction of Caballo Dam, Conchas Dam, and some county courthouses and larger schools. For example, here in Albuquerque, a lot of what was done at the University of New Mexico, including Zimmerman Library, was done as a PWA project. The two-story schools that were built in the 1930s as PWA projects that replaced the earlier ward schools in the heart of Albuquerque were buildings that were designed by Louis Hesselden. These were PWA projects.

Farther south from these projects, where the National Hispanic Culture Center is located today, the core remaining building was the old East San Jose School. That is an adobe school that was constructed for the local people by local people on work relief and was a WPA project. So you have that distinction between the PWA and the WPA.

The other projects that were extensive in New Mexico, of course, were the Civilian Conservation Corps. I think that the CCC is an interesting and perhaps a pioneering example in the history of various bureaucracies being required to cooperate and interface with each other because the idea there was [that] once [the boys'] need[s] and eligibility were determined, they were trained by the army. And then when the army finished with them, they were then sent out to work under the auspices of these various federal and state agencies that were eligible for CCC projects. So it was really an interdisciplinary thing that left a tremendous impact on New Mexico's landscapes.

JL: I know that you've looked at a lot of architectural sites that were born of the New Deal. Could talk you about some of them?

DK: Looking at New Mexico in the 1930s and seeing how little had been done to develop a public infrastructure since the time of statehood [1912] enable us to appreciate how much potential the New Deal held for expanding public buildings and public landscapes in New Mexico. When Clyde Tingley was governor, he kept a series of pictures on his office wall of "before" and "after" depictions of schools. On a percentage basis of WPA money that came into the state, New Mexico was highest of all states in the amount of money that went into public schools. That tells us [that] the state of the schools in New Mexico prior to the New Deal wasn't very good. I've heard anecdotal accounts of schools in chicken coops and other things in some of the remote areas.

Tingley, when he came into office in 1935, wrote letters. In those days, there were more than nine hundred school districts [in New Mexico], many of them closing down after just a couple of months because the district's money was dependent largely upon the property tax. Property taxes in New Mexico, as the price of commodities dropped in the 1920s, had been spiraling downward. At the same time, the amount of unpaid property taxes had been going up. In fact, the property tax itself went up because the value of land had dropped so much that they had to begin to charge more for whatever was being evaluated, and this led to sort of a tax revolt that put a cap on how much of a mil increase you could have on a tax. To deal with that, the sales tax that we have now was done as a temporary emergency tax for schools in 1933, and then it just stayed there.

JL: Is that the New Mexico gross receipts tax?

DK: Yes, that's where that began. Tingley wrote a letter to each of the county superintendents asking them to evaluate their schools. One of the most interesting things about [looking at] the Tingley collection at the state archives is being able to get a sense of the history of public education. Tingley had sort of a boiler-plate letter that he would send to the different school districts, saying, "If you know what your needs are, write to us." His architect was Willard Kruger, who developed a set of blueprints for two-room, four-room, six-room schools, often including an all-purpose cafeteria-gymnasium in back of the central entryway. Once that was done, schools could then submit their applications for WPA funding to build those schools.

Maybe the most remarkable community was Clayton up in Union County, which at that time had a population of about eleven thousand people. Today I think it has five thousand people. The superintendent of schools up there was Raymond Huff, also a Democrat who, like Tingley, understood the potential of federal funding. From 1935 to 1940, I believe, Huff managed to get federal money paid to more than half the residents of Union County for constructing buildings, making ceramics, or making furniture for the library, and little by little the school system up there built an auditorium [and] a football stadium, and gave a face-lift to a three-story brick building and made it Spanish Pueblo revival. Next to it, they built a high school with a landscape among the buildings. They built a boys' woodworking shop. Something new at that time was girls' home economics, and they built a home economics room. They constructed an entire school system complex that is there today and is now a National Historic District.

Things like that happened in every county, but I think that as a single example of what could be done with WPA funds for public education, the Clayton example was a very good one. Many smaller towns built city halls—Tucumcari, Melrose. You can find those buildings, and generally you can interpret them as WPA buildings when you see them, even without a marker.

There was some road construction done under the WPA—not so much on the federal highway system, but, more similar to Texas, on farm-to-market roads over in the eastern part of the state. There were flood-control projects, such as in Silver City, where the former main road had become the ditch, and that was done as a WPA project. Sidewalks were put in everywhere. You can stop today in Magdalena, or you can walk through T or C [Truth or Consequences], and you will see "WPA 1938," or even, earlier than the use of the term "WPA," you'll see "FERA," the Federal Emergency Relief Administration, which was the umbrella under which the WPA was covered. So those kinds of things were done.

Parks were done—some of the finest parks that we have in New Mexico today, municipal parks. Cahoon Park in Roswell. Hillcrest Park in Clovis. Arthur Park in Estancia. Roosevelt Park in Albuquerque. The Alameda in Santa Fe. The Alameda was done in part by [the] WPA and by the CCC. It was during and under the WPA that Steven DeBoer, who was an early landscape architect here in the West, did most of the remote park systems for the city of Denver and worked as a consultant for the WPA here in New Mexico. It was DeBoer's vision that began to foresee how the capitol complex would appear in Santa Fe. The first step in doing that was the construction of the Supreme Court building in 1937. DeBoer envisioned that you would come down from the old commercial part of Santa Fe across the Alameda, where you now had the park, and gradually step your way up toward the capitol, which is now the Bataan Memorial Building.

There are airports. Here in Albuquerque, what we call the old air terminal was a major project. That almost would be one of the exceptions to what I was saying about labor-intensive WPA as opposed to capitol-intensive PWA because that was a three-quarter-of-a-million-dollar project. It was essentially a concrete-reinforced skeleton with adobe wall in between, and then that synergy of bringing in the flagstones, bringing in the vigas, and putting them together to make this airport, which had been a goal [for] Albuquerque to the same degree that straightening Route 66 had been. Albuquerque's chamber of commerce and Clyde Tingley, when he was the mayor here, had wanted to make Albuquerque the crossroads of New Mexico, and they wanted to do that by getting an east–west highway through here, which they did when Route 66 was straightened out of Santa Fe. But then when they built the airport, they also had a facility for east–west planes. By this time, you're starting to fly your DC-3s, and you're going to have night flying, and at that time they also then had the Varney line, which became Continental Airlines, which ran north–south from Denver to El Paso.

And I would argue that it was because of the completion of that airport and the city['s] acquiring that land on the mesa east of the airport that they were in a position by, I believe, 1939 or 1940, to get further federal funding to put in Kirtland Field. I don't think Kirtland Field would have been seen as an attractive army air base had there not already been the WPA air terminal here.

JL: Can you talk about any other types of public buildings that were then part of that, maybe up in the northwestern quarter of the state? Was anything up there?

DK: In the northwestern part of the state, you have the McKinley County courthouse in Gallup. When you go east of Gallup to Fort Wingate, you'll see a lot of the architecture that we identify with the New Deal that was done under the auspices of the Indian Civilian Conservation Corps. So they did do projects on the reservation, but that was done separately for Native Americans.

JL: Could you talk a little bit about that?

DK: What I find most interesting about that is to think of it in terms of John Collier. Harold Ickes knew that even though he was

Republican, Franklin Roosevelt was looking at him for what he could offer the administration. Ickes remembered going in for an interview with Roosevelt just after he'd been elected, and [Ickes] thought that he was going to be offered the directorship of the Bureau of Indian Affairs, and Roosevelt offered him Interior instead, and then Ickes went and got John Collier to head the BIA.

Collier was very much like-minded in terms of that notion of Native Americans holding onto their cultural identity, and I think one of the most important ways of doing that was finding a way to leave those boarding schools behind, which had just been anathema to preserving Native American cultures. People [Native Americans] would be taken to Carlyle or Haskell, and they would be stripped of everything that they knew and marched around in dresses and uniforms and so forth. Collier's response to that was to get the schools back in the communities. One of the things that was done was to look at how architecture influenced people's attitudes and created a comfort zone for them. Collier's reasoning was if the hooghan was the building of the Dineh [Navajo] and that that was what they were familiar with, that maybe the education within that context would be the solution.

So one of the things that occurred under the Navajo CCC was the construction (there are still a few of them left) of these double hooghans that were meant to be community schools where the children would be either with a relative or at home, but that they would come to school, that school would occur within the environment that they were comfortable with, and then they would go home. So if you go out, for example, to Prewitt, out just north of Interstate 40 at the Baca site, there is a double hooghan there. At Tohatchi, there was a double hooghan. Those were all done under the CCC.

JL: Were there New Deal projects in Farmington or San Juan County?

DK: Yeah, we can take a look up here. In Aztec here, you get the nuts and bolts stuff of sewer lines, library construction, city hall construction. There was gym construction in Blanco, irrigation ditches in Bloomfield, excavation and repair work of ruins at Chaco. Farmington had lots of stuff. Five-room school construction, office for the WPA, a junior high school addition, sidewalks, high school construction, airport improvements, library construction, gym construction. But it's not as widespread up there actually as it is in some of the other parts of the state.

Another very interesting thing is what the New Deal did in terms of political alignments in this state. Until the New Deal—the system of the GOP [Republican Party] and the wealthy Hispanos, the patrons who went out and suggested how people might vote—northern New Mexico was largely Republican. When Clyde Tingley was governor, people got in line. [This being said], it's interesting that he thought that he could amend the [New Mexico] constitution in '37 [so] that [it] would permit him to run for a third term, but the state had been growing, and he lost over on the east side, and he didn't get that amendment, so he was finished in office.

One of the things that's dear to my heart in terms of the WPA in New Mexico is the former Carrie Tingley Children's Hospital in the Hot Springs–Truth or Consequences area. I think that if there's any single New Deal story in New Mexico where we can look at the personal interest of Franklin Roosevelt and his connection with Clyde Tingley, it probably is with the Carrie Tingley Hospital. A couple of years ago my wife and I had the opportunity to go to Warm Springs, Georgia, to look at the hospital where "Doc" Roosevelt, as the local people used to call him, had made over a Civil War–era hot springs resort where he would go. He came from a family that had had a tradition of going to Europe and taking baths. He felt that this was somewhere he could go to overcome the paralysis to his muscles [from polio]. He purchased the place in 1926.

He redid the facility down there completely. In order to accommodate people who don't have easy and free movement, you've got to keep things on a single plane. So when they designed Georgia Hall, as the facility is known, it was basically a series of parallel buildings and colonnades going back to a two-story hall, and this became the main facility that really was the leading facility of its kind by the early 1930s when he goes to the White House.

The Tingleys had never had children, but people always talked about Carrie Tingley going down to the stores the days after Christmas and buying half-cost gifts that went to children the following year. Children were taken into care by Carrie Tingley in her own house and looked after when parents were away. I think that was the beginning of the idea of doing something for paralyzed children in New Mexico. I think Clyde Tingley actually gives a talk in Hot Springs and raises the possibility of those thermal waters being used. Within a couple of months, he meets Roosevelt on a navy ship in San Diego. Tingley raises the possibility of a children's hospital as a WPA project, and Roosevelt is quite enthusiastic about it.

He has Tingley take his architect, Kruger, to meet Henry J. Tombs, who was the architect for Georgia Hall in Warm Springs. They visit Warm Springs. Tombs points out the things he would do differently if he were doing it over again, and all of that gets incorporated into the plans for the hospital down there, including, in a distilled way, the sense of the elongated green, broken up now into two courtyards with two single-story wings on both sides. They had a little shop where they could do brace work and everything. The only second-story section was where they kept a room for the Tingleys when they came down and visited. In their correspondence, Roosevelt talks about how little children in need will have a place.

JL: Boy, this is great. We've gone a long way here, David. Anything you want to address that we haven't talked about?

DK: I think that more than most states, New Mexico benefited and was greatly affected by the New Deal. Some of the areas where efforts were being made to shore up or develop infrastructure didn't always have the lasting results that people intended for them. But I think, on the other hand, to create a state park system, get communication with state agencies from county to county to county—those kinds of things did get done. Probably the rate at which they were accomplished was accelerated by the New Deal, so much so that come the 1940s and the war, New Mexico was more in the twentieth century and able to be a place where you could set up Manhattan projects than it might have been had there never been the urgency of combating this widespread depression that came to the country and to the state.

By the time I was born, Harry Truman was president. But I still, with a smile on my face, call myself a Roosevelt Democrat. I think that the world we live in today—not that you would wish an economic catastrophe on this country—but I think that sometimes people need to find a common denominator, and I think we do not have that kind of definable common denominator right now, and I think that we are less for it.

Richard Melzer, photo by author

Richard Melzer

Introduction

Richard Melzer is a professor of history at the University of New Mexico Valencia campus and has served as the president of the New Mexico Historical Society. The author of many books and articles on New Mexico and the Southwest, he is a leading scholar of the history of the Civilian Conservation Corps (CCC) in New Mexico and has written a fine book entitled *Coming of Age in the Great Depression: The Civilian Conservation Corps Experience in New Mexico, 1933–1942* (2000).

In June 2006, I wended my way through the Valencia campus to Melzer's office, where I met a historian with an evolved sense of humor and thought to myself that if I were to begin anew as a history major, I would definitely want Richard Melzer as a professor. During our interview, he not only provided an historic perspective of the CCC in New Mexico, but also colored in the gray zones and made the history real.

The CCC was one of Franklin D. Roosevelt's (FDR) favorite projects. The CCC workers were trained by military personnel and thus were inadvertently prepared to participate in the terrible war that followed the Great Depression. Not only did the CCC help restore natural habitat in New Mexico and beyond, but it also fostered the environmental viewpoints of thinkers such as Henry David Thoreau, John Wesley Powell, John Muir, and Aldo Leopold.

Richard Melzer

JL: Would you give me an overview of your research into the Civilian Conservation Corps, also known as the CCC?

RM: Years and years ago I did research on coal-mining camps in New Mexico, starting with Madrid and then Dawson, and of course the great design was to do Gallup, too, or the small camps outside of Gallup. But I only got as far as Dawson. My main focus was on the Depression in those camps. So my first book is on the Great Depression in Madrid.

JL: Your major focus, as I understand it, is the CCC. I wonder if you could talk about the history of how that came to be in New Mexico and then maybe talk about some of your favorite CCC sites.

RM: I wonder if it would be helpful to mention what I did in the intro to that book, which explained how I got involved in the CCC, which really came out of my studies of the mining camps. I was interviewing a man who had graduated from the high school in Dawson in the late 1930s, and he said that the day he graduated from high school was the darkest day of his life. That's so unusual because that's supposed to be a day full of promise, optimism. Of course, I had to ask why. He said, "There were no jobs." Phelps Dodge wasn't hiring at Dawson, and there weren't any jobs in the local area, Raton, or other places. The only people who were really lucky in that class were the guys who got to join the CCC. So I had heard of the CCC, of course, but never in such compelling terms. That began the pursuit—it lasted about twenty years—[of] interviewing eventually about a hundred fellows from the CCC.

As that generation began to die out, I realized that I needed to put this in writing so that they would have it and share it with their families and their generations. So I finally drew a line in the sand—you know how that goes—and began to write. Got more and more interested in it. Of course, it was *the* most popular New Deal agency. Even conservatives liked the CCC. There's something to like for every political group, it seemed, because it was so helpful to the young men who were involved with it.

Of course, New Mexico was incredibly fortunate. We had two great politicians who were heavily involved in getting federal projects here: Clyde Tingley as our governor and, of course, Dennis Chavez as our senator by 1935. They were just great in getting funding for projects of all kinds—many different New Deal projects, of course, but including the CCC. The CCC was FDR's pet project. It was the first project he proposed during his first hundred days, a period of incredible activity. It had worked for him on another scale when he was the governor of New York, and he tried it out there. It worked so well that he was anxious to try it on the national scale. How many wins was it? A win-win-win situation because the fellows would join, and this was great for them because so many of them, of course, had dropped out of school, given the Depression and given other factors, including discrimination against Hispanics, even in New Mexico. So they had dropped out of school, and they didn't have any work experience or education or training. So they were sort of in limbo. But here was a chance for them to come of age, to go through a process where they could be accepted and have some direction in their lives.

In fact, the two main things that I heard over and over again in all the interviews were, first of all, that this was the turning point of their lives. They didn't know what would have happened to them if it weren't for the CCC. The other thing that they kept on saying was the great lesson in the CCC was how to work with others because they got to work with other people from New Mexico. There was so much work to be done here [that] they brought in fellows from other states, too, including Pennsylvania. That's quite a shock in terms of these fellows getting along. And more of a shock, Oklahoma, and the greatest shock, Texas. Always clashes when the Texas newcomers would come into a camp. There'd be fights. They'd fight each other with fists and bats and knives and forks, and they'd get that over with, and then they'd get along. And they began to know about each [other], understand each other. It's like most young fellows, whether it's in the military or the Los Alamos Ranch School or wherever. They first encounter each other, [and] they've got to somehow adjust. They did that physically in the CCC.

JL: I know that they were trained by army personnel. Was it the Army Corps of Engineers?

RM: No, actually it was the army reserve officers. I guess some naval reserve officers, too, but mostly army reserve officers. That's another win for the CCC because those reserve officers would become officers during World War II, and they'd had this incredible experience in dealing with young civilians in an army setting, so they'd be well prepared for the draftees in World War II. They never knew that, of course. That was a coincidence, we hope. But it turns out that it worked very well. The army ran the camps, but the actual work projects were assigned to various federal agencies—the National Park Service, the Forest Service, and other agencies. So that on a day-to-day basis in camp, the fellows would report to the officers, but when they went on work assignments, they were not under military discipline anymore.

JL: You just alluded to something that has been rumor[ed] off and on. Just how anticipated or unanticipated was World War II from the point of view of the administration? Has any light ever been cast on that?

RM: Just a lot of suspicion by suspicious-natured people. In those days, conservatives feared that FDR was trying to become a dictator, and this was his private youth army. It makes some sense, I guess, if you want to think about it that way, because these are the days of Hitler's youth army. They saw it going on in Europe under the fascists, and they worried about that possibility here. But it didn't happen that way. These fellows, just like the officers, were becoming prepared for World War II. That's another win of the CCC. These fellows knew how to live in barracks, they ate in mess halls, they ate army food because the recipes in the mess halls were from army cookbooks. They learned discipline, saluting, taking orders, but they didn't learn how to use weapons. They didn't learn how to fight, other than [by] fighting each other. When the war broke out, there was even some talk—or complaints, actually—that, Why aren't those CCC fellows training to get in the military? Why don't you give them rifles? But it never happened.

JL: I'm thinking about how in a sense it was necessary that FDR really exponentially increase the sense of bureaucracy in order to make all this stuff happen. Of course, some of that can be seen in what they call the "alphabet soup of acronyms."

RM: Absolutely.

JL: I wonder if you could talk about that a little bit.

RM: It's interesting because, as I tell my students, it was wonderful that all this money came into New Mexico. It helped alleviate the misery in the state. It brought projects here that probably would not have been built for years, if ever. In fact, I was just quoting a [Governor] Tingley letter to Senator Chavez in 1935, saying, "Don't tell the federal government this, but we're probably going to have more people than work here because there are so many people in need." So it was a great opportunity for New Mexico. Especially because—it's so weird, because we had always been in a depression, at least the rural people, so this was something of a heyday for some people at least who benefited from it.

JL: I've done a lot of fieldwork among traditional Navajo people older than me, and I was born in the middle of it [the Depression], in 1936. Some of these Navajos didn't even know about the Depression. It did not affect them at all. A couple of weeks ago my friend Stewart Udall, who was born in 1920, told me about how he went through the Depression, growing up and living in a small town—St. Johns, Arizona. In those days, those parts of Arizona and New Mexico were all interchangeably the same habitat. He talked about how the sense of self-sustainability that existed in the rural Southwest was what kept a lot of people going.

RM: Absolutely. They knew how to be poor. They sure did. And in some cases they didn't even know they were poor. It was just their way of life, for generations if not for centuries. You think about making your own food, getting your own wood from the forests as long as the national forest would let you do it, go out hunting up there and fishing as long as they'd let you do it. Being self-sufficient, building onto the house. Building a house. You could do all those things without necessarily being involved with a cash economy.

JL: Something that's really interesting is how the land grants, the New Mexico land grants, got rearranged and became either public lands or privatized in other ways. My friend Cipriano Vigil wrote a powerful song entitled "Se ve triste el hombre," which talks about how sad the man is at having lost his land grant to the U.S. government. Could you talk a little bit about that? I'd like to see if we could set the cultural stage for when the CCC actually came in and helped provide useful work.

RM: Like you said, so many of the land grants were lost or changed hands over the years, so that what land was left very often was subdivided over and over again among the children and so that there was very little acreage left to really live on. People evidently did it because, like you said, they often survived. But with the loss of land grants, especially in the north, a lot of men had to go out for labor in other states—Nevada, Colorado, Wyoming, Montana—sheepherding, railroad working, working in the sugar beet fields. They'd go off for three, four, five months of the year just to get the cash they needed to send back home for people to survive at home.

It's so ironic to me that New Mexican villages survived off the wages sent by these migrant workers working in other states when now we're talking about Mexican immigrants coming to the United States to get the money to send back for their villages to survive, their families in their villages. It's so ironic because at one point the governor of Colorado sent the National Guard to the southern border of Colorado with New Mexico and made sure that no migrant labor came into Colorado. And, of course, they were concerned about Mexican labor coming into Colorado by way of New Mexico. But when you have a Hispanic crossing into Colorado, how do they [the National Guardsmen] know the difference? [People] didn't have national ID cards or anything in those days. So New Mexicans were discriminated against, and they lost jobs as a result. Thousands of Mexican immigrants were deported in the 1930s. Some New Mexicans didn't leave New Mexico for fear that they'd be grouped with these immigrants and deported when, of course, their family had been here for centuries. It was a different culture, a different group, than the Mexican immigrants.

And then of course we can't forget the homesteaders, who were often poor whites, who tried to come in, especially in eastern New Mexico. If they survived the process of homesteading, especially in the early twentieth century, then they faced the drought and the Depression of the '30s, and that was just another trial for them. Some made it, and some of course didn't. I did an oral history of a fellow in the CCC, Sy Porter. It was published in the *New Mexico Historical Review*. He describes his family's poverty in Corona. They had a little ranch outside of Corona, and they couldn't get by. They had all these kids, and some of them were sick, and they had a really hard time. He tells a wonderful joke, I'm sure it's an old joke, but I like it so much. He said that they were so poor that when the doctor came to their house, he never charged them anything for the house visits because the doctor knew how poor they were. He told them to take this medicine, so he gave them the medicine in the bottle.

They asked how much to take, and he said, "Just enough to cover a dime." So the doctor left, and they realized they didn't have a dime. The most they had was a nickel. So they covered it twice.

JL: I've thought about this, but nobody's really talked about it that much. That is how the economic Great Depression and the great drought hit eastern New Mexico at the same time and how those events melded.

RM: Up in the northeastern part of the state, the Dust Bowl—Union County, right on the border with the Texas panhandle, Oklahoma panhandle, western Kansas, and eastern Colorado, that was the center of the Dust Bowl. Just horrible experiences up there. You might have seen some of those photographs of those enormous dust clouds a mile, two miles high coming in over Clayton and other places in the Dust Bowl. And then you hear all the incredible stories.

The other day I heard of a woman on a homestead who would make lunch for the men who came home for lunch. She'd make sandwiches, and she'd put them on a plate. The first day she did it, the dust blew in and destroyed the sandwiches. So the next day she got smart and she put a towel over it. The dust covered the sandwiches. The next day she covered it with two towels, and dust still covered the sandwiches by the time the men came home. It just permeated everything—the smallest crack. It was so upsetting. Life out there was pretty depressing, anyway; it could be so lonely. But then you would have this constant wind and the dust everywhere. You could take a bath, and five minutes later you were covered with dust. Then the gray skies all the time. Just awfully depressing.

You hear of families where the wives and the children would just move away because it was too much for them. I read an anecdote the other day about a young boy who was traveling in a wagon by himself, and he got caught in one of these dust storms. He found his way to a ranch house, and the rancher was surprised to see anybody out in a dust storm because it was blowing so badly. So he brought the boy in, and the place was a real mess; it was covered with dust. The rancher said, "You'll have to excuse me. My wife got so upset; she said she couldn't stand it anymore, and she left me." So just to make conversation the boy said, "Do the winds blow like this all the time?" He says, "Yeah, it blows like this all the time, day after day after day." Then he hesitated and then he said, "And then it gets worse. It blows like hell."

JL: Is this in part the result of pumping too much water out of the Oglala Aquifer, do you think?

RM: Yeah, I think so. Of course, they overproduced in the 1920s, first in response to World War I and then in response to the demands of the '20s. I've heard it said that they tractored themselves into this situation because they overproduced, and the soil became loose, of course, and with the drought became looser, and then with the wind it blew away. Once a CCC fellow from Oklahoma said he was serving in New Mexico, but he always felt like he was at home because you could always see Oklahoma blowing over his head in the Dust Bowl.

I'm sure you're familiar with the book *Pie Town Woman* [by Joan Myers about Doris Caudill]? And at the very end of *No Life for a Lady*, she [Agnes Morley Cleaveland] talks about the homesteaders coming in and the homesteaders moving out—not being able to survive off the land.

JL: Actually, one of the big issues that is really important is how conservation and preservation occurred through the practices of the CCC in the 1930s because this affected the American West forevermore.

RM: Yeah. I talked about the win-win-win situation. Another great win was for conservation in the West, particularly in New Mexico, specifically in those communities, those areas of the state, that they worked in. Any kind of conservation work you can think of, they were involved in—they planted millions of trees across the country. They were very efficient at it in terms of one fellow digging the hole, [the] next fellow putting the small tree in, and the next fellow settling it down and going on. Just a mass production sort of process, and that's interesting. They learned a work ethic, almost an industrial work ethic in some ways. So that's another way the country won from this program because they became the workers of the postwar period—industrial workers in many cases.

That's another thing. These fellows had such a great appreciation for the environment and conservation; they were determined activists and supporters of conservation the rest of their lives. And I'm not saying that we wouldn't have had a conservation ethic or it wouldn't have been as strong without them, but it was even stronger because of them.

JL: What other kinds of activities did they engage in?

RM: They built lookout towers for forest fires. They fought forest fires. In fact, three of them died here in New Mexico in forest fires. Of course, they built roads and paths into the forests so that the forests could be maintained and they could have access to the forest fires. One of the few criticisms of the CCC was [that] they were too good at fighting forest fires because almost as soon as a fire would break out, they'd have a crew going out there, and I guess it's a natural process that there need to be some fires.

JL: I know they also did a lot of stuff like riprap to try to keep erosion in control. Could you talk a little bit about that?

RM: They built thousands of check dams, especially in the southern part of New Mexico, but all over the place. It was a humble organization. You're probably familiar with the WPA [Works Progress Administration], and everything they did, they put "WPA" [on it]—a cornerstone, even sidewalks, they put "WPA" and the year that they worked on that particular sidewalk. But there are only a couple of places in the whole state where you actually see the marking "CCC," and it's usually very small. Of course, it seems appropriate, out in the wilderness, when you do a check dam, you're not going to put "CCC" or something on it because there are so many of them. And of course they helped in floods, too. In the Pecos River valley and the Río Grande, they were always there to help ranchers and farmers in small towns. In the archives, you see letters over and over again from mayors and chambers of commerce to the camps thanking them for their help in the floods.

JL: You know, apropos of that, there's this wonderful corrido [narrative ballad] written by Reymundo Luna, "El corrido de San Marcial." It's my understanding that the Elephant Butte Dam was the first of the big dams constructed in the West. It was completed by about 1916, and its primary objective was to make it possible for people in the Mesilla Valley to successfully farm. But is there any indication [that] it was also in part to be a flood-control dam? There was this great irony: in part, because of its presence, the town of San Marcial was flooded out [in 1929].

RM: Sure. It's just a crazy situation. In fact, I did write an article for the *New Mexico Magazine* about the floods of San Marcial. I think it came out [in], what, 1990, '91.

JL: Could you talk about that a little bit for me?

RM: San Marcial was such an important railroad town. It was a small town, but it was an important town just south of Socorro. It wasn't there that long, but the people who lived there felt such an attachment to that little community—especially the Hispanics, and anyone who lived there or grew up there felt an incredible attachment to the place. So they mourned the passing of that, just like they do at Madrid and at Dawson—any other little community, I guess. But this one was such a terrible situation because it wasn't just one flood; there were two floods. The first flood was terrible enough. All the silt and everything came into town. Whole [railroad] engines were turned over. At the Harvey House at San Marcial, the flood came up to the second floor. The Harvey girls and the guests were all up on the second floor, the thing was so high. So they'd just begun to recover from that. It was like a boxer taking a real hard hit. They'd just begun to recover from that, and then you get this second flood, and they knew they couldn't recover. They had doubts about being able to dig out and survive from the first one, but after the second one they knew they were doomed. They'd have to take off.

It was a real tragedy, of course, the water flooding the area and the threat of disease, the problems of getting supplies in [even] on a miniscale compared to what New Orleans has gone through [because of levy breaks caused by Hurricane Katrina]. But there were some of the same dangers on a smaller scale. People not wanting to leave, but of course having to.

JL: Is there any evidence at all that had Elephant Butte Dam not been there, the flood might not have happened?

RM: The flood was because of heavy rains, especially in the north. That certainly caused it. But it was compounded by Elephant Butte, it sure was.

JL: There's real irony there.

RM: There sure is. Floods were so common in the [Mesilla] Valley before those days, and the first thing they wanted of course was Elephant Butte [Dam]. But because that was not working as well, especially for the middle Río Grande, they had to have the other solutions, including [forming] the Middle Río Grande Conservancy District.

JL: Are there any other dam projects that were accomplished by the CCC—bigger dams?

RM: No, not in New Mexico. They had these thousands of check dams and some slightly larger ones, but nothing on a very large scale at all. One of the beauties of the CCC was that it was so mobile. They would do small projects and move on. The barracks were transported all over the state. In fact, some of the barracks are still around. One rancher called me up the other day down in Silver City, and he thinks his barn was the old mess hall. And sure enough, a bunch of CCC guys went down and said [that], yeah, it used to be a mess hall.

They did soil studies, especially in conjunction with New Mexico State [University]—New Mexico A&M in those days. They did a lot of erosion control. You hear of the problems with the prairie dogs today, and they were involved with a lot of that. They used to spread the poison over the fields. They went on rabbit hunts. They'd spread out over acres, and they'd just swoop right through an area and kill any rabbits in their path. It sounds brutal today. But I guess they thought it was necessary in those days.

JL: What other projects come to mind here? Maybe mention some of the more visible sites that still exist.

RM: Like I said, the projects are everywhere. [They're] not as conspicuous because they [didn't] mark the projects. But let's start from the south at Carlsbad Caverns. They built the first concrete steps down into the caverns. Then at White Sands, they built the visitor's center. Bosque del Apache [National Wildlife Refuge] is a CCC program, including the main building, the headquarters, and the paths. Bandelier [National Monument], the visitor's center and the inn or the cabins there are CCC. A lot of the trails back into the ruins—CCC. The National Park Service building in Santa Fe.

Another win for the CCC is that they hired local people to supervise and help the fellows. At Bandelier, for example. These fellows, without any training or experience, could not have built those buildings or the vigas or any of the beautiful furniture there. They couldn't have just made that up. So the CCC hired local experienced men. They were called LEMs. They served as the foremen and the experts in teaching the fellows these things. You look at them [the CCC workers], and you say, "How could they have done that, first time out?" They didn't. They had plans, and they followed the plans, and they took the instructions from the LEMs, but we don't know how many things they did that were thrown out and tried again until they got it right. It was a great learning experience for them.

I was talking about Bandelier, and so much of the furniture and everything was made by the CCC. But they brought in other artists, including Indian artists, to do the murals and paintings there—so it was a real mix of the cultures. The WPA would build a post office, and they'd bring in the artists to do the murals that would reflect local culture, whether it was Indian culture or Hispanic culture or whatever.

JL: Was there much activity up around Farmington in San Juan County?

RM: Not a lot up there. I think some of it might have been political. One of the most famous New Deal scandals in the whole country was right here in New Mexico. Scandals of accusations that you had to be Democrat—you had to be friends of a certain wing of the Democratic Party. The trials actually involved accusations against Dennis Chavez's wing of the party. As many as seventy-five men and women were put on trial. Most of them were acquitted, but it was a struggle within the party for control of the New Deal programs. Tingley was always conscious of how many Republicans were involved in the administration and running of the programs. There were rumors that you had to be a Democrat to join the CCC, so whether they were or not, they always said they were Democrats. There were accusations that on election day the Democrats would go down to the camps and round up the guys to bring them into town to vote.

JL: More than once?

RM: Probably more than once, right—several times. (Laughs) But you know, this is all machine politics, and that's what Tingley wanted. He created a political machine in Albuquerque, and he was determined to do it in the state as a whole. Certainly that's what Chavez wanted to do as a base of his career.

Another result of the New Deal is that incredible shift to the Democratic Party that would not have happened except for the New Deal. A downside of the New Deal in New Mexico is the increased dependency on the federal government. And that trend continues and enlarges in World War II and to this very day. We're so dependent on the federal government in making decisions, critical decisions, about the environment, about employment, about money and projects—whatever, coming into New Mexico. In good years, when you agree with the administration, that's OK. But in other years, it can be disastrous, especially for the environment and the culture.

JL: Can you talk a little bit about the CCC and the Indian people?

RM: There was a separate organization, the Indian CCC. For the mainstream CCC, I guess you could call it, these fellows left their homes and were sent into these camps, two hundred in each camp. But in the Indian CCC, they did projects on their reservations, and they stayed home, so they'd report to work in the morning and be shipped out in trucks or whatever to the project sites. And again more in conjunction with their culture and their needs. I mentioned before about that trend, especially by the '20s, of men in northern New Mexico migrating out to other states for work. So that became part of the culture, that it was OK and expected for one to leave home and be gone for months at a time. So when the CCC came along, just by accident [it] fit into that pattern. It was a responsibility of a young man, men of whatever age, to go off and make money and send it home. So the CCC fit into that custom without ever intending to. When you signed up for the CCC, you got a dollar a day, and you had to designate someone that the money would be sent to. Five of those thirty dollars [each month] you could keep, but the other twenty-five dollars were automatically sent to whomever you designated. So another win would be for the families back home. They needed that money.

Now for the fellows it sounds terrible—they got only five dollars a month. But they were living in the middle of nowhere; their room and board and clothes were taken care of; they went to town maybe two or three times a month on a Saturday night, so it was just extra money. Some of the families even saved some of the twenty-five dollars they got every month, so when the fellow ended his enrollment in the CCC, he'd have a sort of a nest egg, some way to get started in life.

JL: Was there any restriction as to how many people per family could be CCC people?

RM: No, there wasn't. Although the rumor was that you could have only one per family. So you hear stories about brothers changing their names and moving to Arizona to live with relatives and sign up over there. There [were] all sorts of rumors, and every time they heard one, they tried to deal with it—the rumor that you had to be a Democrat or only one person per family. Of course, there were requirements about height and weight, and for some fellows that was a problem in New Mexico because of the Depression and not weighing very much. Probably the funniest requirement—and sad, too—is [that] you had to have three serviceable teeth, two of which had to be on the top or the bottom and the other one in the other direction so you could chew. But some of these guys didn't even have teeth. So when they went to the CCC, another win was they got medical attention. There was a camp doctor and a camp dentist, and usually these men circulated among the camps, but at least the fellows got to see them.

Some sad stories. One fellow went to see the dentist, and the dentist said, "Even your three remaining teeth aren't good, so we'll take them all out and be back next month with your false teeth." So the fellow waited the month, and of course the doctor didn't come back for six months, but he eventually got his teeth.

JL: Was he able to work then?

RM: Yes.

JL: Were there any sort of menus? Can you recall what they were fed?

RM: Yeah. They were fed off of the army cookbooks, and there's another one for the country leading up to World War II because you had cooks who were trained to cook army food for large numbers. So a lot of these guys became cooks in World War II because they were all prepared. They knew the recipes; they could deal with large numbers and lots of complaints.

       A lot of the CCC guys became the noncoms of World War II because they had had this experience. They went to boot camp, and the drill sergeants noticed these guys right away. They knew how to live in barracks and how to make a bed, the cot, and the whole routine. So they'd pull them out, and they progressed a lot faster than the others, so a lot of them became the corporals, sergeants, or officers in World War II.

       It's said in New Mexico that everyone knew of a friend or a relative in the CCC, it was so prevalent, and they were so awfully glad to get the jobs.

JL: Could you talk about anything that persists in New Mexico today, seventy-some years later after the CCC?

RM: Yeah, there is a youth conservation corps run out of Santa Fe, and they do a good job. They get proposals for projects from communities around the state, and then young volunteers, boys and girls, work on the projects. It's remotely tied to the CCC concept. By the way, I should mention there was a female version of the CCC. Eleanor Roosevelt saw how successful the male version was, so she complained to Franklin, as she was known to do, that there should in all fairness be a female version. So it was created. It was part of the NYA, National Youth Alliance. They were scattered all over the country, not as many by any means.

The CCC, you're talking about more than three million guys, and here in New Mexico it was fifty-four thousand. But not as many women were involved with this project. But probably the most successful program for women in the whole country was right here in New Mexico out by Fort Stanton.

JL: And what did they do?

RM: They had various projects. They didn't work in most places. The girls didn't like to go out in the middle of wilderness and be that far from their families and from towns, but apparently this camp was run so well. It was a home economics sort of thing in terms of cooking and sewing. They even had their own catalog—a catalog of the things they had made that people could order. In particular, I remember aprons. I guess there's one catalog from it up in the Smithsonian.

JL: What would you like to talk about that we haven't talked about?

RM: I've covered all my win-win situations, including, of course, the families back home. Local communities benefited. Usually local communities were real leery about the news that a CCC camp was coming in. They didn't know what to expect—all these young males sound[ed] like trouble. Sy Porter, in his interview, said that his sister was sure she was going to have to carry a knife around to defend herself against all of these guys because a lot of them they expected from Texas—Tejanos. Well, the camp comes in, [and] they get along real well with the fellows. It really helped the local farmers because some of the supplies and food would be bought from the local community. They became friends with them; they invited CCC enrollees over for dinner. And that girl who said she had to carry a knife around? She married one of them.

JL: We've covered a lot of ground here. I'm really stoked. This has been a super interview. I had a good time.

RM: I did too.

PART III

Seeking the Path
of Common Sense

The Great Depression came to an end on December 7, 1941, when the Japanese bombed Pearl Harbor. Franklin Delano Roosevelt proclaimed it a "day of infamy" and launched the United States of America into the deadly morass of World War II. America rallied valiantly, and adults of that era proved their merit by defeating the dread Axis by 1945.

New Mexico served up a disproportionately high number of young men, mostly Hispanos, many of whom met their destinies during the Bataan Death March in the Philippines, thus irreparably rending the fabric of Hispano culture. Navajo code talkers greatly aided the Allies by conveying secret messages in the Navajo language, befuddling those Axis enemies who were listening in on shortwave radios. Citizens who remained in the United States conserved gasoline through rationing and by observing a thirty-five-mile-per-hour speed limit. Food tokens were second only to the coin of the realm, and oleo margarine required that a colored pellet be squeezed and mixed into the lard-looking grease to give it the hue of butter. The ball-point pen had yet to be introduced to the marketplace.

With the end of the war, America entered its golden age as the most powerful nation on the planet, and economics came to dominate collective attention. The threat of nuclear annihilation became the psychological "white noise" of two generations, when we stopped thinking in terms of future generations. Science and technology came to be regarded as the means to "save all" in spite of a profound history of scientific misapplication.

Yet, somehow, certain "malcontents" rose to the occasion by openly criticizing what we were becoming and at what expense to our planetary habitat. By the 1960s, such dissenters as Robinson Jeffers, David Brower, Allen Ginsberg, Gary Snyder, Edward Abbey, and many others reinvigorated and evolved points of view professed earlier by Henry David Thoreau, John Wesley Powell, John Muir, and Aldo Leopold. Their work nurtured the modern environmental movement, which is now a major factor in the cultural system of checks and balances vital to the health of the planet. The cultural attitudes and practices of enduring Native American cultures provide a level of wisdom that harkens back to a time when landscape was perceived as sacred terrain rather than as real estate.

The interviews in this section are intended to help bridge the boundaries wrought by cultural biases that are contrary to common sense as we address overpopulation, waning natural resources, rampant consumerism, global warming, and climate change.

Melissa Savage, photo by author

Melissa Savage

Introduction

Melissa Savage is a biogeographer who received her Ph.D. from the University of Colorado and thereafter joined the geography department faculty at the University of California at Los Angeles (UCLA). After retiring from UCLA, she returned to her home in Santa Fe, New Mexico, and founded the Four Corners Institute, whose mission is to partner with local communities in the Southwest in the restoration of natural ecosystems. Its mission statement says, "The Four Corners Institute works to bring together the diverse voices of the Southwest, people with a stake in the health and integrity of the environment, to collaborate in their recovery. Current scientific knowledge can assist partners in making resource choices that restore and revive our natural places."

Melissa Savage has followed her imagination around the world, exploring the flow of Nature through myriad ecosystems. She always returns to the American Southwest, where she continues to devote her life to restoration of habitat, preservation of wildlife corridors, and vigorous defense of endangered species. She is deeply committed to her science and concurrently follows her evolved intuitions as she passes through the natural world that she loves.

I interviewed Savage in 1999 as part of a project for the New Mexico

Wilderness Alliance. Herein she reveals her passion for wilderness preservation throughout the American West and beyond.

Melissa Savage

JL: One thing that many people don't know yet is what *biogeography* is.

MS: Well, it is a very broad term and an old discipline. Aristotle was a good biogeographer. It really means knowledge of all the natural communities on the face of the Earth, how they are organized, how they work. And geographers especially, unlike ecologists, have spent their whole careers looking at the way that people and human communities interact with natural communities. Natural communities are usually thought of as whole communities without the touch of people. But, in fact, the human influence goes back so far that there are no pristine landscapes. There are no communities that haven't been touched, even well before the industrial age. Human use of fire goes back half a million years, and there is no more single powerful influence on the shape of the natural landscape than the use of fire. So that is one of the distinguishing characteristics of the practice of biogeography. Looking at what people do to natural environments.

JL: Do you think that the word *bioregion* really does have currency, or do you think that there is a better word?

MS: I think *bioregion* is a very useful idea. It is easy for people to understand what it means. You can always use better words. But bioregion speaks to people. Since human communities interact with natural communities so much, often people create a bioregion by what they do. Look at Europe. That kind of characteristic use of the landscape has produced a kind of large bioregion that would be different without people. So bioregions, yes, but in terms also of human uses of it. You can think of it at different scales. You could think of the scale of Europe, for example, where the kind of use has been consistent across the whole landscape of the whole region of Europe. But you can also think of the bioregion of the Rhine Valley, for example, or the bioregion of your own community of people. Santa Fe is a bioregion, or the Santa Fe River bioregion, which is very small, but it is very easy for people to grasp what is going on in the places that they are most familiar with. So I don't think that you need to belabor what the scale of the bioregion is. The term works at many levels.

JL: I have a tendency not to think in terms of geopolitical boundaries, but within this particular context I [instead] think of New Mexico as a mosaic of bioregions. Does that ring true to you?

MS: Well, yes. New Mexico is at the congruence of two or three natural bioregions. The plains, the southern deserts, the mountains, the Great Basin all meet here.

JL: The New Mexico Wilderness Alliance is working very hard to effect legislation that would preserve more than forty proposed areas as wilderness areas. How would you define a wilderness area within the context of today's culture?

MS: Wilderness is a place where the human touch has been very light. I think it is quite desirable to say there are places where we can close the roads. And the main message about natural places is that we are losing them. And losing them. And losing them. People are busy in their own lives and just don't have the time and the energy to pay attention to what is happening. And what is happening is extremely serious globally. And it is extremely serious in New Mexico. We are losing species; we are losing viable water systems. We are losing forest systems. We are losing grasslands. You know, every natural community has lost so much of its area, and even places that are semiwild have lost so much quality that we can't afford to lose any more. And there is this movement in the West to retain the very last scraps. Most natural areas have to be pretty big chunks in order to retain the species of animals, for example, that need room to move around. A thousand acres is not enough for almost all mammal species. So we are at a very critical time, I think. And if these last scraps don't get put into some kind of wilderness area now, we will never have them again. They are gone forever. There have been, over geologic time, five gigantic species-extinction episodes. For example, we can document that at one time 96 percent of marine species went extinct, a fairly catastrophic event for life on Earth. But we are now in the middle of the sixth giant catastrophic species loss, and it is completely due to human activities. Most of the people can't relate to that. You read these articles in the newspaper, and it becomes part of the background of the terrible things that are happening everywhere. But this is completely irreversible. We can probably reverse many things, but we cannot reverse species loss. It takes millions of years for diversity to recover. So this little map of proposed wilderness areas with its boundary lines drawn in may seem like some kind of political struggle. It is not just a political struggle. I believe that the single most important thing happening in the West right now is the protection of the[se] remaining areas. Most of our wilderness right now is rock and ice. It is in high-elevation areas that nobody has wanted to claim, where it is easier to designate wilderness. And a lot of these areas proposed for protection are at low elevation. They are riparian areas. They are grasslands. They are communities at low elevation, so they have had a lot of impact. These areas are absolutely critical to the species that remain. So without them, those species will just go. And we will see it soon, in twenty years, ten years. We will see them go. So that is why I think it is really important to make these wilderness proposals happen, not only in New Mexico, but throughout the West.

JL: Absolutely. You've visited some of these areas, including the Peloncillo Mountains around the bootheel of New Mexico?

MS: Yeah, I have been to the Peloncillos. They don't look like much. They're extremely dry. They have been heavily used. They have been overgrazed. They have been beat up. There is not a beautiful forest there or little Alpine lakes. There are no big animals walking around that you can see. It just doesn't look like much. People often go to a place like that, and they say it is a wasteland. In fact, that is how the Navajos got their reservation. Everybody thought, "This is a wasteland with no use whatsoever." But E. O. Wilson talks about the little things that run the world, and so many of these places that you go to, you just can't see what makes a really active biological network that is happening at a ferocious degree. For example, if you sat up all night in the Peloncillos, you would see animals. It is an ideal place for desert sheep and tortoises, and it has thousands of species in a natural community that has a lot of integrity, and even though those areas have gotten beat up so much over the years, it's really important to protect them.

JL: That's where Warner Glenn saw a jaguar. He got photographs of a jaguar. The Peloncillos are part of a proposed wilderness area. They make up a wildlife corridor. Could you talk about wilderness areas as corridors for migrations?

MS: First of all, I have to say, isn't it miraculous that such a large, beautiful, noticeable mammal would be using a place that looks this austere to us? Yeah. There has been a lot of work on the use of the mosaic of the landscape at a scale that we don't see. For example, spotted owls. There are maybe thirty places in the Southwest, in Arizona and New Mexico, that spotted owls can use. And spotted owls can disperse for quite a long way, maybe two to three hundred miles. And so when they reproduce, [the offspring] need to get away from the nest and find another place. People have mapped out the kinds of patterns across the landscape that these birds fly from one place to another, disperse. But those habitats have to be within a certain range. They have to be able to find suitable habitat that is not too far away. And one by one, those nesting places for spotted owls, as you know, are winking out. As soon as one habitat becomes unsuitable, it is no longer available to them. It is just one less node in the network that they use to disperse to.

Other animals need to use land corridors. Mountains and riparian areas are the two really important dispersal routes for animals like [the] jaguar. That jaguar was coming up from Mexico, where there is a small but viable population. If we could get those animals to disperse to southern Arizona and New Mexico, they could establish a viable population there. This is an opportunity for a large beautiful animal that people care about. It is just fantastic to think that they could reestablish a population in southern New Mexico. It also says that the communities that support jaguars are healthy enough, which is very encouraging. The fact that it could come into this country at all without being killed is very encouraging. If we designate these [corridors] wilderness areas or protect them in another way, we might see the recuperation of a lot of big, beautiful animals. Of course, it also means that these species are like umbrella species. If they are there, then there is a natural community below it that is unseen to us that is really healthy. So it is an exciting event. Everyone used to say, "If the canary is alive in the mine, it means that everybody else in the mine is OK." So if the jaguars can survive there, it is one good measure of a good habitat. Corridors are important, very important. They have to be continuous, and that is hard to achieve because sometimes land can be very expensive, sometimes being very desirable places, like river corridors.

JL: Trying to figure out means of getting privatized land within the context of a wilderness corridor is a very major thought. Any ideas on that?

MS: I think that the private landowners, ranchers in the West, are beginning to realize that what they want to do with their land, what they need from their land in terms of ranching or whatever they are doing, doesn't have to [be in] conflict with wildlife needs. And if only they were told what those needs are, they would be happy to accommodate wildlife. I see a shift from what has been a conflict, and we still see the tail end of that cultural conflict, especially around the wolves. People fear wolves and fear their reintroduction. These wolves are a different species than European wolves that attacked people and that led to the fear of wolves that infuses Grimm's fairy tales, a fear that we learned when we were children. These wolves rarely attack human beings. But they do impinge on ranching. If the ranchers are sure that they will be compensated for what wolves do to livestock, a number of them have shown that they are willing to accommodate wolves. And we also have very large landowners in the Southwest, like Ted Turner, for example, and the Animas Foundation on the Gray Ranch, who have worked very hard to accommodate wildlife needs. They still have cows out there. But they also care enough to find out what is needed for the wildlife. I am very encouraged about a new ethic in the use of private land.

I have to point out, it is really important for ranchers and other private-property owners to get the information they need. It seems to me that they are making a big effort. They are saying, "We are willing to commit resources and money and time to this." And they need to get the kind of information that it takes to take care of the land in a different way. Rangeland and natural systems in New Mexico have been getting better for a hundred years. A hundred years ago was the very bottom. The grasses were gone, and [now] the ranchers have been taking care of the land enough to bring it back to this point.

Biological systems are so complicated. There are so many interacting features of biological communities that it just takes years and years and years to begin to have any kind of understanding. Biological scientists are reductionists because you can't study a whole biological system all at once. In the end, hopefully we will not have a reductionist view, but will take all the understanding that we have had from studying all the single parts of these systems and be able to put them together. We can't do that yet. It is going to take a long time. But it is what everybody cares about now. We need desperately to understand the biological system that is the Earth, so that we can head off some of these really terrible trends.

JL: Would you define *reductionism*?

MS: Reductionism involves having chosen to study one element of a system. For example, if you study just tortoises, tortoises don't make the community work. And you can't study tortoises without studying the cactus that they eat and the ravens that pray on baby tortoises and all the other parts of the community. Tortoises don't live in isolation. But you can't study everything at once. So a scientist chooses one aspect of the community to study.

JL: I want to go back to the example of spotted owls. The Ladrone Peaks near Socorro are one of the proposed wilderness areas. Do you think that the top of the Ladrone Peaks would be a suitable place for spotted owls?

MS: Yes. I don't know a hell of a lot about spotted owls. As a matter of fact, nobody does. We don't even have a good handle on what it is that they like for breeding territory. We always thought it was spruce fir, dense spruce fir. But now it appears that maybe they actually nest in riparian areas a lot. Peter Stacey has been studying them in the Manzano Mountains and elsewhere. So this is true about a lot of components of natural communities. We study for years, we think we know what is going on, and then we find out to our surprise that it is not true. The good thing about science is [that] it is highly revisionist. Scientists have been trained to say, "OK, I have known this all along, but now I have found something else, and I have to revise what I have thought about what I was doing before." And wildlife communities especially are difficult to study. So we must be in the frame of mind where we say, "We think we know what is going on, but we are really not sure." We have to build into protecting the systems a big buffer of uncertainty.

JL: Could you please talk about the "sky island" concept? About Ladrone Peak as a sky island and how that actually is a place where biota can breed and be happy and survive?

MS: Any place that you study has a whole set of diverse kinds of ecosystems. Those mountains are especially diverse because they start out at the bottom of deserts and go up to what is essentially a kind of Canadian community at the top, through many other kinds of communities. But anywhere you look, it will be that kind of situation. The unusual thing about the sky islands is that they are very isolated. Every community that is not a desert community is really stuck on that mountaintop because it can't come down. Mice in the ponderosa pine forest zone can't get down across the desert and go up another sky island. So those are isolated communities. We know that, biologically speaking, isolated communities are very unusual and unique because of evolutionary trends. Because they are isolated, their genes don't mix with anybody else's. You get very special communities that you find nowhere else and a lot of endemic species that don't occur anywhere else except in that one spot. So those places have always had a special reason to be preserved—because they are unique.

JL: One of the things that I love to think about is the shift from the Pleistocene to the Holocene, when actual forests migrated up the mountains.

MS: This is actually another important understanding that needs to be communicated more broadly—that what we see on the land right now is not what occurs on this kind of place all the time. Over time, these systems are tremendously dynamic and changing and won't stay this way in the future, even without human impact. We have to factor in the natural dynamics of climate.

The end of the Pleistocene, or the last [most recent] ice age, happened about ten thousand years ago. And that coincided with the rise of human species as a dominant feature on the face of the Earth. Over the past ten thousand years, people have been affecting natural community patterns tremendously. Ten thousand years ago the Southwest was covered with spruce fir [in] places that are now full of sagebrush and cactus. Natural communities move and fluctuate with time on very large scales. So that kind of background is something that all human activities are operating within, these big climate shifts. And you know that the climate is shifting dramatically right now. The whole planet is warming up. In fact, I've heard some facts lately that are just staggering. The arctic polar cap has thinned 40 percent in the past twenty years. That is a huge number. The arctic ice cap is already floating in water, so the water level doesn't change. But that same kind of impact is also going on in the Antarctic, and we have a tremendous concern over that because those ice sheets, which are very thick, are sitting on land, and they could slide off into the ocean. Catastrophically. And they probably will at some point if current trends continue. And the oceans could rise eighty or a hundred feet. And that is a big effect. But that big effect is also happening in slow motion in the Southwest. If, by the middle of the twenty-first century, temperatures go up three to five degrees Fahrenheit, it will result in huge changes in the patterns of natural communities. And this is especially important when we have a situation like this, where protected areas are just small isolated islands. Not only sky islands, but every refuge is isolated because it is an island of a natural community, sitting in a matrix of heavily used land. Ranching, urban areas, and roads fragment natural communities. When communities shift against this climate background, you may find that a patch of ponderosa pine forest that is sitting in a sea of ranching will need to move if things get hotter, and [it] probably won't be able to. And this is even more true of animal communities, which are stuck in these little protected islands. They will go extinct if the climate changes very seriously. That is a really big issue in designing natural reserves that we have not solved. We are creating these refuges as if the world were static, as if climate were static. And it is so much more important that we think about corridors and dispersal routes and large chunks of protected area so that animals can safely move across private land in case that they need to move. And they will need to. Things are not going to stay the same here.

JL: One of the things that fascinates me is the notion that major human impact on our planet is only about five hundred human generations long, since the advent of the Holocene, and that the warming trends that are occurring during the Holocene have metaphorically baked civilization into being.

MS: The concern is this, yes, we have seen huge natural changes in the past. We have seen big extinction events, and we have seen rapid climate changes. The concern now is that the rate of change is something that has never been seen, or rarely. And of course, also, it is against a background of patterns of use that put natural communities at greater risk. The rate of extinctions, for example, is enormously fast right now, so fast that even if we recognized what was going on, it is doubtful if we could do anything about it fast enough to save some species. We really need to pay attention to what is going on in the really short term.

I believe the more people know, the more ethically they will act. I think that a lot of people are living their lives in ordinary ways that just don't allow them to understand what is happening. If they knew, they would care. Whenever we look at polls of Americans who are asked if they want to preserve natural areas, 80 percent or more would like to do it. But they don't have the information that will tell them how to do it, how to do it in their own region, and how to do it now. I think that if they knew how, they would act. There is an overwhelming support for protecting wild areas. There is a small vocal minority that I think has got wrong information, and you hear them a lot, especially when it comes to changing very traditional ways of life. But I think that most people understand what needs to be done. They just don't know how in their own lives to affect what is going on. I think they need the information to do that, and it would happen.

JL: Something that we face here in New Mexico is that we live in a very arid state. We have less surface water than most. We have a small river that goes right smack through the middle of what is currently known as New Mexico. Could you talk about the human impact on the watershed that is encompassed by the Río Grande del Norte? By that, I mean extending from the San Luis Valley in southern Colorado down to where the Río Conchos comes in from Mexico. Another factor is that our aquifers are being depleted at a terrible rate. Would you talk about the importance of preservation of water habitat to the biotic community of New Mexico, of which we are a part?

MS: Rivers are like the heartbeat of a landscape. Where would we be without our rivers? The Río Grande means so many things to so many people. It is so big. It is so complex. It really underlies life in our watershed. And the need for water in the river is apparent, and sometimes the Río Grande actually becomes dry in places. The riverbed becomes dry. And, of course, then it supports no life as a river. No natural community life. The main reason for this is that so much water is drawn out of the Río Grande for agriculture. The city of Albuquerque actually doesn't draw that much river water compared to the agricultural community. And again I think that this is an area in which people haven't known what has been going on, haven't thought about what has been going on. Agriculture in New Mexico is a livelihood that we would like to continue. We would like to see small farmers be able to survive and grow the crops that they grow in the middle Río Grande area. But there hasn't been any systematic thinking about what is happening to this water. Most of the water is still drawn off in dirt ditches, acequias. We lose tremendous amounts of water to the ground, to the air. Nobody is thinking about the conservation of agricultural water. In California, the vast majority of water is used for agriculture. And only now are people beginning to reassess the use of that water. Is that the best use? Is the best kind of conservation being applied to that? These are old systems of water use that haven't been rethought in the context of today's needs. And pressure groups, like environmental groups [that] were trying to keep some water in the river, are partly responsible for pushing our awareness of the use of the river. But the river has to be thought of as a whole organism, where some water needs to go to agriculture, some needs to go into people's houses, and some needs to be used by the natural community. The allocation of that water needs to be rethought at a whole watershed scale so that all parts of the natural and human communities can be sustained. And I think that they can, even on the water that we have now.

JL: We should consider that at some point the human population will exceed the carrying capacity of the watershed.

MS: Always with these issues of how many people can be supported, the most important issue is, At what quality of life? We could probably support four times as many people in this state if everyone conserved water, if people had no lawns, had no golf courses. But the use of that as an absolute measure—how many people can we support and at what level—is really the wrong way to approach this problem. The question is, As an integrated community of plants, animals, and people, what is the best use of water? Clearly at this point we should have many fewer people in New Mexico. This is because of how people use water, how it is allocated. The lion's share of water currently goes to agriculture, which is a very small proportion of New Mexico's economy.

The unappreciated message is [that] we are losing the natural communities. And twenty-five years from now, fifty years from now, we may look back and think we live in such a desperate world, compared to what was here twenty-five and fifty years ago. Just the way we can look back twenty-five and fifty years ago, and realize the integrity of the natural communities that we have lost. Just think of those big old cottonwoods. Twenty-five years ago there were big old cottonwoods everywhere, and we have starved them of the water that they needed, and now they are going or gone. I watch them die every year. And it will take another couple of hundred of years to get them back. I really miss those cottonwoods so much. So thinking ahead, let's not get in the position where we look back with so much regret and say, "We could have protected, preserved our natural communities, but we weren't paying attention. And now we have lost so much."

Daniel Kemmis,
photo by Jean Larson

Daniel Kemmis

Introduction

In 1996, I was producing a thirteen-part documentary radio series entitled *The Spirit of Place*. I traveled throughout the American West in the
old Chevy pickup truck that served as my home away from home. In my
kit, I packed a small library that included one of the most provocative
books I've ever read. It was entitled *Community and the Politics of Place*
(1990), by Daniel Kemmis, then mayor of Missoula, Montana.

On the eve of my sixtieth birthday, I camped on the eastern aspect
of the Continental Divide near Missoula. I awoke to the new decade
intent on celebrating this "youth of old age" in finest fashion. I bathed
in a creek, brushed my teeth, and drove into Missoula to city hall. There
I found Daniel Kemmis, who was willing to be interviewed, and thus I
had my intellect torqued by this brilliant man.

Only rarely have I met politicians whose vision has had more than
moderate scope. Mayor Kemmis's sense of history and mental facility
invigorated me enormously, and I came away with a sense of hope for
the biotic community of the North American continent. His other books
include *The Good City and the Good Life* (1995) and *This Sovereign Land:
A New Vision for Governing the West* (2001).

Daniel Kemmis

JL: In your book *Community and the Politics of Place*, you do a superb job of defining the sense of the *public*—the word itself and the notion of the *republican* in the traditional sense, not the current political sense of the word. I'd like you to please define your sense of *public* as you did in your book.

DK: Well, as with a lot of other words, I tend to try to go back to the roots and understand what we can learn from that. My understanding of the roots of *public* is that it has something to do with the people, that what is public is of the people, and therefore it immediately evokes something of the communal in us. What is public is not mine or yours, but ours. Then what I did was to move from that to the sense of the *republic*, which in Latin was the *res publica*, the "public thing." That phrase is, on the face of it, fairly meaningless, but if you start digging into it, you start to realize that those things—those real physical objects, tangible, touchable things that we care for together—maybe do have something to do with the way that we are together.

      I came across a wonderful little image in the work of Hannah Arendt where she talks about the "public thing" in terms of a table and says you can imagine people seated around the table, and then you can imagine the table just suddenly vanishing. And these people are then unrelated to each other. They suddenly are out of relationship with each other. Her argument, which I believe is sound, is that we have come to be out of relationship with each other because we've ignored the importance of those things that hold us together and that we hold together.

JL: Apropos of the table and the things that have brought us together in the context of the body politic, so to speak, the political body serving the public has taken on many connotations, and unfortunately a lot of Americans are now very cynical about public office. I think that this is one of the great tragedies of our time. You really address well in your book the sense of responsibility that must be maintained not just by the elected political official, but also by the individual citizenry and how it becomes a collective event to really participate within a community. I'd like you to talk about that if you would.

DK: My political career has stretched over a period of about twenty years now, and the last half of that has been spent in local government and specifically in city government. As I got to know more about my own city and started paying more attention to other cities, I became fascinated by the physical being of a city. I became drawn more and more back to the old idea of the city as a living thing, as an organism. We know that it has systems within it, circulatory systems, and so on. You don't have to do city work for very many days in a row to come to feel that the city really is like a living thing. And that in turn began to bring home to me the possibility that maybe that old phrase "the body politic" was meant to be much more physical than we now take it to be. We still use the phrase, but we mean very little by it. We mean something you might come in touch with by public-opinion polling, which in my opinion is precious little.

But in the life of a city, the idea of the body politic becomes much stronger. And, among other things, what I came to believe is that the idea of citizenship is deeply rooted in that almost physical sense of the city. Citizenship is of the city. To be a citizen is really to be a denizen of the city, to be shaped by the city, and to give shape to the city. And when you start thinking about it that way, then the sense of caring that goes with citizenship comes back into focus. The way in which people might actually take care of a specific place and what they have built together on that place begins to reinform citizenship in a way that we've pretty much lost track of. We don't call ourselves citizens anymore; we call ourselves taxpayers, which says a tremendous amount about how far distanced we are from that living sense of the body politic.

JL: I wish that more mayors in cities around the United States would come to understand this. You very clearly differentiate or discuss the differences in thinking between Thomas Jefferson and James Madison, which I think are profound differences. I would like to ask you to address those.

DK: Of course, Jefferson and Madison were great friends, and they had a great deal in common. But their politics, at least at one point, diverged pretty sharply. And that point was really at the point of adoption of the U.S. Constitution. Madison is, in many ways, the father of the Constitution, and he came to see that what it was going to take to make the nation work, which was really being created by the Constitution, was a kind of abstraction of people from place and from the immediacy of the concerns that are tangibly in front of them. And so the whole system of checks and balances that is built into the Constitution is really meant as a way of keeping people apart from each other and keeping them from engaging directly in face-to-face problem solving. Now, there were some very good reasons to do that, but Jefferson was very worried about it. He had the strong sense that democracy finally works only when people are face to face with each other, and then they themselves have significant responsibility for solving problems among themselves. He therefore was doubtful whether a large nation could work as a democracy and remained doubtful about that throughout his life. I think that some of those doubts are coming back to us now as we begin to see how that system of checks and balances has alienated people, has moved them away from taking responsibility for solving problems themselves. Now we find ourselves with a system that we know doesn't serve us very well, but with no very clear sense of what the alternative might be.

JL: Decentralization as an ideal seems to me to be much more workable because a smaller group of people functioning in a cooperative fashion would be more likely to be successful. So I'd like to ask you to talk about what you would regard to be an ideal in the context of democracy and how it can work in a nation and whether or not decentralization from the point of view of respective communities might be a workable factor in that. Does that make sense at all?

DK: What I have come to believe more and more strongly is that we're now passing through a period in political history that is much more profound than we're generally aware of. What I believe it really amounts to is that, well, for two hundred years we have lived under the sway of the nation-state as the defining political entity; that that period of history is ready to pass, as all periods of history do pass; and that we're moving now in the direction of the recognition of organic forms at all different levels. The most important of those levels is the most local, and that localism comes down, I think, finally to very small units, to neighborhoods at least. What you recognize about neighborhoods immediately is that they are organic. You can't tell something by drawing straight lines on a map, "This is going to be a neighborhood." You can only ask it, "What is the neighborhood here?" and then it defines itself. And you move up from there to the city and then the organic relationship between a city and its surrounding countryside. There again, you can't tell an area what that organic relationship is going to be, but if you ask, if you pay attention to how city and countryside relate to each other, you see an organic form emerge. I think politically we're going to see that happen all the way up through the continental level and finally to the global level. I think we have to be willing to exercise citizenship and politics at all of those levels, but I also believe that the way in which nationhood has defined our political thinking and acting is ready now to soften, if not dissolve.

JL: That's an interesting thought. Earlier on you talked about systems. I'm a very strong proponent of systems thinking, actually. A person for whom I have great respect intellectually is Garrett Hardin, who wrote *The Tragedy of the Commons* and whom

I've had the good fortune to spend some time with. He wrote an essay called "An Ecolate View of the Human Predicament," devising the word *ecolate* as a Hardinism. It's a definition, basically, of understanding the thought patterns within the context of systems and understanding the ramifications of individual actions. I find this to be particularly appropriate when looking at an urban or a community environment in the context of its surrounding habitat. I think that this is probably one of the most important things for all citizens to understand and one of the least addressed. Could you delve a bit into the importance of that from your own perspective?

DK: It's such a subtle matter, or it seems that way to me. You know, we've come to think of politics and political systems almost entirely in terms of people, and so we devise our systems entirely around people, essentially having ignored place, so where it is that we live is kind of factored out of the political equation to a large extent. Or when it is factored in, it's factored in in an arbitrary way that I think somehow gets in the way of a workable politics. Now, in the West we had a great warning of this from John Wesley Powell, who said, "If you're going to inhabit this arid landscape of the West, you're going to have to do it on the land's own terms," and that means you ought to create your political subdivisions according to the way the water flows and the way the landscape organizes itself. If you try to create them in other ways, you're going to get into a lot of trouble. We're finally, a hundred years later, realizing that. I think [that] on a lot of different levels we're now realizing that somehow, in order to do well politically, in order to do well as a species, we have to pay attention to where we are, and we have to let the landscape determine our communities and recognize that those communities are real living things on the landscape and that politics is not a matter of figuring out what each individual wants and then adding that up, but figuring out what this living body on the landscape wants and needs and how it can best prosper. It's a form of thinking that is just very alien to us. But I think now it's become crucial to learn it.

JL: That's well stated. Adjacent to that, a thought that comes to mind frequently, that has been well articulated by people like Gary Snyder and Edward Abbey and certainly a lot of Native American people, bases itself around the reality that our species is simply a constituent member of the overall biotic community. I think that's one of the biggest thoughts right now.

DK: I do too. And again it's a very hard thought for us to incorporate because we have become so anthropocentric in all of our thinking, and we've just assumed that all that really matters politically is us. But if you start giving reality to the idea of place and the inhabitation of place, then you can't very long ignore the fact that we are only one species that inhabits any given place and that inhabiting it well even on our terms finally means that we have to be inhabiting it well in terms of those other species.

That's why in a place like this I've come to believe that wolf reintroduction has a lot more political significance than we imagine, and we play out the politics of wolves here in sort of political terms of "us against them," the people who are in favor of reintroduction against those who are opposed to it.

But the real question is not that. The real question is, What's the role of the wolves here? What is the importance of them being brought back into our community?

JL: I totally agree. Years ago, I worked on a wolf recovery project of the *Canis lupus baileyii*, the Mexican wolf, in the Sonoran Desert and environs—actually, a little farther east. And it's a tough problem. At one point, there were only thirty-three Mexican wolves left in the species, and the gene pool was scarily diminished.

DK: I was delighted to hear that New Mexico was talking about that. I think it's an easier proposition up here. But I hope it will work there.

JL: So do I. One of the wondrous characteristics of this area is the abundance of water, which we don't have in New Mexico. As a matter of fact, I recently read that New Mexico has less surface water than any other state, proportionately speaking. Obviously a community must rely to a tremendous extent on the natural resources available to it. Again, obviously one of the real systems of balance that must be maintained is the relationship between community and available resources without overwhelming the availability of the resources. There are a couple of issues here that I'm going to ask you to address, the first being your perceptions regarding the human carrying capacity of an environment such as your own, and the other being how one deals with the carpetbagger, a phenomenon that has been taking place ever since the Civil War.

DK: I guess I bring to this [issue] as to many other things a kind of hopefulness or optimism in spite of everything that seems to be going wrong. I find great hope in what I think is deep attention that is now being paid to the idea of sustainability. You can think of something like sustainability as an issue of public policy, as something that we deal with kind of on the surface of things. But my sense of it is that it is much more fundamental than that. That there is a way in which our relationship to the Earth itself is being redefined almost from the bottom up, and that there's a growing sense that well-being in the deepest sense, in the daily sense of what it means to live well and to live a satisfying life, can't be divorced from some sense of sustainability. Gary Snyder speaks of this so wonderfully to my mind when he talks about living now as if you were laying the base for future generations to live even better.

    I think there's a fundamental human instinct in that direction, and I think, with a little encouragement, people can come around to see that their own lives are going to be more satisfying to the extent that they are living in such a way that life can go on and [will] not decline, but get better and better. You know, in a way, I think that our generation—the generation since World War II—has had a scare, a scare of a lot of different kinds. We had the immediate scare of the bomb and grew up under the bomb, and we had the scare that nobody else has had for a long time, that our children's lives might actually be a lesser thing than our own lives. And that's finally not acceptable to people, I don't think. They can live with it for a while, but not for long.

JL: Apropos of that, I was in the army in the late '50s as a musician. I was a corporal with a trumpet. My job was performing the "Stars and Stripes Forever" at the Nevada Proving Grounds seven miles away from detonating bombs. I saw three of them go off. That profoundly affected my thinking because of the absolute nonselectivity of what is destroyed within that realm. And it certainly shaped my thinking. I have one child—hoped she wouldn't be born with two heads, and fortunately she wasn't. But nonetheless, it turns out that one of the bombs that I played for was the very bomb that dumped on St. George, Utah, to the extent that so many people became very ill with cancer. It actually dumped on the car of the family of Terry Tempest Williams, the writer. One time she and I were having a discussion and discovered this mutual experience. It was a very profound thing, really, because the bomb truly has shaped our entire generation, and I think it's probably caused many people to not think in terms of future generations, which is what culture has traditionally done. And that has created that level of cynicism that I find so dangerous in our own culture right now. It's to me one of the most deadly serious things. How to regenerate a sense of continuity and a sense of optimism? Any light that you can cast on that would be greatly appreciated.

DK: First of all, I think you're exactly right. I think the sense that so many of us have that there may not be a future led to living life in a very different way and a very, very sick way, and that our political cynicism is absolutely inclined with that sense that there may not be a future at all. I hope and believe that we've begun to emerge from that. I think that the end of the Cold War has made people believe once again on a sort of species level that in fact there may be a future. And now my sense is that the best way to begin to dissolve that cynicism is to draw on those experiences that people have that are in fact life affirming. Many of them exist on a very small scale, but they exist everywhere. Everywhere people put energy into nourishing life and nourishing the good life, especially within their own communities. Drawing people's attention to how satisfying that is, how deeply, fundamentally, satisfying it is, is the best way I know to begin to crack and break up that concrete of cynicism that has so overlain the landscape.

JL: I've been influenced by Peter Kropotkin's work, by *Mutual Aid* and others of his books. His greatest contribution, I think, or at least certainly one of them, was based on his own work as a geographer in Siberia. He was born into Russian nobility and relinquished his noble status. He was largely influenced by Charles Darwin, and in the late nineteenth century he went to Siberia to map some mountain ranges and, armed with Darwinian thought, observed natural history. Five years later he had come to the conclusion that evolution of species owes far more to mutual cooperation than to mutual antagonism. That became fundamental to his sense of anarchist thought. It was anarchism in the communalist sense, where people do assume responsibility.

One of the things that you brought out in your book was that Wallace Stegner talked about how the rugged individualist might have to dilute the sense of rugged individualism in order to become more communally oriented—that with the closing of the frontier of the American West, a level of rugged individualism, which has been very much a part of our culture for the past 220 years, has had to redefine itself. Missoula, Montana, is still regarded as frontier by many, and vestiges are still here in amazing ways. How do you imagine people resolving that sense of rugged individualism with the sense of community and place?

DK: One of the things that drove me to write my second book, *The Good City and the Good Life,* was just trying to pay attention to life within the city of Missoula, and then from there I began to pay attention to the life in other cities. And one of the things that really has struck me about cities—and here I've been guided so much by the work of Jane Jacobs, who was, I think, our great contemporary observer of cities—but one of the things that Jane Jacobs has always been so sharply aware of is the rule of entrepreneurship within a city. You can convert that, I think, fairly easily to ecological thinking. If you think of the city as [an] ecosystem, then what you begin to see is that it's a whole layer and [a] kind of covey of niches that are waiting to be filled—an almost endless availability of niches to be filled, which is one of the ways that I always think Darwin thought. That there are all of these niches, more and more niches. Once you've filled up the daytime, then fill up the night, and this sort of thing.

The same is true in a city. The way that that "nichemanship" expresses itself very often is through entrepreneurship. People are sort of driven to find their own niche, and that's good. That form of individualism is fundamental to the life of the city. But in the end the city can't work simply in those terms unless there is along with that, over that, through that, some way in which people also come together and recognize the life of the whole community and the good for the whole community—then nobody does well individually, either. So what I became fascinated with is this way in which this particular political entity, the entity that we call the city, expresses the drive to life that we know as individuals, but at the same time the larger drive to life of the larger body, the larger community. They're not finally and can't be antagonistic to each other.

JL: One of the things about the American Southwest that fascinates me is that one can see remnants of cities of other cultures—Chaco Canyon is spectacular that way, probably to me the most easily defined. Some people have hazarded that it was basically an entrepreneurial enterprise, and it was not necessarily a city where people lived all the time. It was a place where trade took place. A system of roads has been discovered. The system includes many, many smaller communities throughout the area, and it's thought—by some, at least—that Chaco may well have been a center of commerce that would have had to be abandoned around the year A.D. 1300. Many think that it was abandoned because of drought and the fact that human overpopulation had resulted in necessary natural resources being used up.

I'd like to get your opinion on this. I personally believe that the ramifications of human overpopulation extend into virtually every area of discontent and problem that we face today. I want to ask how you feel about that.

DK: I think that that's almost certainly true. If you try to draw back and just look at things in global ecological terms, then it seems pretty clear to me, at least, that somehow our species has taken up more than its fair share of ecological space and that that's not finally a sustainable relationship to other species. I'm a lot less clear about what to do about it. I've come to believe that to a certain extent you have to let these things play themselves out and that public policy is only going to have so much effectively to say about something like that. It really is finally a biological and a systems issue. So I try to be alert not only to the ways overpopulation has created problems, but also try to watch what's going on and see: Is there any new species wisdom that is coming to the extent that we're forced to be closer together and are adapting in some way? It would be surprising if we're not. And the question is, you know, What kinds of species wisdom might be arising there that might be useful to us?

I guess what I'm really saying is, with this as with so many other things, I think it's a little too easy to fall into black-and-white thinking and simply to say, "The problem is population, and it is simply a problem." I believe it's a problem, but most of these things, I think, operate more dialectically than can ever be resolved into a simple black or white.

JL: I totally agree with that. I recently read a very provocative book, *The Diversity of Life* by Edward O. Wilson, a Harvard entomologist who is a terrific thinker. Have you read that book?

DK: No. I have read one of his books, *Biophilia*, but not that one.

JL: I haven't read *Biophilia*. One of the things Wilson addresses in *The Diversity of Life* is that over a span of 660 million years, there have been five major spasms of extinction of life wrought by the presence of asteroids or volcanoes or events of that magnitude, the most recent having been the end of the dinosaur period about 65, 66 million years ago. Wilson is now contending that evidence strongly suggests to him that over the past few human generations, our own species has probably initiated the sixth major spasm of extinction, which is a terrible thought, but nonetheless many biologists are concurring with this. Some of us now contend that one way through the dilemma has to do with vigorously restoring the right of cultural diversity and biodiversity to exist within any given habitat and [with] nurturing cultural evolution within the context of a given habitat. Do you have any thoughts on that issue?

DK: When you deal with problems like global overpopulation, in some ways it has the same numbing effect as the bomb has had. The problem can be so large that it can sort of stop you in your tracks. Or to the extent that if you try to react to it at all, you're always subject to the sense that maybe it is too big, and maybe you're not able to think clearly about it. I think we have to think as clearly as we possibly can, but part of that involves a kind of humility about how much we're able to see. But I'm absolutely convinced that part of coming to clarity is getting clearer and clearer about how those relationships are within our grasp, and what I mean specifically is that I can't imagine how we could begin to correct this kind of global misdirection except by learning very clearly what it means to live well on specific parts of the Earth, getting clear about what inhabitation is all about, and doing that in fairly localized ways and always with an alertness to what we can usefully extrapolate, then, to larger and larger senses of inhabitation. So wherever we see, for example, people understanding that they dwell in drainages, that they dwell in river basins, wherever we see people saying, "I don't care where the county lines are. I don't even care where the state lines are. But this bioregion, this basin, matters. This is where the question is, How can we live here in a sustainable way in a sustainable relationship to the landscape with the other species?" [then] that's good work, and it has to be finally Earth-redeeming work. Wherever you see something like the Colorado Plateau, where a whole bioregion across several state lines is saying, "This is a real place, and the question is, How do we live well here?" then that's good work, and that needs to be encouraged.

The people who are engaged in that work, then, I think, have to start to ask themselves, "Now to what extent can we carry what we're learning here to the continental level? How can we start to understand that the artificial lines that we've drawn across the continent don't serve us and can't serve us?" And then from there to the global level. So I guess what I'm saying is, I think we really have to get back into our species being, and so much of that means just paying very close attention to what it means to live well in the very specific places that we find ourselves.

JL: I'm really fascinated to see how people who come from apparently disparate backgrounds are coming to the same conclusions concerning the relationship of our species to the habitat that we inhabit.

The mood of Missoula as I wander the streets feels really positive. I would imagine there is a fair amount of citizen participation in the way the city is evolving. Can you describe how that has come to be?

DK: Being mayor of Missoula has been wonderful work for me, partly because I have always loved politics and have always wanted to do it, and this has given me a chance to do it every day all day for several years now. But part of what's so satisfying about it is that I've been able to do it in a town that has such a high level of genuine citizen involvement. I almost hate using those words because it still sounds so dry and forbidding. What I mean by it is actually something very different than that. What I've come to appreciate is how many different ways so many people in Missoula find to contribute to the life of the city, to continually making it better. And they've come, I think, to kind of pride themselves on it in a deep way that finally becomes a matter of political culture. They love taking on tasks that should be too big for them and figuring out how to get it done. That to me is the essence of democracy. It has almost nothing to do with voting. It has almost nothing to do with going to meetings. It has to do with coming to know that nobody else is going to take care of this place. There isn't anybody else. There's only us, and we have it within us to do great things here, actually to create a civilization. To have been able to be part of a community with such a broad and deep sense of that and at the same time one in which those strains of cynicism, of anger and alienation, are very much present and in which it's necessary every day to work against them—that's been good work.

JL: We've addressed many issues. Is there anything that you would particularly like to address? Things that you might see evolving on the horizon? Anything that is provocative?

DK: I've spoken before about the optimism that keeps me going, and I've come to have a sense of a kind of emerging understanding that seems to me to be deeper than the rational systems of thought that we have engaged in. I believe evolution goes on and on, never stops—never stops the work of adapting to whatever it is that we're facing. And I'm convinced that within our collective unconscious there is tremendous work now going on, tremendous adaptive work, creative work; that it is readying new forms, including new political forms; and that the real work of leadership is to be alert to those emerging forms and to be prepared to assist them in their evolution—not to make things happen, but to help things happen that are arising and emerging.

William deBuys, photo by author

William deBuys

Introduction

Over the years, my friend William deBuys and I have gone awandering through the West in wondrous conversation. Several years ago I was producing a six-part documentary radio series entitled *Moving Waters: The Colorado River and the West*. Bill had recently written *Salt Dreams: Land and Water in Low Down California* (1999), a wonderful book that includes photographs by Joan Myers. I read *Salt Dreams* and realized that the radio series would be wildly incomplete without an interview with Bill.

William deBuys is one of the West's great writers and environmental activists. He earned his Ph.D. in American studies from the University of Texas and is the author of several books and many articles. He is currently a member of the faculty of the documentary studies department at the College of Santa Fe. He has also ridden many miles on horseback through southwestern rangeland and is handy in the art of wilderness survival.

Bill's fourth book, *Seeing Things Whole: The Essential John Wesley Powell* (2001), focuses on one of nineteenth-century America's great men. Bill rightly regards John Wesley Powell as America's first "bioregional" activist. In the interview, he characterizes Powell and provides a sense of the breadth of Powell's perspective. Indeed, Powell lays groundwork for dealing with the dilemmas that face all of us who live in the arid habitat west of the hundredth meridian.

William deBuys

JL: What inspired you to write your book *Seeing Things Whole: The Essential John Wesley Powell*?

BD: I'm trying to remember when I got the idea to do the Powell book. I think it must have been in the middle 1990s. At that time, I was writing a good deal about the environmental history of the Southwest. And I kept meaning to consult Powell's final advice about how the West should be settled. That advice is contained in three articles that he published in *Century Magazine*, I think in 1890. It's been a little while since I looked at all of those dates. I had these rather bad photocopies of the articles in my files, and I would dig them out much too frequently. It became kind of a chore to find them each time I needed them. I thought, "These articles are too important to exist only in archived copies of *Century Magazine*, now more than a hundred years old. They should be in print." That led to thinking, "Goodness, there's a lot of Powell's work that isn't in print now and should be."

   Later I made the mistake of mentioning this to a friend of mine, Walt Coward, who was then a program officer for the Ford Foundation. Walt said, "How much money do you think it would take to get that material in print?" I said, "Oh, for my part I could probably pull it all together for ten thousand dollars." Actually, that was a laughable amount, just enough to create an obligation to finish the book. I spent a whole year as a fellow at SMU [Southern Methodist University] writing my contribution to the book, and that involved a lot more than ten thousand dollars of expense.

JL: You got deeply into Powell's life and probably read everything that was written about him and also everything that he ever wrote. He was actually one of the most fascinating people to come out of the nineteenth century. I wonder if you could physically and spiritually and intellectually characterize the way Powell actually was.

BD: Powell was a fascinating character. He was truly an American original. He was the first fully realized combination of explorer, government bureaucrat, and scientist all rolled into one. He wasn't a very big man: medium stature, not very heavily built, but very wiry, very strong, and, as most people know, he lost the greater part of his right arm at the battle of Shiloh in the Civil War. But that never slowed him down. He would have probably plucked out the eyes of anyone who said that he bore a handicap. In fact, it was with only one arm that he descended the Colorado River twice, rode all over the Colorado Plateau, engaged every Indian group in the region in conversation, recorded their languages and many of their folkways. We think of Powell as an explorer. He was also a geographer. After Clarence King briefly held the position, Powell was the second director of the U.S. Geological Survey. A lot of people forget that for twenty or twenty-five, maybe thirty years he was also the founder and first director of the Bureau of American Ethnology, the purpose of which was to capture and preserve information and artifacts and whatever knowledge could be gathered about the lifeways of North American Indians.

JL: One of his most significant contributions, at least the way I perceive it, is his deep study of the arid lands west of the hundredth meridian. He was born east of the hundredth meridian, so this must have been quite a staggering moment to actually visit this arid landscape. Could you talk a little bit about that?

BD: I should probably go back to something important about his makeup. You speak of his birth. He was born in western New

York State near the Finger Lakes and grew up in the Midwest. His father was a Methodist exhorter, hence the name for his son, John Wesley Powell. His father was a passionate, religious man, much like the father of John Muir, who was almost a contemporary. Their lives did overlap quite a lot; they were almost of the same generation. I think in the way that Muir's father's passionate sense of mission metamorphosed in his son to a defense of wild lands, Powell's father's passionate sense of mission metamorphosed in Powell to an equally powerful commitment, not to defend wild lands so much as to use land wisely and see its various features as an integrated whole rather than looking at one resource in an isolated manner at a time—one use of the land at a time. Powell genuinely saw things whole.

JL: That's amazing. The other way of seeing then would sort of be pre-reductionist?

BD: Yeah, very much so. So when it came to looking at the West, Powell was a fine student of American history, really, and he fully appreciated that American settlement had proceeded with a kind of westward-moving agricultural frontier based on small homesteads, small farms, and that occurred in its fullest development in the Midwest, separate from the plantation South, which was a different kind of frontier and a different-moving agricultural line. But Powell recognized that the fundamental difference between the West and the East was the aridity of the West and that that yeoman-based, family-farm, westward-marching frontier would necessarily break down when it reached the arid lands. The arid lands he essentially defined as the lands west of the hundredth meridian, which received less than twenty inches of rain and snow equivalent per year.

JL: Could you talk a little bit about how Powell gained his scientific knowledge?

BD: He was a completely self-taught man. He had some important mentors along through his childhood and youth, people who would point him in the right directions. But there was an inner fire burning in Powell, and in the same way that Henry Thoreau or John Muir would go on long rambles through the countryside, so would Powell, and he would collect snakes and rodents and plants and so forth and identify them and analyze them, try to figure out how the natural history of his little universe worked. And as he grew older, he ranged farther and farther afield. At one point in his youthful life, he got on a small boat and descended the Mississippi River—I'd have to look this up, Jack, but I think all the way to New Orleans—a journey much like Huck Finn's. He was making his natural-history collections along the way and just out on his own, alone. He would have been in his late teens, probably, when he did it.

JL: I did a bit of research about [Thomas] Jefferson's agrarian vision. I know that many early-nineteenth-century Americans were still very caught up in that. Basically, his agrarian vision had been subsumed by the Industrial Revolution. Is there any light you can throw on Jefferson's general sense of what his agrarian vision would be, or was?

BD: I'm by no means a Jefferson scholar, but my sense of Jefferson's vision is that he placed great faith in the household unit, the nuclear family, of property-owning individuals who worked the land—people who were literate, who read newspapers, who kept themselves informed, and who participated in democratic processes. All of those factors were important: staying informed, working the land, and owning property—not necessarily owning large amounts of property, but owning property. Those were the ingredients that made a good, exemplary democratic citizen—someone who would not be vulnerable to demagogues, someone who would be a steady, conscientious participant in the processes of democratic political life.

JL: Was it 160-acre hunks that he was thinking about? Does that ring a bell?

BD: The Homestead Act and its predecessors, the Preemption Acts, went through various manifestations, but in 1862 when the Homestead Act was enacted, well after Jefferson, this sort of standard of the family farm had been defined as a 160-acre farm unit. The Preemption Acts, I think, had also sort of enshrined that number. When the Homestead Act came along, it was in a sense a consolidation and reaffirmation and expansion of legislation of land law that had already been in place. But those previous acts had to do with this or that specific area or specific class of people who would be able to file for farmsteads. And the Homestead Act said, "We're opening this up for all the public domain in the United States, and we're opening it up to all citizens." So no longer were the laws for settlement specific to this region or that region or to this class or that class. It was all land that belonged to the government that was opened for settlement, and it was open to all people.

JL: Another thing that Jefferson instigated was surveying much of the United States. As I understand it, he was deeply into wanting to see the whole country, the whole landscape, surveyed.

BD: That's right, yeah. I don't think it was just Jefferson. In a way, you can think of the Aloquit Parts survey that is enshrined in the Northwest Ordinance for the settlement of Ohio, Indiana, and Illinois as an expression of the Enlightenment philosophy. The rational mind could organize the surface of the Earth in a way that people could access it, and land could become real estate, could become an economic commodity rapidly for the good of people. We think rather negatively of the grid survey system today because of its very significant faults when it comes to working with the land itself, but from the point of view of that system's creators and applied to generally flat and homogenous landscapes, it was a brilliant creation.

JL: Something that has struck me over the past few years, having spoken with so many Native American people who still have their traditional recollections at least, is that I've never met a single traditional Native American who didn't regard the land as sacred. And it seems to me that first with the coming of the Spaniards from the south in 1541 with [Francisco] Coronado and then really big time with [Juan de] Oñate in 1598 and then thereafter with the northern Europeans coming from the east, thus was born this secularization of the landscape, which then made a clear path to commodify it.

BD: Yes, I think that's exactly right. I recall a term I heard first from Polly Schaafsma years ago. She was inveighing against concepts of God in a box, which the three great monotheisms [Judaism, Christianity, Islam] really express in an extreme fashion. If your God is transportable, then you take that God with you as you move across the land, and wherever you are, you create your sacred space in a church or a synagogue or a mosque, and that becomes sacred space. If God is not in a box, if the spiritualism and the divinity existing in the world resides in place and is specific to place, then you can't carry that God from place to place. That God has to be there, and the presence of the God, the numinousness of the God, is to be found in the landscape— in some places more than others, but in places in that landscape, not [in] places that people construct anew in a kind of random pattern.

JL: Ed Abbey pointed out that when gods were taken out of Nature and made extraterrestrial, the landscape suffered a great deal.

BD: That's right. If you remove the spirit from the land, if you eliminate its divinity, then you license yourself to be able to do anything with it you please.

JL: That's precisely what the commodification of the landscape and the waterscape has become.

BD: That's right.

JL: Could you talk about when Powell came to the arid West, the way he regarded landscape, not necessarily within the context of a geopolitical survey, but rather within the context of the watersheds?

BD: First and foremost, when Powell got to the arid West, he saw it as a setting for an enormous human tragedy because he foresaw, quite correctly, that the continuation of the homestead pattern of settlement would guarantee misery and suffering for the people who tried to make it on a 160-acre farm west of the hundredth meridian. Because he knew that with less than twenty inches of rainfall, agriculture would fail. The 160-acre farm wasn't large enough for stock raising. It wasn't big enough to be a ranch, a livestock ranch. It absolutely could not support a family through farming based upon rainfall. Powell saw the immediate need to approach the West for settlement in a manner completely different from the approach that had been used rather successfully in the East.

       And the approach had to change in a number of ways. The surveys had to be different. This land was not uniformly flat, and it was not homogenous. It was broken and mountainous, and there [were] timber and grazing there, and water over there, and so forth. The elements that people needed in the landscape were not uniformly distributed as they had been in other places, or roughly had been. Powell also saw that the units of land needed in order to survive were very different depending on the type of activity. Someone who was going to make a go of it with a ranch needed a lot of land. If a person was going to be a farmer west of the hundredth meridian, that person, that family, needed to irrigate their land. So (a) that farm needed a source of irrigation water, and (b) it didn't need to be 160 acres because with irrigation one could produce the food for a family and a surplus for selling at market on a good deal less than 160 acres. So all of these things had to be adjusted from the original Homestead Act vision.

JL: I have a copy of that map you gave to me—I love that map, Powell's map where you colored in the various—

BD: *Powell* did. They're colored in the original.

JL: They are? Wow. Could you talk about how those zones are defined? What did he see them as?

BD: Well, the longer Powell studied the lands of the West—it might be fair to say that he studied them more exhaustively, certainly as exhaustively, for as long a time as any individual ever has—the longer he studied the lands of the West, the surer he became that the right way to organize them—politically, economically, and socially—was by watershed. He saw that the grid survey overlying the West chopped the land up into units that were not functionally whole because the watersheds do not follow the grid. If you want to establish a just and prosperous society in the western part of North America, he thought the best way to do it was to organize people so that they had access to the timber, the water, the grazing, and the farming lands more or less equally, and so that the use of the timberlands would be in part controlled by the people who were farming with irrigation downstream.

The purpose behind this [way of organizing things] was that the people downstream would want to have a good water yield, and they'd want to have reasonable flows; they would want to have good clean water. And because of this, they would manage the timberlands in an appropriate way. Not that they wouldn't cut timber, but they wouldn't abuse the land. They wouldn't follow the cut-and-run, rape-and-ruin timber practices that Powell was seeing so much in those days. They also wouldn't overgraze their grazing lands for the same reason—because they needed to keep the landscape intact. Widespread erosion would have ruined their agricultural operations down at the bottom of the watershed.

So, for these reasons, Powell saw a kind of system of checks and balances that would naturally occur among the people who shared a given watershed. Because of this, he said the watershed is the right unit for organizing the political, social, cultural, and economic life of these western lands. So he set about, through the U.S. Geological Survey, which he was then directing, to map the watersheds—the major and the minor watersheds of the West—and produced this glorious map that you've referred to, which actually, in different colors and shades, identifies about 150 separate watersheds in the West. Powell argued that these watersheds, rather than counties, should be the basic administrative unit[s] of western government.

Powell's idea almost made it through. Powell was a good bureaucratic infighter and a good legislative lobbyist, but in the end he was defeated with this plan. But if his plan had been effective, the effects would have been certainly very, very interesting. It's hard to say what would have transpired. But his idea was that each of these watersheds would be a more or less autonomous commonwealth. And if you just think about the amount of individual experimentation and adaptation that would have occurred in each of those 150 commonwealths scattered around the West, with people controlling the use of the lands—the people who lived on the land controlling the use of the land—the amount of experimentation would have produced some disasters, but also surely some very, very interesting new institutions for the stewardship of western land.

JL: One of the things that we've talked about in the past that I would like to ask you to talk about is how John Wesley Powell actually was the very first bioregional thinker, at least as far as we know, in the United States.

BD: If Powell were alive today, I think he would embrace that word *bioregional* with full enthusiasm because he did see the landscape—its topography, [its] geology, its hydrology, its vegetation, its wildlife, the people living within it, its climate, its potential to produce food and timber and wool and all those other things—he saw all these factors as deeply intertwined and in fact viewed things in a very ecological manner, although the word *ecology* had scarcely been coined in his lifetime. He saw all these things as interconnected, that you couldn't try to maximize just one of those factors without influencing all the rest, and that in order to care for the land in a way that would allow it to support a humane and just society, you had to think about all those elements of the land together as a unified whole. And that's the essence of bioregionalism today.

JL: Garrett Hardin wrote this wonderful essay—in 1984, I think—"An Ecolate View of the Human Predicament." His ecolate view is very much a bioregional view, basically trying to gather together as many clusters of related factors as possible and then trying to extrapolate future possibilities or probabilities therefrom. It would have been interesting to hear a conversation between Hardin and Powell.

BD: Wouldn't it! That would have been a great conversation. What Powell understood was that all these factors are specific to place: how the grazing over *here* is not necessarily what it is over *there*, and that the potential for irrigated agriculture in *this* watershed may be completely different from the potential for it in *that* watershed. So all these decisions, this sort of nudging [of] this bundle of interconnected factors one way or another, the nudging of it had to be done on a place-specific basis.

JL: Something that's of great interest: as you said, he visited virtually every group of Indians west of the hundredth meridian. And each of these groups of Indians highly revered the local deities. I wonder if he picked up on that.

BD: Well, I think he appreciated that. I never was able to discern that Powell himself was religious in his later life. I think his religion was really science and planning. And I don't know to what degree he really respected the Indians' belief. I think he felt that their lifeways were soon to be extinct and that his mission was to capture their language and to record their lifeways to the greatest degree possible before they should be lost. I think he believed that the best hope for Native Americans was, as the missionaries in those days were saying, to convert to some form of Christian religion and to become farmers. I don't think Powell's view of their best prospects was much different from that. But the fact was that he got on well with Native people on a person-to-person basis. He gave them personal respect, and that's something not very many people did in those days.

Another interesting thing about Powell is that he was roving all over the wildest parts of the West in the wildest days of the so-called Wild West, and Powell never, never wore a side arm. He never went armed. He saw no need for it.

JL: That's wonderful. One of the people successful in challenging Powell's whole notion was a man named William Gilpin. He [and] others were instrumental in trying to basically commodify the West and imagine the West as something that could be greened up and turned into money. It was that sense of development that really created an economic imperative that came to dominate the westward expansion. Is there anything you would have to say about that?

BD: That was basically the struggle that Powell was engaged in. Powell was trying to slow down the pursuit of fortune long enough that the development and inhabitation of the West could be well planned and organized. In the end, he was unable to slow it down, but that was the basic tension that he was fighting with. So since it never did slow down, the settlement of the West was kind of a rush for not just gold, but for farming land and timberland and economic opportunities of all kinds, and in the chaos of that effort a lot of patterns were set, a lot of actions were taken that chopped up the land and impaired the ability of the land to support people. You think about the rampant overgrazing of the open-range years, the great die-offs in the bad winter of 1890, the thousands and probably tens of thousands of farms that failed, the ghost towns that were abandoned and blown away, and so forth. This great tide of human suffering and failure that also accompanied the rush to riches was part and parcel of that.

JL: Looking to the future for the West, which is kind of tough to imagine because there are so many different variables that didn't even exist—I was just thinking about the fact that [Thomas] Malthus had written his essay on human population not too long before Powell was born.

BD: I think that's right.

JL: In other words, these are the overlaps that are interesting. The population of the planet at the beginning of the twentieth century was about 1.5 billion, and it's currently about 6.5 billion.

BD: I remember when I was in grade school in the 1960s, it was about 3 billion, and it's more than doubled in my lifetime.

JL: It was about 2 billion in 1936 when I was born, which is really scary.

BD: Well, you know, a couple of things that Powell never really anticipated was the degree to which the West would become industrialized, let alone the degree to which it would become urbanized. The West is today the most urban area of the United States. More people live in cities in the West than [in] any other part of the country. And those cities are growing, and they're growing on a land base and more particularly [on] a water base that [are] *not* growing. In fact, the water base is probably, with climate change, shrinking. Quite a few models of the future effects of climate change predict that the middle latitudes of western North America will experience a significant decline in precipitation and consequent streamflow over the next fifty, sixty, eighty years. That bodes very ill for the West of the United States.

JL: Looking at New Mexico, which I'm made to understand has less surface water than any other state—

BD: Does it?

JL: Yeah. In a good year, it has about 231 square miles of surface water out of 120,000 some-odd square miles of landscape.

Subsequently, we're pumping out of our aquifers at an inordinate rate in New Mexico to make up for the lack of surface water. So you can extrapolate the future there pretty readily. Does looking at the ecological point of view versus the economic view make sense to you as something to think within?

BD: Well, in a way, separating those two, I think, is a good path toward failure. It's like separating heart and mind or body and soul. These things come together joined in important ways, and to look at the world strictly through an economic lens will lead to ruin. Looking at it strictly through an ecological lens at the same time I think is impractical because we are economic beings, and humans dominate the life of this planet to such a thorough degree that you can't neglect how you look at things, to take into account how people are going to survive. That's both an economic and ecological question. So somehow we've got to find a way to unify those lenses, look at things binocularly, and to look at them in a time frame that is long. So many of our problems arise, as Powell would have argued in his days, from looking at what the game is going to be in the next three months or six months or year, rather than looking at how things are going to be twenty or thirty years down the line. Certainly our foresight is fallible, but we've got to try.

JL: The tricky part to me is trying to amass the clusters of factors that have to be looked at and the lenses to look at them through. Do you have any final thoughts?

BD: My foggy crystal ball for the West—I think probably the two biggest factors that our society needs to prepare for are, on the one hand, increasing aridity of an already arid region because of climate change and [on the other] also to think humanely and wisely about cultural change. Because the movement of people from South America, Central America, and Mexico northward into North America is not going to slacken because we try to build bigger fences along our international border. This is a demographic trend of people on this planet that is powerful, long term, and not soon to change. And so if we really want to think about how we continue to abide here in the West, we need to think about those water resources, we need to think about the flow of population in this direction coming from the south, and, for goodness sake, *we need to think about what the land really can support.*

Frances Levine,
photo by Blaire Clark

Frances Levine

Introduction

Dr. Frances Levine, an ethnohistorian who has lived in New Mexico for more than three decades, is the author of *Our Prayers Are in This Place: Pecos Pueblo Identity over the Centuries* (University of New Mexico Press, 1999) and presently the director of the Palace of the Governors New Mexico History Museum in Santa Fe. The Palace of the Governors is considered by many the oldest continuously used public edifice in the United States.

Fran Levine has a profound insight into the intercultural relationships within the upper Río Grande watershed and how the watershed itself continues to influence these indigenous cultures. As vigorously noted by John Wesley Powell, aridity is the most prevalent characteristic of the American landscape west of the hundredth meridian.

Culture groups of myriad persuasions have been passing through the region of the Río Grande Rift for many millennia. Some have followed megafauna such as the woolly mammoths into oblivion; others have lingered, evolving agrarian practices that allowed them the cultural leisure to reflect on their presence within the flow of Nature and to celebrate the local deities and spirits in ceremonials that continue to endure, even in this age of technofantasy cum legalistic bureaucracy in which territorial disputes are settled in the courts rather than in the field. Thus, we set ourselves apart from our fellow species, unless, of course, we elect to ignore man-made law and go atavistic.

A few years ago I interviewed my friend Fran Levine regarding her perceptions of intercultural contact along el Camino Real de Tierra Adentro, the Royal Road to the Interior, during the sixteenth and seventeenth centuries. I asked her if I might include an edited version of that interview in the present work. She asked that instead we consider including an essay she had written that provides a perspective of intercultural relationship enacted within the habitat of the northern Río Grande watershed. It is fitting that Fran Levine's essay conclude a work that attempts to cast some light on what it takes to survive along the Continental Divide or anywhere else.

Listening to the Land

Tradition and Change in the Northern Río Grande

Frances Levine

Which comes first: the blessing or the prayer?
It is not easy in this landscape to separate the role of man
from the role of nature.
—J. B. Jackson,
A Sense of Place, a Sense of Time (1994)

Introduction

Days after I moved to New Mexico in the early summer of 1976, I attended the first of many ceremonials that would teach me about the connections between the past and the present, and between the secular and the spiritual in this fragile environment. It was June, and so hot I could believe the tall tales people told about frying eggs on the sidewalk. It was the season when Pueblo and Hispanic communities prayed for rain. Throughout New Mexico, community members walked in solemn processions to their fields carrying bultos (statues of saints). There they prayed and watched the billowing clouds for signs of an approaching shower.

In many Hispanic communities on the feast day of San Ysidro (May 15) and on the feast of San Juan Bautista (June 24) the saints are carried from farm to farm. San Ysidro blesses the spring planting, and San Juan Bautista's purity is said to bless the waters of streams and acequias (irrigation ditches) as well as those who bathe in the holy waters. In one hymn to San Ysidro, verses seek protection against thieves or bad neighbors, hail, and drought:

From the accustomed thief
Who is never afraid of the Lord
Please protect our plants
We ask this favor of you
The destructive hail
Let it not damage our crops
We ask you with fervor
To have a bountiful harvest this year
In all your goodness, kindness,
I ask you from my heart
To send my plants and crops
Favors and your blessings

Del ladrón acostumbrado
Que nunca teme al Señor
Nos libre nuestro sembrado
Te pedimos por favor
El granizo destructor
Que no nos cause su daño
Te pedimos con fervor
Tener cosecha este año
En tus bondades confiado
Te pido de corazón
Le mandes a mi sembrado
Favores y bendición.

The dance I saw was a matachines dance. It was held in the community of Three Rivers, a small Hispanic community on the edge of one of the southern Apache reservations. Matachines, danced in both Pueblo and Hispanic communities, symbolize the fusion of indigenous and Spanish traditions. The dance is performed throughout the year, but most often during the Christmas season and on New Year's Day in several villages. Men dressed in black pants and white shirts wear tall, crowned headdresses with flowing lace and bright-colored ribbons. They are often accompanied by a quartet of fiddle and guitar players;

their dance is an intricate pattern of paired dance steps. There are many levels of meaning to the dance and role playing. In the dance, an Indian girl is symbolically married to a Hispanic man, signifying the Conquest and the assimilation of cultures that characterizes the Southwest.

This was not the usual matachines. There was no complex foot-work, no melodious fiddle playing, no pantomime or burlesque depicting transgressive behaviors. There was an intensity here that matched the heat of the day. The matachines had been brought to the banks of a dry, dusty stream bed to perform a miracle. They were going to pray for rain and dance to save the withering crops. I did not entirely understand then the implications of the matachines, but I watched every move as they first dug a small hole in the dry stream bed and then filled it with water carried from the well in the churchyard. Now, nearly thirty years later and after working in many New Mexico communities, I understand more about the significance of ritual in bringing rains to save crops.

Background

The northern Río Grande, that area between Albuquerque and Taos, contains some of the oldest cultural landscapes in North America. It is a region of uncommon physical beauty as well as startling contrasts of ancient and modern cultures. The regional landscape records both the persistence of traditional ways of life and the onslaught of change. Spectacular ancestral archaeological sites provide enormous time depth to contemporary Pueblo Indian and Hispanic communities. Along the northern Río Grande and its tributaries, ancient cultures continue to exist near bunkers where the first atomic bomb was developed. Pueblos, kivas, and centuries-old adobe churches survive next to casinos and golf courses built recently in several Pueblo Indian communities. Centuries-old adobe houses, constructed of earthen bricks baked only by the long months of sun and heat, stand next to prefabricated trailer houses, the only affordable housing left for many whose families have been native to this land for centuries.

The land itself along the northern Río Grande records the antiquity of land tenure and inheritance practices, patterns clearly visible in aerial photographs and land-tenure maps. In many Pueblo communities, lands are titled to individuals for their house sites, whereas some plots of agricultural land and grazing lands are held in common by religious societies or kiva groups. This division of lands permits a pattern of land use and land tenure that support social sodalities and make it possible to separate the many colors of corn grown in the Pueblos for food and ceremonial purposes. Along the Río Grande, between Española and Taos, another land-use pattern is also evident. The distinctive pattern of narrow fields fronting on the river is called *long lots*. It is a land-use and land-tenure pattern introduced into New Mexico by Hispanic settlers in the beginning of the seventeenth century. Each strip runs from the river to the uplands and a community's common lands. It affords each landowner river frontage and a share of all the ecozones and biozones in the community.

Northern New Mexico is alternately described either as a region where traditional cultures are endangered by development or as a refuge region where older cultural forms persist. It is a region in which social tensions are palpable and change is often a threat to older cultural practices. Pueblo Indian communities, Spanish and Mexican land-grant communities, vast tracts of federal land, and rapidly expanding Sunbelt communities demarcate the land holdings and in many ways separate the region into competing interests. Productive land and water resources are scarce in this semiarid region, and they are the currency and the subject of increasing competition. The value of land is being redefined throughout the region as the traditional basis of the economy has shifted away from agriculture, largely small-scale crop farming and livestock production, to a base of light manufacturing, tourism, and retirement.

Throughout northern New Mexico, there is a palpable sense of loss that recurs in the popular press and scholarly writing, as well as in the oral traditions of the Hispanic and Pueblo Indian communities. The losses include the loss of indigenous languages and regional variants of the Spanish language; the loss of *ejido*, or common, lands on which traditional communities gathered subsistence resources and building materials, for centuries in many cases; and the loss of cooperative relations among the Hispanic and Pueblo Indian communities. Within that palpable sense of loss, however, centuries-old customs persist, reflecting an adherence to traditional ways of life and a belief that these ways are still relevant.

No contemporary issue is as emblematic of the struggle between traditional and modern lifeways as the water rights adjudications currently under way in much of New Mexico. I have served as an expert witness in water rights adjudications throughout New Mexico for more than twenty years. Water rights adjudications are legal proceedings in which the rights to acequias, deep water wells, and other uses of surface and ground waters are legally defined. My involvement has been primarily that of an ethnohistorian assisting community acequia associations or the state of New Mexico in documenting the use dates that establish the antiquity of water rights. In other cases, I have worked with community acequia associations in documenting the customs that community acequias have used to share available water. Many of the issues addressed directly or indirectly in water rights adjudication lawsuits are related to the tensions between sustaining traditional ways of life and meeting the needs and demands of a rapidly expanding and more urban population in the region.

The community acequias of northern New Mexico serve some of the oldest European settlements in the United States, dating back to the earliest years of Spanish settlement in the late sixteenth and early seventeenth centuries. Pueblo Indian communities have lived along the Río Grande and its tributaries since at least the mid-fourteenth century. Pueblo people have farmed portions of their traditional use areas even longer, using a variety of water-harvesting and soil-conservation techniques. In recent years, water rights adjudications have heightened concerns in these communities over scarce land and water resources. Pueblo Indian communities and the centuries-old Hispanic communities of the region would theoretically seem to have little to fear in the process of determining water rights. New Mexico is a prior appropriation state, meaning that rights are determined in part by seniority in years when water is scarce. As the oldest titleholders to these lands, Pueblo and land-grant Hispanic communities should have the most secure titles. In reality, however, some of the oldest communities often have the most to lose in the adjudications.

Water Rights Adjudications—The Legal Steps

There are at least three classes of participants or parties in water rights adjudications. The state of New Mexico, through the State Engineer Office, participates in the process as the stakeholder of all the water in the state. Communities often see the State Engineer as withholding or denying water through adjudications. The State Engineer, in contrast, maintains that the office is mandated by statute to perform an independent analysis of claims and available water supply and to ensure that adjudications proceed on a correct factual and legal basis. The U.S. attorney, within the Justice Department, participates in suits as the protector of federal rights, including those of American Indian tribes, the National Park Service, the Forest Service, and other federal agencies. In addition, American Indian tribes usually have their own attorneys. Individuals and groups of water users, such as mutual domestic water systems and associations of community ditches, also participate to protect their interests. The State Engineer Office is usually the plaintiff, bringing suit against non-Indian defendants or against the United States as trustee for Indians. In some cases, the United States and the Pueblos have joined the state as plaintiffs against all other users. As a result of the alignment of the parties, public perception seems to be that the only issues involved in adjudications are the definition of American Indian rights versus those of non-Indians. The adjudications feed interethnic and intracommunity conflicts over scarce land and water resources, as well as less overt interethnic tensions that have simmered in many New Mexico communities for generations.

The Acequia: A Metaphor for Resource-Based Relations

Through the adjudication process, water rights are prioritized, quantified, and privatized as individual property rights. The privatization of rights changes a fundamental principle of traditional water use, in which water is a shared resource and carries with it obligations for shared labor and wise-use responsibilities. Traditional water use does not assume that that use is a fixed individual property right. Use rights are usually maintained only as long as the *parciantes* (use-right holders) perform their communal obligations and exercise responsible water use. Local customs of water sharing and distribution and the traditional understanding of land use and settlement practices in a particular community are among the most important issues that traditional users seek to protect. Local customs can be considered by the courts when these practices bear on the definition of rights.

For many contemporary community acequias, the strict application of the priority system anticipated by the adjudication process is a threat to the practices of water distribution and water sharing by which community acequias have functioned for centuries. The switch to a priority system represents a loss of local control over resource allocations and can be detrimental to the social fabric of a community. There are alternatives, but they demand a very different alignment of the parties. In many ways, the acequia is a metaphor for the shared traditions and shared values of rural life, especially among the Hispanic communities of northern New Mexico. To be a parciante, a mayordomo, or a *comisionado* is to accept a place in the life of the community and a set of responsibilities to the land, to the people, and to the very fabric of community life.

The local perspective of the acequias has a contribution to make to regional, national, and international issues. Water-sharing agreements recorded in northern New Mexico legal cases are similar to agreements found throughout the world. Increasingly, public-policy administrators are turning to indigenous peoples and local perspectives in drafting resource-management agendas. Stanley Crawford, an eloquent writer and himself a parciante in Dixon, New Mexico, pleads urgently that we recognize the contribution of acequias before they are lost and with them the lessons of communal responsibility for the land. The acequias contribute richly to the diverse social and physical landscape that makes the northern Río Grande a diverse bioregion of the United States. They distribute water to make a broader riparian zone and provide habitat for birds and trees that might not exist without these sustaining waterways. Acequia associations have served for more than four centuries as local land managers, and there is much to be gained from implementing in modern land uses the shared perspectives of traditional resource users.

Water Rights Proof—An Allegorical Case

La Acequia de la Cuchilla in the northern reaches of the Río Grande drainage dramatically illustrates the basis of claims made by Pueblo and Hispanic communities to the same water source. In water rights adjudications, the courts look for finite historical proof that one community or one person made the first use of irrigation waters along a particular stream. The rights to this precious resource are then owned by the party or parties that can show continuous use from the first user. In the case of the Cuchilla Ditch, rights are being adjudicated to landholders in the community of Des Montes, New Mexico, located about five miles northeast of the town of Taos, just on the edge of Taos Pueblo reservation lands. It is not where the water is used in this case that is of greatest interest. The intrigue lies in how the water arrives on the land and the stories that Taos Pueblo and Hispanic residents of the Taos Valley tell about this miraculous ditch.

The Cuchilla Ditch diverts from the Río Hondo, in the deep valley near Valdez, New Mexico, about twelve miles upstream from the town of Taos. From the bottomland farms in this beautiful village, the Cuchilla Ditch appears to run uphill, surely a miraculous occurrence. Taos Pueblo elders interviewed in the 1960s and an oral history recorded in Valdez in 1939 give very different accounts of how this miraculous ditch came to into existence. The stories are important in comprehending the ways in which two cultures with ancient roots in this land assert their claims to precious water resources and demonstrate their bonds to the land.

The Hispanic version was recorded by a New Deal historical researcher named Simeón Tejada. Although he does not name his sources, he evidently interviewed several elders in Valdez when he recorded the story in 1939. The WPA translation relates the villagers' folk history of how the Cuchilla Ditch was surveyed:

> Immediately after the settling of the town of San Antonio [1894], now Valdes [sic], the residents gave thought to making a ditch so that they might irrigate the plains of Desmontes. They made use in their survey for this ditch of an instrument made in the form of a triangle with a thread fastened to one of its corners and a piece of lead fastened to the other end of the thread; this gave them their level for the flow of water. The tools they used were of wood and with these and the level, give rise to admiration of the engineers of today at the true course of the ditch. To the naked eye it seems that the water runs uphill. This ditch is a mile long; at first an axle bushing from a wagon was used to measure the water—today it irrigates a large acreage with an abundance of water.

The Taos Pueblo version of how this ditch came to assume its astonishing course was recorded very briefly in the land claims case that Taos presented before the Indian Claims Commission. Anthropologist Florence Hawley Ellis was employed by the U.S. Attorney's Office to establish the antiquity of Taos Pueblo and the extent of their aboriginal use lands. She conducted archaeological excavations establishing that the Pueblo has existed on its present site since at least the mid–fifteenth century. Although Valdez is currently outside the boundaries of land held by Taos Pueblo, it is well within their traditional-use area defined by Pueblo elders in land-claims testimony.

In the Tewa language of Taos Pueblo, the name for the Cuchilla Ditch is Eagle Feather or Eagle Feathering Ditch. I have also heard Taos Pueblo people refer to it as Eagle Tail Feather Ditch, a reference to the way in which Eagle used his tail feathers to establish the uphill course of the ditch. In Taos legends, Eagle is credited with founding Taos Pueblo and with humans' ability to speak, if one knows when to listen. In a land-claims study, Taos elders identified two supernatural beings as the creators of the ditch. The elders claimed the Cuchilla as a ditch irrigated farms of the Taos Pueblo people long before the Spanish came to the Hondo River valley.

In both the Pueblo and Hispanic stories of the origin of the Cuchilla Ditch, the miraculous image of water flowing uphill is credited to ancestors. In the Taos Pueblo versions, supernatural beings, or perhaps eagles, are responsible for laying the course of the ditch. In both versions, the people's needs are sustained by heroic efforts.

Listening to the Past, Planning for the Future

These stories are examples of ways in which cultures construct "place" from a specific set of cultural references that often mix the historical and the allegorical. Both stories demonstrate core traditions of Pueblo and Hispanic people who have farmed this arid land for centuries. Each culture identifies specific agents who established their place on the landscape. For Taos Pueblo, the supernatural and the spiritual beings established this place. For the Hispanic storytellers, their antecedents, the *ancianos*, were the founders of this place. Both stories relate to the larger cultural and community values that can be learned from listening to stories tied to the landscape. For the Hispanic residents of the Taos area, the Acequia Cuchilla came to exist by the careful engineering and hard work of the *pobladores*, first settlers. The oral history is specific in describing the crude but careful hand-eye leveling of this ditch. For Taos Pueblo elders, the ditch is also ingenious. The agents in the Taos version are the supernatural and the spiritual beliefs that deeply root Pueblo people in this place. Taken together, the versions of the Cuchilla story illustrate the miraculous forces and the laborious practices that sustain communities on the arid landscape of northern New Mexico.

Land-use and water-use competition are not recent problems in New Mexico. Court cases are among some of the oldest documents found in the Spanish Archives of New Mexico, which date from the late seventeenth century. Perhaps more answers for sustaining diverse cultural landscapes in the future may be provided by reexamining our heritage of customs and traditions. It is time to incorporate traditional processes as well as technologically based solutions to find a way to balance the old and the new, the traditional and the innovative.

Traditional Hispanic and Pueblo communities practice customs that are centuries old, sustaining a tie to their land base. Court records and stories of the elders often reveal that the resolution of conflicts was based on principles of sharing. The resolution in many cases stemmed from a core principle that each land and water user depended on the production of the land. The process of resolution invited accommodation. Each side yielded a little, each side gained a little, but ultimately the parties knew that water and productive land were finite. They had learned this in many cases by listening to the land, by knowing how their homelands came to be, and by knowing how their resources could best be shared.

Postscript

This tiny glimpse of intercultural fabric that spans the southern stretch of the Continental Divide is like looking at the larger picture through a pinhole. For me, having conducted and edited these interviews, it has been a revealing glimpse, brightened by Fran Levine's essay.

Preparing this book allowed me to contemplate, intellectually grasp, and intuit something of the fellow participants' points of view. In so doing, I stepped out of range of the white noise of mass media and whole-mindedly listened to human intelligence at work. After each interview or conversation, I came away refreshed in mind and spirit for having experienced true cognitive diversity.

After a long lifetime of wandering the American West and Mexico, I am convinced that biodiversity and cultural diversity are intertwined. Indigenous cultures are shaped in large measure by their geophysical and biological habitats. Our planet teems with cognitive diversity, each community resonating to the timbre of respective homeland.

I have come to know and befriend people of many indigenous origins, mental capabilities, spiritual proclivities, and physical abilities. The people I know who have handcrafted their own lives and who recognize themselves to be rooted in Nature are conscious people. I personally think that the purpose of life is evolution of consciousness. Our species, the human species, is capable of great consciousness and is perhaps part of the mind of our planet. At our best, we develop and use our intellects to understand the nature of that universal system that encompasses both the microcosm and the macrocosm. By peering through the lenses of mythic perspective and metaphor, we gain intuitive insight as to why we are here. We strive to define ethical standards that are interculturally acceptable and biologically sound. Compassion is an evolved attribute. Compassion combined with consciousness must blaze the trail through the next stage of the great adventure.